Lives at Risk

Lives at Risk

Hostages and Victims in American Foreign Policy

Russell D. Buhite

A Scholarly Resources Inc. Imprint
Wilmington, Delaware

© 1995 by Scholarly Resources Inc.
First published 1995
Printed and bound in the United States of America

Scholarly Resources Inc.
104 Greenhill Avenue
Wilmington, DE 19805-1897

Library of Congress Cataloging-in-Publication Data

Buhite, Russell D.
    Lives at risk : hostages and victims in American foreign
policy / Russell D. Buhite.
        p.   cm.
    Includes bibliographical references and index.
    ISBN 0-8420-2552-9. — ISBN 0-8420-2553-7 (pbk.)
    1. United States—Foreign relations. 2. Hostages—
Government policy—United States—History. I. Title.
E183.7.B84   1995
327.73—dc20   95-5688
                                                          CIP

For Gracie,

who came first

and took us all hostage

Acknowledgments

I am deeply indebted to a number of individuals who have assisted in the completion of this study: James Harrell, my research assistant at the University of Oklahoma, helped to locate documents and secondary sources for me in the initial phase of the project. My administrative secretary in the History Department at Oklahoma, Martha Penisten, not only handled her official duties with incredible efficiency but also "processed" words and edited some of the early chapters. Gary Vaughan has served as my research assistant since my move to the University of Tennessee. He represents a model for his position—he is intelligent, painstaking, mature, and professional in every respect. His contribution has been enormous. My former student, Mary Brennan, gave the manuscript a careful reading. Her years of experience in military intelligence and her eye for infelicitous phraseology and imperfect logic have made her a compelling critic.

I have also imposed on the friendship of professional colleagues to critique the work. Jonathan Utley, a longtime member of the faculty at Tennessee and a distinguished diplomatic historian, challenged me on nearly every page, to my great benefit, if not delight. David Levy, my collaborator on the publication of *FDR's Fireside Chats* and an outstanding teacher/scholar and editor nonpareil, offered insightful comments on both style and content. Richard Hopper of Scholarly Resources gently pressured me to expedite completion of the manuscript, then helped to shape it into the kind of book he wanted.

Finally, I wish to thank my wife Mary for her love and encouragement. Her support has been far greater than I can adequately convey.

About the Author

Russell D. Buhite, a native of Pennsylvania, earned his Ph.D. at Michigan State University, where he worked with Paul A. Varg and Warren Cohen. His publications include *Patrick J. Hurley and American Foreign Policy* (1973); *Soviet-American Relations in Asia, 1945–1954* (1982); and *Decisions at Yalta: An Appraisal of Summit Diplomacy* (1986), as well as numerous articles and essays on American foreign relations.

He is professor of history and head of the History Department at the University of Tennessee.

Contents

Introduction

Terrorism and American Foreign Relations

This study of American foreign policy focuses on the issue of how the United States dealt with the holding of its citizens as hostages on foreign territory and how it responded in other cases in which Americans were victimized while living or conducting business abroad. The episodes of victimization in the nineteenth century are covered not only because they are of interest, but also because they reveal how U.S. officials reacted to the most notable instances of lives at risk during that era. Similarly, the post-World War II prisoner repatriation dispute with the Soviet Union provides evidence of the use of Americans, not technically as hostages but as pawns, in the early period of the Cold War and thus as a factor in the origin of that conflict.

The work has several primary purposes: to identify the most important terrorist episodes; to provide the appropriate context in each instance; to characterize the individuals kidnapped or otherwise victimized in order to bring them to life; to indicate how the unfortunate people involved were treated; and, most important, to demonstrate how each case affected American foreign policy as well as how attitudes and actions informing policies reflected U.S. history in the larger sense. A corollary objective is to show what these cases might suggest for action in future incidents. This study's main significance, then, is that, unlike any other work on the topic, it not only engages some major historical questions but addresses critical contemporary public policy issues as well.

In large part this is an account of terrorism, acts of which come in a variety of forms: car bombings, assassinations, contamination of water supplies, release of deadly toxins into the air, subjection of people to nuclear radiation, sabotage aboard in-flight aircraft, and kidnappings. Experts have attempted to define terrorism and explain its root causes; they also have sought to preempt, simulate, and squelch it. Indeed, scholars have churned out voluminous literature on its many facets.

Hostage-taking is only one variety of terrorism, which is best and most simply described as "a process of deliberate employment of psychological intimidation and physical violence by sovereign states and subnational groups to attain strategic and political [or economic] objectives in violation of law."[1] Because this work is not a conventional study of terrorism, however, the term itself assumes less importance than it would in many examinations of the subject. Hostage-taking, this study's main concern, may be defined, in accord with a United Nations convention on the subject, as "the seizing or detaining and threatening to kill, injure, or continue to detain another person to compel a third party to do or abstain from doing any act as a condition for the release of the hostage."[2] Victimization requires no formal definition; it may or may not constitute terrorism. In this work it usually does not.

Democracies and constitutional monarchies engaged in the slave trade on a massive scale through the eighteenth century. The United States did not terminate slave ownership until the Civil War despite the "self-evident" truths enunciated in the Declaration of Independence. European imperial behavior and American policies in the Philippines, the Caribbean, Central America, and on the North American continent included the arbitrary incarceration and disposition of native peoples. Thus, democracies historically have not been innocent of trading in human flesh. On the other hand, owing to their values and institutions, democracies have not engaged in hostage-taking to a degree even approximating that of authoritarian and dictatorial regimes, and in the twentieth century one finds few such examples.

To say that democracies have had a particularly difficult time in responding to acts of terrorism is to understate the case. Among the options generally accepted as the most efficacious for them none is ever fully effective; none has provided any better than imperfect security for citizens of democratic states. Most experts cite the need for international cooperation among like-minded nations as one important counterterrorist step—that is, cooperation among democracies and other states that have a great deal to lose in terrorist attacks. Cooperation starts with the acceptance of a common definition of terrorism and ends with an agreement to share intelligence, provide technological support to major airports and other international facilities, cut off trade with countries that harbor terrorists, and prosecute or extradite those terrorists taken into custody.

That some of the options have proven far better in theory than in practice seems axiomatic to even the most casual observer. When national or special economic interest is involved, cooperation in economic sanctions against those allowing terrorist operations from their territory may prove impossible, as the world learned in observing the passivity of European countries and Japan toward oil-producing states in the Middle East. Good intelligence may prove equally difficult to obtain because terrorist groups are notoriously suspicious and cautious about revealing their secrets or sharing their membership: the Shining Path guerrillas of Peru, for instance, have required that their initiates kill a policeman or a judge before granting them full standing in the organization. Technology has a critical part to play in the struggle against terrorism but is usually extremely expensive and often, as in the case of detection devices at busy international airports, cumbersome and time-consuming. Periodic pronouncements celebrating the end of hijackings have been about as meaningful as confident evangelical assertions concerning the end of the world.

Central to the functioning of democracies is law, and in an ideal world domestic and international law would deter terrorism. That it has not done so—not in any event during the twentieth century and particularly during the Cold War—is testimony to the power of revolutionary ideology and to the blocking of a United Nations agreement on terrorism. Third World nations during the 1960s, 1970s, and 1980s as well as their Soviet and Chinese sponsors consistently opposed international sanctions against violence, even acts against innocent civilians, if such behavior could be construed as furthering opposition to "racism" and "colonialism." This obstructionism and the sometime reluctance of democratic states to extradite persons accused of political crimes meant that for several decades law had little practical effect against terrorism.[3]

A distinguished diplomatic historian, Michael Hunt, whose work, including an insightful book on the symbiosis of the American historical experience and the country's foreign policy, is pertinent to this study, argues that the core elements of the national ethos manifested in U.S. external relations have been 1) national greatness tied to the promotion of liberty, 2) a firm belief in racial hierarchy, and 3) a profound distrust of revolution.[4] As he points out, an elaborate "scientific" and folk wisdom on race took form in the eighteenth and nineteenth centuries and carried over into the twentieth. The work of ethnographers, historians, geographers, and other scholars, most of it half-baked and contradictory, gave motor force to the idea that culture, civilization, and national character were determined by race. At the top of the hierarchy of race, of course, were the white people of the world and at the bottom the black. In between were Mongolian, Malay, American Indian, and racial-ly mixed Latin American peoples, none as backward, ignorant, or slothful as blacks but, at the same time, none quite capable of achieving at the level of whites. Graphic depictions of racial types appeared in many American textbooks used well into the twentieth century, and teachers held forth confidently on the differences in capabilities among the races. A sort of national preoccupation with race not only helped define the American perception of other peoples but informed foreign policy as well by reinforcing and rationalizing U.S. actions abroad.[5]

Easily yet curiously coexisting with this ideology of race was the practice of an expansionism closely linked to liberty. The United States became a "dynamic republic," spreading civilization across the North American continent while taking the blessings of freedom with it, then moving farther westward toward Asia and southward toward the Caribbean, all the while justifying a severe racial hierarchy and, for a good part of the time, slavery. By the turn of the twentieth century the United States had eagerly joined the European nations in an imperial drive for greatness, largely for many of the same economic and psychological reasons that motivated the Europeans but also, it was alleged, on a type of benevolent crusade to extend liberty.[6]

Despite an avowed interest in the external extension of liberty, Americans, after an initial flush of enthusiasm for the French Revolution, developed a decidedly skeptical view of revolution. Initially this doubtfulness rested on philosophical principles: people should rise up only against authority rendered illegitimate by persistent usurpations of individual and property rights and should normally follow a moderate—and constitutional—course. In practice, therefore, neither officials nor the public could muster much enthusiasm for the rise of Latin American peoples against their Spanish masters, the Poles against the Russians, the establishment of the French Republic in 1848, or many other uprisings of the nineteenth century, the rebellions of the Greeks against the Turks in the 1820s and the Hungarians against the Hapsburgs in 1848 and 1849 being notable exceptions.

By the twentieth century the philosophical objection was reinforced by possible challenges to American strategic and economic interests. That revolutionary activity almost always brought a new form of tyranny justified American opposition on the more practical grounds of self-interest. Thus, the United States found itself against revolution in Russia, China, Iran, and other spots around the world. Opposition became particularly pointed during the Cold War competition with the Soviet Union.[7]

Although these components of ideology do not fully explain the responses to the victimization of Americans and the responses do not fully confirm the ideological underpinnings, the episodes studied herein do fit reasonably well into the interpretative framework outlined above. While American opposition to the revolutionary regimes in Russia, China, and Iran offers one explanation for the endangerment of Americans in those countries, it does not justify the taking of hostages; and these new regimes—all of them brutal, repressive, and tyrannical—have tended to prove the prescience of the conservative philosophical assessments of revolution. Yet, interestingly, despite its antirevolutionary attitude, the United States, for the most part, reacted less aggressively to violence against its citizens in the twentieth century than it had in the nineteenth.

The United States has been a target of terrorist groups and other victimizers throughout much of its history. Although the new nation followed an isolationist course in its political relations with Europe, its commercial activity took it to all parts of the globe through the late eighteenth and nineteenth centuries. By the early twentieth century the United States had become a commercial empire, with domination and control established in the Western Hemisphere and a colony set up in the Eastern. American traders accepted few geographic constraints. Missionaries and other purveyors of American culture proved equally farsighted and determined.

As the twentieth century wore on, what began as a commercial empire became a commercial/political one. Moreover, after World War II, as a result of its competition with the Soviet Union, the United States developed a gigantic infrastructure of international power, a power that intruded into all parts of the world and often made Americans unpopular with other peoples. It was not just that American capitalists sometimes unfairly exploited other nations' resources. Americans inspired envy because they were rich; they inspired animosity because they were insensitive to other races and cultures; they engendered hatred because they took sides in other countries' domestic disputes; they were taken hostage because they were available and vulnerable; they were victimized because their ideological baggage included liberal-democratic ideals alien to indigenous peoples. They were seized because their government became the primary benefactor of Israel in its conflict with aggrieved Arabs. By the last half of the twentieth century the United States had become not merely a target of terrorist groups but the most inviting of targets.

Two important and closely related questions require attention in this work: What were the responses to violence against Americans in the eighteenth and nineteenth centuries? How and why were the responses different in the twentieth? An examination of developments during the nineteenth century in particular reveals a tough, physically aggressive approach and several prominent explanations for U.S. policy. Among the most compelling are the greater latitude enjoyed by naval commanders and the slowness of communications. These commanders often acted in accord with their own conceptions of national honor, unrestrained by officials in Washington. Both the former and the latter understood that commanders exercised what often amounted to sovereign power in dealing with other peoples. Moreover, primitive communications not only meant that orders could take weeks or months to arrive but also that a naval commander's independent behavior could go unreported in the United States until months after he had acted. Public opinion thus influenced policies only indirectly, if at all.

Racial attitudes began to change by the middle of the twentieth century, but, for most of the nation's early history, both American officials and laymen assumed that the dark-skinned populations of Asia, Africa, or Latin America were ipso facto inferior. This automatically rendered any violent action against Americans committed by such people unwarranted, immoral, and subject to the harshest retribution. It made definition of the term "barbarian" relatively easy, and it encouraged in Americans a sense of unity on certain international issues; resistance to the Barbary pirates became, in consequence, a way to define national interest despite the generally divided opinion of the Northern and Southern states about that concept during the late eighteenth and early nineteenth centuries.

An equally compelling justification for severe reaction to any victimization of Americans was the sense of national greatness that became part of the nineteenth-century attitude. The conquering of a continent and the increase in wealth associated with industrialization, combined with the maintaining of democratic institutions, convinced Americans of their superiority and of the fitness of the United States as a world model. As a result of this swelling nationalism, Americans did not shrink from international competition that manifested the accepted masculine values of physical strength, vigor, assertiveness, and violence.

The turn of the twentieth century, and more particularly the administration of President Theodore Roosevelt, brought a dramatic change in the American response to terrorism. Significantly, the Roosevelt years saw an alteration in the way public opinion was formed and in how the president reacted to and was influenced by the views of the people. One prominent American historian has observed that Roosevelt had "the first major career in American politics to be conducted wholly within the era and under the influence of modern journalistic media."[8] From the midnineteenth century through the early twentieth century, American newspapers experienced a major transformation in technology, including the everyday use of Linotype machines and photoengraving, and adopted modern business techniques. Journalistic coverage of public figures and government agencies suddenly subjected policymakers and their proposals to greater scrutiny than ever before. While President Roosevelt often made himself the beneficiary of this attention, he sometimes became its victim.

As the twentieth century progressed, what began as primarily a print phenomenon became a multimedia process, and public opinion played an even greater constraining role in hostage and victimization cases. Radio, and later television, provided nearly instantaneous coverage of developments. Families and friends of victims, not to mention a more informed citizenry, often circumscribed government action. In the name of humanity, policies of negotiation and conciliation replaced the mailed-fist approach to hostage crises.

Other factors contributed to the different approaches employed in the nineteenth and the twentieth centuries. In the period after World War II, weapons and explosives became more widely available. Terrorists had greater mobility and could strike at distances farther from their home bases, and audiences, about whom terrorists were always concerned, were increasingly accessible through modern technology. Furthermore, terrorism against Americans accordingly became more common than ever in the nation's history. But the Cold War and Soviet support for some of the countries sponsoring kidnappings, hijackings, and other brutal acts tended to prevent forceful countermeasures. Fear of Soviet power thus determined American behavior.

The incidents examined in this study suggest several other generalizations about American foreign policy, particularly concerning the relative importance to policy formulation of national interest, national honor, partisan politics, and individual personalities, as well as about what happened historically when the welfare of hostages tended to conflict with national honor. A brief review shows that national honor, while always a heady sentiment among articulate critics of an administration in power, seldom determined policy. President Lyndon B. Johnson experienced personal embarrassment and the serious compromising of his country's prestige at the hands of the economically backward and militarily inferior North Koreans rather than risk the lives of American hostages (Chapter 6). President Harry S. Truman suffered similar grief during the holding of Angus Ward by the Chinese Communists in 1948 and 1949 (Chapter 5), as did President Jimmy Carter while Iranian militants imprisoned Americans in Tehran in 1979 and 1980 (Chapter 7).

Apart from the fitful efforts of John Adams and Thomas Jefferson in dealing with the Barbary states (Chapter 1) and in President Andrew Jackson's response to Malay "pirates" and Argentine challenges to U.S. rights in the South Atlantic (Chapter 2), one finds few examples of national honor as a factor of major influence in the forming of U.S. policy.

On the other hand, the careful and cautious assessment of the national interest tends to stand out as a major component of decision making. Hence, neither President Woodrow Wilson nor President Warren G. Harding chose to follow the French and belligerently challenge the Soviets while the latter held Westerners, including Americans, hostage; likewise, both President Franklin D. Roosevelt and President Truman, who desired Soviet cooperation in forging the post-World War II peace, eschewed a quid pro quo as Joseph Stalin held Americans as pawns in 1945 (Chapter 4). Indeed, all of the administrations after the onset of the Cold War took measured looks at U.S. interests given the nation's large-scale global commitments (Chapter 8). The bellicose rhetoric of Theodore Roosevelt during the Ion Perdicaris affair of 1904 (Chapter 3), and before that the U.S. intervention to free Americans held during the Boxer Rebellion (Chapter 2), do not mask the careful determination early in the twentieth century of the comparatively minor importance to the United States of the Northeast Asian and North African regions of the world. The Barbary kidnappings of a century earlier also show American officials as ever mindful of the relative costs of military action and paying ransom.

Interestingly, public opinion usually produced conflicting responses during hostage incidents, particularly during the twentieth century. As previously noted, public opinion focused attention on events and forced policymakers to take action. However, at the same time, Americans tended to express concern about the lives of the victims and, in consequence, kept officials from answering too aggressively, except in the episodes of the nineteenth century.

What may be said of public opinion also may be said of partisan politics. Politicians whose party happened to be out of power did not shrink from seeking political advantage from hostage situations. Thus, Republicans worked to embarrass President Carter during the Iranian crisis, President Johnson during the *Pueblo* affair, and President Truman during the holding of Ward, while Democrats derived some political satisfaction from the hostage predicament confronting President Ronald Reagan. In Jackson's time, political opponents called attention to his ham-handed action toward the Malays, and even Jefferson's congressional allies criticized his naval-building proposals. But where hostages' lives were involved, politicians usually took pains to remain studiously vague in their policy prescriptions.

After the turn of the twentieth century the personalities of presidents and others responsible for policy seldom managed to turn the U.S. reaction in an aggressive direction; there were simply too many constraints even for those determined to promote an activist agenda against terrorists and other victimizers. Thus, President Truman railed privately about his desire to bomb Chinese cities and blockade Chinese ports but had to retreat to negotiation in the Ward case; and President Reagan, although he reacted instinctively in pronouncing himself unalterably opposed to dealing with terrorists, dealt with them.

One of the obvious restrictions facing even the most aggressive of U.S. policymakers was the source of the victimization of Americans. Many of the incidents were perpetrated by extragovernmental groups not easily influenced by pressure from any quarter, particularly from outside national borders. The Boxers were a quasi-independent, antiforeign organization wreaking mayhem, at least initially, without the official sanction of the Chinese government. Likewise, neither the Turks nor the Bulgarians were responsible for holding Ellen Stone (Chapter 3), but rather a ragtag band of Macedonian rebels; and Perdicaris fell victim to a bandit leader seeking revenge against the ruler of Morocco. The Malayan killing of American pepper traders did not fall in the category of government-sponsored activity, nor did Chilean violence against American sailors in 1891.

That a number of the incidents were government inspired did not necessarily make them easier to resolve. The Soviet Union, the People's Republic of China, and North Korea all held Americans as either hostages or pawns in the furtherance of some governmental purpose, while the Iranian regime of the Ayatollah Ruholla Khomeini quickly placed its imprimatur on the seizure of American embassy personnel. With the notable exception of the Barbary kidnappings and the Austrian holding of Martin Koszta (Chapter 2), most of the governmentally directed episodes of hostage-taking occurred during the twentieth century, and after the United States had become the most powerful nation in the world.

Ironically, in the first hostage crises (the holding of Americans by the Barbary pirates in the late eighteenth and early nineteenth centuries) U.S. policymakers, until the conclusion of the War of 1812, pursued a flexible approach not unlike those adopted in such crises in the twentieth century. The nation paid ransom and negotiated with kidnappers until it accumulated sufficient military might and could join European collaborators in forcing a showdown with the North African marauders. Once such power existed, those responsible for its exercise did not shrink from action out of fear for the loss of either foreign or American lives. Thus, one sees a continuum in U.S. policy from the period of the early republic until the era of Theodore Roosevelt, when a new irony emerged—a president with a chauvinistic, bellicose, saber-rattling reputation who pursued policies more in accordance with those of his late twentieth-century successors than of his nineteenth-century predecessors.

NOTES

1. Yonah Alexander, foreword to Donald J. Hanle, *Terrorism: The Newest Face of Warfare* (Washington, DC: Pergamon-Brassey's, 1989), ix.

2. Geoffrey M. Levitt, *Democracies against Terror: The Western Response to State-Supported Terrorism* (New York: Praeger, 1988), 14.

3. Abraham D. Sofaer, "Terrorism and the Law," *Foreign Affairs* 64, no. 5 (Summer 1986): 901–22.

4. Michael H. Hunt, *Ideology and U.S. Foreign Policy* (New Haven, CT: Yale University Press, 1987), 17–18.

5. Ibid., 46–81.

6. Ibid., 19–43.

7. Ibid., 92–124.

8. John M. Cooper, Jr., *The Warrior and the Priest: Woodrow Wilson and Theodore Roosevelt* (Cambridge, MA: Harvard University Press, 1983), 28.

Chapter 1

The Barbary Pirates: Terrorist Tormentors of the Early Republic

Conventional wisdom holds that the first major American experience with hostage-takers, the Barbary pirates, consisted of a melodramatic confrontation in which the United States finally prevailed after constructing a naval force commensurate with its commercial and political aspirations. Having built a rudimentary navy, so the story goes, American officials forced a showdown with the "barbarians" of North Africa, following which the United States paid no ransom or tribute and no American seamen faced the indignities of imprisonment and torture.

Such an interpretation, although not entirely inaccurate, leaves out much of the story. Villainous as they may have seemed, the roving corsairs from the North African countries of Morocco, Tunis, Algiers, and Tripoli did not act entirely without provocation, and the Christian states of southern and western Europe played a part in perpetuating the centuries-old tradition of brigandage carried out in the Mediterranean and eastern Atlantic. Moreover, a number of questions about U.S. domestic policy are neglected in the standard accounts of this episode in American history. The evidence suggests, for instance, that both John Adams and Thomas Jefferson believed that an external enemy could help promote unity within the United States; both saw merit in war with the Barbary pirates. It also seems likely that proponents of a stronger federal government favored the creation of military power capable of compelling support for such a government. Finally, that the end of the menace from North Africa coincided with Great Britain's decision following the Napoleonic Wars to stop buying off the Barbary states and to confront them with its naval power seems more significant than most historians have acknowledged.[1]

To understand the American difficulty with the Barbary states it is necessary to examine their religious and economic motivation within the context of their long-standing rivalry with pirates commissioned by Christian states of Europe. The absence of peace

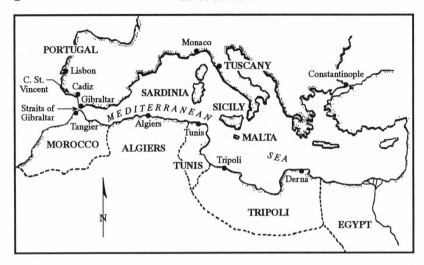

between the maritime countries of Europe and North Africa was, in the eighteenth century, as much a responsibility of the Europeans as of the North Africans.

In the late 1600s, England, France, and the Netherlands, in turn, applied pressure on the Barbary countries and made "peace" with them. In exchange for naval stores, cannon, ships of various sizes, and other types of assistance, these major commercial nations of Europe received friendly treatment for their own seamen and traders as well as assurance that piratical depredations would continue against their competitors. These maritime powers were not hostile in principle to the Barbary states; they were out to make a profit through either military resistance or accommodation.

On the other hand, the states of southern Europe, allied with the papacy, sought the total subjugation of the infidel on the African rim of the Mediterranean. As they had done since the time of the Crusades, they utilized whatever means deemed necessary, including military, in the proselytizing of the Christian faith. While the activities of the Islamic corsairs are generally well known, most Americans are not aware of the existence of exact Christian equivalents licensed and sanctioned by, among others, Spain, Sardinia, Monaco, Tuscany, and, most especially, the pope. Of these counterparts the Order of St. John of Jerusalem, stationed first at Rhodes and then at Malta, preyed on more Muslim shipping, captured more booty, and took far more hostages than the North African pirates ever did. At any time in the 1720s and 1730s, as many as six to ten thousand Muslim slaves were held at Malta, most of them taken from vessels of Tunis, Algiers, and Tripoli, and when Napoleon seized Malta in 1798, he released over two thousand North Africans. To say that Christian pirates kept the coasts of the Barbary states in constant turmoil and insecurity throughout the eighteenth century is to understate the case. When the Barbary pirates took American hostages, they were acting in accord with generally accepted practice, both Christian and Muslim.[2]

All of these North African states owed allegiance and paid tribute, more or less, to the Ottoman Empire. By the end of the eighteenth century the empire had been in existence for five hundred years, for three hundred of which it dominated nearly all Arab countries. However, by the 1790s it was clearly in decline, especially in Tripoli, Tunis, Algiers, and Morocco, where military commanders originally under the sway of Constantinople (now Istanbul) gained a great deal of independence and began to create dynasties. These semiautonomous regimes not only determined internal policies but also conducted relations with foreign powers, often in the form of authorizing privateers to capture foreign ships and hold them and their crews for ransom, with the privateers keeping a percentage of the booty. The degree to which the regime itself became directly implicated in initiating this activity depended on the country in question and the circumstances of the time.[3] During the period of American difficulties with the Barbary pirates, the rulers themselves were nearly always responsible for the seizing of seamen, cargoes, and ships.

Although the first American ship had been captured as early as 1625 and during the seventeenth and eighteenth centuries numerous cargoes and crews had fallen victim to Muslim piracy, Great Britain, for the most part, provided secure protection for its North American colonies in their trade in the Mediterranean. Indeed, prior to the Declaration of Independence, as many as one hundred American ships each year took products such as grain, rum, flour, and fish to the various ports of the region in what can only be described as a very lucrative trade. Nearly one-sixth of all American wheat and flour and one-fourth of all dried and pickled fish had gone to the Mediterranean. That the leaders of the new nation expected this trade to continue and that the nations of Europe, particularly Great Britain, would not support a commercial competitor against the Barbary states seems clear in view of later events.[4]

Aware that exit from the British Empire also would mean the withdrawal of maritime protection, American statesmen turned to the French for assistance against the Barbary pirates. In the interest of reducing the power of Great Britain, France in February 1778 signed treaties of amity, commerce, and alliance with the United States but would do no more than promise to use its "influence" or "good offices" with the states of North Africa. Still, American leaders saw grounds for optimism. In the late winter of 1778, Muhammad XVI, ruler of Morocco, foreswore any hostile intentions toward U.S. ships and invited them to visit Moroccan ports. He followed up this invitation with an agreement to send a consul to Philadelphia. This consul, D'Audibert Caille, a French merchant who had lived in Morocco for several years, came to the United States, where he worked to foster friendly relations between the two countries. One of his actions was to urge Benjamin Franklin, then minister to France, to arrange a present for the Moroccan emperor for which purpose Franklin assiduously sought funds from Congress.

Paralyzed by the absence of authority under the Articles of Confederation and preoccupied with the conclusion of the War of Independence, Congress failed to do anything about relations with Morocco or any of the Barbary countries until May 1784. It then issued a resolution thanking Muhammad XVI for his friendly approach and commissioned Jefferson, Franklin, and Adams to negotiate agreements with the Barbary states. With scant congressional instruction, these three peace commissioners acted alone to formulate U.S. policy toward the Barbary countries.

Not long afterward the United States suffered its first hijacking by Muslim pirates. Incensed that he had not received presents despite his expressions of goodwill, the emperor of Morocco permitted the seizure of the *Betsey* on October 1, 1784. Although the Moroccans did not enslave the ship's crew, they held the men prisoner for over nine months, permitting their release only after intervention and mediation by the government of Spain and the payment by the United States of ransom in the amount of $30,000. Having lost their own ship on account of its unseaworthiness, the captives upon release traveled to Cádiz on July 18, 1785, aboard a Spanish vessel.

After three years of discussion the United States and Morocco signed a treaty in January 1787. Several features of this agreement held special meaning for the United States, including provision for the respect of neutral rights and the repatriation of captured seamen. The treaty stipulated that the latter would not be enslaved and that the United States would not have to pay ransom or tribute.[5]

Unfortunately, the agreement with Morocco had no impact on the other Barbary states. Algiers soon became a problem when it concluded a peace treaty with Spain, thereby ending a war between these two countries. The pact lifted the Spanish blockade of the Straits of Gibraltar and gave Algerian pirates access to the Atlantic. On July 25, 1785, only seven days after the crew of the *Betsey* had arrived in Cádiz from Morocco, Algerian pirates, sanctioned by their government and manning a fourteen-gun vessel, approached the schooner *Maria* near Cape St. Vincent, boarded it, and took it and the crew of six captive. On July 31 another Algerian ship captured the Boston-based vessel *Dauphin* as it sailed toward Lisbon. Within a week, Algiers had captured two American vessels and enslaved twenty-one men. These actions were quickly followed by the brazen announcement that Algiers was at war with all countries unwilling to pay tribute and that the American seamen would be released only when the United States ransomed them and agreed to purchase a peace treaty.[6]

Although Algiers was a small country with limited resources, its naval power should not be minimized, certainly when compared to the virtually nonexistent American force. Algiers may have had as many as nine warships in 1785; it may have had either sixteen, if one accepts Jefferson's estimate, or as many as forty-seven, if the *Massachusetts Centinel* were to be believed. Whatever the correct number, the force would prove formidable.[7] Some of the vessels, including many that attacked American ships, were xebecs, small three-masted vessels with triangular and square sails. Others, of which Algiers had several, were barques, which were three-to-five-mast sailing ships with all of the masts square rigged except the aftermast, which was fore-and-aft rigged. The Algerians, like the other Barbary corsairs, were not especially good seamen and could have been thwarted fairly easily if the countries they preyed upon had acted in concert, but that was clearly a central problem for the United States. Furthermore, the Algerian pirates were not perceived as particularly pleasant people. Generally speaking, they were shabbily clothed, turbaned, fierce-looking, saber-wielding thieves with little regard for human life, except for what it would fetch in negotiations between their rulers and other countries.

As the men commissioned to deal with the Barbary pirates, Adams and Jefferson (by this time Franklin had left for home) had two major goals: to secure the early release of the American prisoners and prevent a recurrence of these incidents. Since the immediate concern was the fate of the hostages, they asked John Lamb, a sea captain of Norwich, Connecticut, with prior experience in dealing with the Barbary states, to go to Algiers to ransom the prisoners for no more than $200 per man. In September 1785, Lamb, with congressional authorization, arrived in Paris to begin his quest to gain the release of the Americans.

When Lamb finally reached Algiers in March 1786, after lengthy malingering in Spain that evoked the contempt of both Adams and Jefferson, he faced a formidable task.[8] He learned that the treatment accorded the American hostages, both aboard the sloop transporting them to Algiers and in captivity within the country, was bestially abusive, meaning that there was a sense of urgency about his assignment. The Algerian corsairs stripped the Americans of most of their clothing, put them in irons during the trip back to North Africa, and fed them a diet of stale bread, black olives, and polluted water. Once they arrived in Algiers, most of the men faced hard labor, with few amenities of civilized life. If they rebelled or sought normal human contact with their compatriots or captors, they were beaten mercilessly, especially on the soles of their feet, on their thighs, and on their buttocks. They lived in an overcrowded, rat-infested, stench-ridden, windowless slave prison where they slept on the floor like animals.[9]

After several days of maneuvering, the dey of Algiers finally agreed to meet with Lamb on April 1, but only on his own terms. (The rulers of Algiers held the title "dey" because at one point in the past the term reflected a looser relationship to Constantinople than the title "bey," used in all the other Barbary states, but the distinction had become unimportant by the 1780s.) He demanded ransom and promised no treaty. Jefferson and Adams had authorized the expenditure of $4,700 for the twenty-one Americans. Lamb exceeded his instructions and offered $10,000. When the dey insisted that he would take no less than $50,000, Lamb offered $30,000, and then raised the offer to $50,000 as it became apparent that nothing less would suffice. But the U.S. envoy did not have $50,000, and he knew that Congress would have to authorize such a large expenditure. He asked for time to raise the money; left Algiers for Spain, where he resigned his commission; and never returned to North Africa. In the meantime, he did not inform his government of his promise to the Algerians, a mistake of the worst sort given the position of the hostages. After a further period of strained relations with Jefferson, Lamb finally returned to the United States in the early summer of 1787 to face a reprimand from an annoyed Congress.

Several months before Lamb's return, however, a despairing Jefferson had turned to a French religious order known as the Mathurins for assistance. This organization, the Order of the Holy Trinity and Redemption of Captives, worked for a fee and for many years had engaged in the business of negotiating the return of hostages from Barbary countries. (The order went out of existence during the French Revolution.) Unfortunately, this attempt to free the Americans was also unsuccessful.[10]

If Jefferson and Adams were troubled by the plight of the captives, they were equally vexed with the larger policy questions raised by the seizure of U.S. vessels. The United States had no navy, no available revenue to build one, no strong central government able to give direction on national security matters, and no will to project power into other parts of the world. Always small, the American navy had come out of the War of Independence with only five warships, and within two years Congress had auctioned these off.[11] But the prospect of an indefinite circumscription of its commerce by distant pirates, whose sole motive was the acquisition of ransom and tribute, seemed too painful to endure. Something had to be done. Adams worried about the cost of a navy and about the willingness of Congress to appropriate money for a war, which he saw as considerably more costly than the short-term payment of tribute. However, expressing concern that the United States would become "prey to every robber, pirate, and cheat" unless it developed the power to resist, Adams was prepared to fight if the various American states, especially in the South, would go along. The Barbary pirates issue offered "a good occasion to build a navy."[12]

Of the two men, Jefferson comes across as the more militant on the issue of pirates. His predilection was toward "neither commerce nor navigation, but to stand with respect to Europe, precisely on the footing of China." He knew, however, that his countrymen did not agree; they were a venturesome, commercial people whose interests in world markets would require protection. Certainly, Jefferson believed, no American going abroad on legitimate business should face imprisonment at the hands of rapacious, ransom-mongering barbarians.[13] His solution was war, an opinion he expressed most forcefully in a letter of July 11, 1786. Arguing that justice, honor, and respect among the nations of Europe required it, he further stated that building a navy capable of coercing the North Africans would represent the least expensive course in the long run and would "arm the federal head with the safest of all instruments of coercion over their delinquent members." Although Jefferson worried about the threat of a standing army to democratic institutions, he was not overly concerned about the creation of a navy, which could exercise its power only indirectly on American citizens. Nor did he object to the establishment of a strong federal government at this point in his life.[14]

Jefferson's desire to punish the Barbary states was not limited to unilateral action by the United States. He went on to suggest the conclusion of a naval alliance with other less powerful maritime nations in the hope that together the countries might create "a perpetual cruise" that would force the pirates to let them alone. Since money and fear were the two influences of consequence in the Mediterranean area, it would be necessary for the United States to choose. Unfortunately, as Jefferson understood all too well, paying tribute probably meant paying more tribute, and he emphasized "our determination to prefer war in all cases to tribute under any form and to any people whatever." Only force would suffice.[15]

Jefferson took a market-oriented position toward the hostage issue as well. He worried that if the United States offered too much money for the prisoners, or if by chance it offered more than the European countries, such action would encourage the seizing of more Americans. Likewise, he refused to allow the Spanish representative in Algiers to give American hostages any more than a small allowance, thinking that this also would trigger the targeting of Americans. Jefferson followed a similar policy in writing to the hostages, in the belief that any hint of overeagerness to redeem the men would make matters worse.[16]

As the Articles of Confederation gave way to the Constitution and the new government it mandated, Adams, Jefferson, and other national leaders assumed that greater federal power would enable the country to settle the Barbary problem. It was not so easy. Six of the twenty-one prisoners held in Algiers had died by 1789, while the others awaited a similar fate unless Congress appropriated funds to redeem them. During the first year of George Washington's administration, nothing was done about the problem, owing largely to the host of other issues requiring attention. Finally, in 1791, Congress appropriated $40,000 to ransom the remaining hostages (but nothing yet to build a naval force). The money was inadequate to the task. In 1792, Congress came up with $50,000 and commissioned naval hero John Paul Jones to negotiate with the Algerians, but Jones, already wracked by kidney and liver disease, contracted pneumonia and died in Paris before even learning of the assignment. His successor, Thomas Barclay, the U.S. consul in Morocco, also died before undertaking the trip to Algiers.

Although public opinion did not influence American policy in the late eighteenth century in the way it would in the twentieth, its impact was not totally absent, and both Congress and the Washington administration had to pay some attention. In 1794 a Republican society in Baltimore urged that something be done to relieve the suffering of Americans in Algiers. The *Boston Gazette* expressed criticism for the increased cost of living in New England caused by Algerian piracy, and citizens in both the northeastern and southeastern parts of the country wrote letters to the president and Congress asking that the prisoners receive greater aid and that further insults to the nation be prevented.[17]

Efforts at negotiation continued. In the spring of 1793 the Washington administration appointed David Humphreys, then the U.S. minister to Portugal, to secure the release of the prisoners, only eleven of whom remained alive because of the ravages of the bubonic plague and the mental and physical cruelty of captivity. Negotiating a treaty with Algiers became more difficult in 1793 after that country signed a truce with Portugal, thereby once again allowing the Algerian corsairs easy access to the Atlantic. Within only a few months, Algiers seized a number of American vessels, taking over one hundred hostages in the process. These men petitioned Congress for funds to secure their release, usually in the most forlorn and pitiable terms, and some of them did arrange ransom through private sources. Most of them, however, remained prisoners into the mid-1790s.

Meanwhile, on March 17, 1794, Congress moved to create a navy to punish the corsairs and protect American interests. Unfortunately, this action would have little immediate effect both because it took time to construct the six vessels authorized and because the United States soon became entangled in the war between France and Great Britain that followed the French Revolution. The most important result of Congress's decision was the anger that the naval authorization caused among some of its Republican opponents. Their opinions received particularly forceful expression from William Maclay of Pennsylvania who worried about the threat to liberty in the creation of an external enemy; war with the Barbary pirates, he thought, would be little more than a pretext for building a strong central government capable of dominating the states. "War is often entered into to answer domestic, not foreign purposes," he stated. "I fear such was the design of the present report."[18]

Given the number of men in captivity and the impossibility at that time of securing their early release with military force, the Washington administration had no choice but to buy a deal with the dey of Algiers. To this end, the U.S. government appointed as its representative Joseph Donaldson, Jr., of Philadelphia, who arrived in the North African country on September 3, 1795. Described as "a remarkably surly man" possessed of "a forbidding countenance," Donaldson found himself in an assignment certain to try the patience of the most even-tempered and warm-humored of envoys.

Donaldson's first contact with the Algerians produced a bilious outcry from the U.S. "diplomat." Debarking at the harbor in Algiers on a hot and humid summer day, Donaldson had to make his way into town on foot, a long trek made most disagreeable by the pain from his gout and the press of a large crowd of curious onlookers and children who kept running across his path and bumping into him. Moreover, his appearance was hardly likely to win over his Muslim hosts, as he was wearing a cocked hat and had his right leg wrapped in flannel and the gouty toes of his right foot encased in a large velvet slipper. When he finally arrived at his quarters, according to an eyewitness, "he uttered a string of ejaculations and execrations so equally mixed together that I could not tell which predominated."[19]

Despite the Muslim Sabbath, the dey initiated negotiations with Donaldson on the following morning. He offered to release the American prisoners and sign a peace treaty for $2,247,000 in cash, two 35-gun frigates, a large amount of naval stores, and presents of various sorts. When Donaldson countered with $543,000, James Cathcart, one of the hostages employed as personal secretary for the dey, expressed his fear that the volatile Algerian ruler would roast them both alive. However, after an initial paroxysm of rage, the dey came back with a demand for $982,000, which Donaldson, either out of dauntless courage or blind ignorance, rejected.

When Donaldson made preparations to leave on September 4, the dey responded by agreeing to accept a payment of $585,000 plus naval stores and presents. This package comprised the settlement terms, and a peace treaty was signed on this basis on September 5, an agreement replicating the language of an accord between Algiers and Sweden of 1723. Although the treaty resulted in a twenty-one-gun salute to the American flag and other ceremonial presentations, it did not bring the immediate release of the seamen. Donaldson, irascible and cranky in the extreme, decided that the sailors, given their years of captivity, would cut loose in an orgy of drunkenness if set free immediately; incredibly, he recommended only the release of the captains. Infuriated by this decision, the sailors, whose bonds of captivity the dey had temporarily loosened, occupied Donaldson's residence until the U.S. envoy asked the Algerian gendarme to remove them. This action concluded with the beating of the "offending" sailors for no other reason than the crotchets of the man sent to secure their release.[20]

Having thus concluded the peace treaty with Algiers, Donaldson sent it to the United States for ratification. Arrangements also went forward to transfer the money, although the latter proved much more difficult than the former, largely because the war between France and England had created a scarcity of gold in European banking houses. Finally, payment was arranged (all the specie did not reach Algiers until January 1797) and the hostages released. They arrived at Marseilles on July 20, 1796; then, after a quarantine period of nearly three months, sixty-five of them sailed for Philadelphia, where they landed in February 1797. The remaining men had died either of the plague or of hardships related to their captivity, or had taken jobs on other sailing vessels.[21] By 1797 the United States had paid over $1 million in ransom and tribute to rescue American seamen. It had secured the release of 112 men and had bought precarious "peace" with the governments of Morocco and Algiers. Yet difficulty with the Barbary pirates was far from over.

In January 1797, two months before the Washington administration turned the presidency over to John Adams, U.S. envoy Joel Barlow signed a treaty with Tripoli in which the United States bought peace for $56,486. A similar treaty with Tunis cost $107,000, owing in large measure to the seizure of an American ship by Tunisian pirates, which gave them greater bargaining power. Although this latter agreement gave the United States formal treaties with all the Barbary states, Tripolitan anger over having received less money than did their Tunisian counterparts soon led Tripoli to declare war. "Peace" with Algiers proved equally ephemeral.

The absence of appropriate naval power, not to mention the preoccupation with events in Europe, continued to plague the United States. When the resolution to build a navy came before the House of Representatives in 1794, some of Jefferson's staunchest friends opposed it, despite his own pro-navy stance. James Madison, for instance, led the opposition, arguing strenuously that it would be cheaper for the United States to buy Portuguese protection than to build a navy and that a navy would threaten the young nation's democratic institutions as well as its purse. The resolution passed by only two votes, while the bill authorizing the actual building of six vessels passed in March by a margin of only eleven. It probably would have failed without a provision specifying that if peace could be arranged with Algiers, the naval building would cease. Accordingly, in the spring of 1796, when Congress heard of the treaty with Algiers, anti-Federalist leaders, at the insistence of Albert Gallatin, began urging the discontinuation of the naval program. Only the intervention of President Washington and strong support from naval proponents in Congress succeeded in saving three frigates.[22]

Although the Department of the Navy came into existence in 1798, the Adams administration could not use developing American power to discipline the Barbary pirates, given the need to preserve the nation's independence against the British and French. Both of the warring European countries tried to take advantage of U.S. shipping, and both compromised America's neutrality by impressing its seamen and seizing cargoes bound for the other belligerent. The main concerns from 1798 to 1800 were French attacks on American shipping; the XYZ affair, in which three representatives (later designated as X, Y, and Z) of the French foreign minister, Charles-Maurice de Talleyrand, demanded a bribe in the fall of 1797 and a loan from President Adams's delegation to Paris as a precondition to the improvement of Franco-American relations; and, finally, the undeclared war with France. The latter resulted in the building of a U.S. navy, but, with the resolution of the French crisis in 1800, pressures again mounted for dissolving the force.

Before Adams left the presidency, he made a number of recommendations on the navy, only some of which were adopted. He urged the selling of small or poorly built vessels and the retention of thirteen ships, six of which would remain in constant service with the others in reserve for emergency use. In addition, he asked Congress to appropriate funds for twenty-five new ships and for all the supplies needed to keep them in good repair. The bill that Congress ultimately passed in March 1801 required the president to sell all but thirteen ships and to keep only six in regular service. Jefferson moved forward with the implementation of this law until faced with new challenges in the Mediterranean.[23]

In February 1801 the pasha of Tripoli, angered that both Tunis and Algiers had signed more lucrative agreements than he, repudiated his treaty with the United States and demanded a one-time payment of $250,000 and tribute of $20,000 per annum. When in May he perceived that the payment was not forthcoming, he chopped down the flagpole at the American consulate and declared war. This action prompted Jefferson, now president, to send four naval vessels commanded by Commodore Richard Dale to blockade Tripolitan ports. When Morocco declared war on the United States because the blockade interfered with Moroccan-Tripolitan trade, Jefferson dispatched a reinforcing squadron under Commodore Edward Preble to the Mediterranean, a show of force that quickly led Morocco to drop its war declaration and return to the terms of the 1787 treaty. But the war with Tripoli did not end so easily.

At one point during the conflict, Tripoli gained tremendous leverage from American misfortune. Captain William Bainbridge of the frigate *Philadelphia*, one of the blockading vessels, began pursuing a Tripolitan cruiser, got too close to the shore, and ran his ship aground on a reef just outside the harbor of Tripoli. On October 31, 1803, he and his 307-man crew became prisoners and slaves of the pasha and endured captivity for over eighteen months. Furthermore, Tripoli seized the *Philadelphia* and incorporated it into its navy. For a while the only real "victory" Americans could celebrate was the sinking of the *Philadelphia*, an act arranged and carried out by Lieutenant Stephen Decatur and a handful of his seamen in a daring raid during the night of February 16, 1804. But while this denied Tripoli the use of the ship, it did little to win the war. To that end, the blockade had a much more telling effect.

The United States also attempted an overland offensive to put pressure on the pasha. William Eaton, former American consul at

Tunis, adventurer, and glory seeker, made contact with Hamet Caramanli, the pasha's elder brother living in exile in Egypt, who wished to seize the throne of Tripoli for himself. With the approval of Secretary of State James Madison, Eaton organized a group of American marines and sailors to join Caramanli for a five hundred-mile trek across the Libyan desert for an attack on Tripoli. They succeeded in capturing the city of Derne in April 1805 with the assistance of a couple of American naval vessels.

Efforts to achieve a negotiated settlement proceeded simultaneously with the military action. Tobias Lear, the U.S. consul general at Algiers, began discussions with the pasha over the monetary terms for releasing the American hostages, with Lear offering $60,000 and the Tripolitan ruler demanding $130,000. For reasons presumably related to the two-pronged military action and the capture of Derne, the pasha settled for $60,000, thus giving the United States the release of its prisoners and a generous treaty containing provisions for commercial privilege and the rights of American seamen. The agreement of June 1805 also specified that the United States would not only withdraw its support from Caramanli but also would persuade him to leave Tripoli. Therefore, just as the pretender to the throne seemed on the verge of success, he was to be discarded. To placate him the United States provided hush money in the amount of $200 per month for two years and a final lump-sum payment of $2,400. Eaton, largely responsible for the military leverage, was not so easily mollified and spent the rest of his days attacking Lear for undercutting him. He believed that a military solution would have obviated the payment of ransom and settled the difficulty with Tripoli once and for all.[24]

During the war with Tripoli, the United States clashed with Tunis when three vessels of that country tried to run the American blockade of the Tripolitan ports and fell under the control of the U.S. navy. The bey of Tunis threatened war unless the United States returned these vessels, which it had taken to Malta for safekeeping. As the crisis deepened, the United States moved a large fleet consisting of nine frigates and eight gunboats to Tunisian waters.[25] Impressed by this show of force, the Tunisian ruler temporarily backed off and decided to send a representative to Washington to negotiate the return of the vessels. This envoy, Sedi Soliman Mellimelli, became the first Muslim official to visit the United States and, in the opinion of most Americans with whom he came in contact, preferably the last. Comporting himself aggressively, crudely, and ostentatiously, he and his retinue quickly wore out their welcome; in the end he failed to work out a solution to Tunisian-American differences. Mellimelli's return to North Africa in the fall of 1806 after a year abroad coincided with the beginning of war between Tunis and Algiers, which precluded conflict with the United States, a country whose size and strength the bey, given his envoy's reports, apparently now comprehended. The United States signed an agreement with Tunis in the winter of 1807 whereby the former agreed to pay $10,000 as compensation for the captured vessels and received "peace" from the Tunisian ruler.

Owing largely to the resumption of war in Europe in 1803 and the struggle to maintain American neutrality in the face of challenges by both the British and the French, President Jefferson withdrew most of the fleet from the Mediterranean in 1806 and 1807. Although no definitive proof is available, this action seems to have encouraged Algiers to move boldly against American shipping, as did the tardiness of U.S. tribute payments, which by 1807 were in arrears by about twenty months. Algiers seized three American vessels in the fall of 1807, holding the crews and cargoes of two of them until the United States resumed tribute payments. The other ship escaped after the captives overwhelmed their Algerian captors, threw four of them into the sea, and held one young Muslim boy as hostage. Apparently recognizing the inability of the Americans to play the hostage game, the new ruler of Algiers demanded an indemnity of nearly $20,000 in March 1808 for the "inhumane" acts perpetrated by American sailors. The United States paid the money.[26]

In the context of America's world relations, the Barbary pirates simply did not assume primary importance from 1807 to 1815. Jefferson and Madison worked assiduously to build respect for their nation's rights and to avoid entanglement in the European war, all the while knowing that conflict could occur with either Great Britain or France. In 1808 they implemented the Embargo Act, which cut off all trade with other nations and almost bankrupted the United States. They then replaced the embargo with the March 1809 Nonintercourse Act, which forbade trade with Britain and France but permitted commerce with the rest of the world. Neither of these acts nor the measures that followed them worked satisfactorily, and the impressment-maritime rights issue brought a breakdown in relations and, in 1812, war with Great Britain. Only afterward could the United States confront the Barbary pirates head on.

Meanwhile, the North African countries, particularly Tunis and Algiers, took advantage of the American preoccupation to seize numerous merchant vessels and their crews. In 1810 the dey threatened to imprison Americans in his country unless the United States turned a vessel of disputed ownership over to him, a demand with which the American consul quickly complied. From 1809, when the Algerian navy seized the U.S. merchantman *Sally* and took it and its crew of fifteen men hostage, until 1815, Algiers stole cargoes and enslaved dozens of American seamen with impunity. Some of these men received provisions and money from private sources through the American consul, and for some of them Congress authorized ransom payments.

The conflict with Great Britain having happily concluded on the basis of the status quo ante bellum, the United States declared war on Algiers on March 2, 1815. Two formidable fleets, one under the command of Decatur and the other under Bainbridge, arrived in the Mediterranean in late June of that year preparatory to an attack on Algerian and other Barbary shipping. Within days the U.S. naval vessel *Guerrière* attacked and captured an Algerian warship with over four hundred men aboard. Shortly thereafter, other vessels of the U.S. fleets seized an Algerian brig carrying 180 crewmen. Using the captured ships and men as leverage, Decatur and William Shaler, whom Secretary of State James Monroe had sent along as consul general to the Barbary states, negotiated a treaty with Algiers calling for an end to the hostage/ransom/tribute system.

In July and August, U.S. naval power settled some old scores with Tunis and Tripoli. Both countries had released to Great Britain prize vessels that American ships had captured from the British during the War of 1812 and taken to Tunisian and Tripolitan ports. The presence of superior naval force facilitated pledges of compensation, $46,000 from Tunis and $25,000 from Tripoli, in agreements that Decatur helped to negotiate. Neither country thereafter posed a serious threat to American shipping and neither took further hostages.[27]

American naval power, which in the aftermath of the War of 1812 consisted of dozens of warships and gunboats, clearly played a part in subduing the aggressive behavior of the Barbary states.[28] Before ascribing too much influence to this force, however, one should note two important points: the international community had clearly become exasperated with the North African countries and upon the conclusion of the Napoleonic Wars decided to put a stop to their piratical activity; and the mercantilistic practice of using the pirates to reduce the commerce of competitors no longer served the individual interests of the major western European nations. Accordingly, the Congress of Vienna created an international commission with the power to recommend termination of the tribute system. This body then quickly turned to Great Britain, the world's greatest naval power, as the executor of a plan to teach the Barbary states a lesson in modern diplomacy. The initial unwillingness of Algiers to accept a British demand for an agreement abolishing tribute and the enslavement of Christians evoked a harsh reaction: in 1816 a combined British-Dutch fleet destroyed the bey's navy and bombarded Algiers until the dey finally agreed to terms. Thus, it was the international community and not just the United States that checked the Barbary menace.

The activity of the pirates did not cease in 1815–16. The United States kept a patrolling force in the Mediterranean until the French occupied Algiers in 1830 because some piracy continued informally throughout this period. In fact, it persisted until the late nineteenth century when the pirate ships of North Africa became no match for the modern, technologically superior merchant craft from the West.[29]

THAT THE CRISIS with the Barbary pirates has become little more than a footnote in American history is evident in the amount of time and attention given to this episode in classroom lectures and textbooks. Its significance should not be minimized, either as a factor in the national experience down to 1815 or as a segment of the nation's past with meaning for the present, given the terrorism of the twentieth century.

From 1784 to 1815 the Barbary countries captured over thirty-six American merchantmen and one naval ship, imprisoning and enslaving in the process roughly seven hundred sailors. Of these men, either the U.S. government or private agencies managed to secure the release of all but sixty-seven, a fairly impressive record when compared to that of the last half of the twentieth century when the United States had become the world's preeminent military power. It is true, however, that many of the men imprisoned in North Africa gained their freedom only after years of enslavement and brutal treatment at the hands of their captors. At least twenty-eight, and probably many more, died in the pestilent prisons of Algiers, Tunis, and Tripoli.[30]

As might be expected, the existence of U.S. hostages in a foreign land elicited the same range of emotions among the American people in the eighteenth and early nineteenth centuries as in the twentieth: feelings of outrage, contempt for the kidnappers, frustration, and helplessness. When it became apparent that Congress had limited ability to deal with the Barbary states, citizens' groups arose to protest and lobby, especially in cities along the seaboard. Societies comprising thousands of people came into existence not only to raise money to ransom the hostages but also to apply political pressure on those responsible for American foreign policy. A typical letter from a concerned citizen in Connecticut to President Washington began: "I have lately travelled through the N. England states. . . . The Generale topick was the times but principally the sufferings of our citizens among the Algerines." Newspapers took up the cause, and a large group from Philadelphia demanded that the federal government do more to protect American commerce.[31]

One of the greatest problems that faced the Founding Fathers, in view of the divisive political and economic issues of the time, was fashioning a foreign policy that embodied the national interest. The Northeast, South, and West held dramatically differing opinions on the economy. Those Americans living on the seaboard, particularly in New England, recognized the need for credit and trade that only could come through satisfactory relations with Great Britain. People from this region, generally speaking, allowed their economic interests to override old political hatreds. In fact, such interests led them to return to their prerevolutionary interpretation of the virtues of the English system of balancing political power as superior to that of any other country, including France. This perception became particularly true after the excesses of the French Revolution. Great Britain not only had much to offer economically, but it also represented a stable and well-ordered society when compared to the France of the revolutionary and Napoleonic eras.

The South and West, by contrast, held the British in supreme contempt. These regions had become heavily indebted to Great Britain owing to their reliance on English manufactured goods, their dependence on its merchants to market their goods, and their ties with its carrying trade. This resentment was reinforced by the Revolutionary War experience during which Great Britain engaged the Americans in a disproportionate number of battles in the South. The agricultural regions of the country, moreover, did not perceive British political institutions as sufficiently superior to those of the French to overcome their deeper aversions to the former mother country.[32]

In a sense the cleavage occurred because of a revolutionary ideology that promoted a "two worlds" concept of international relations. The earlier consensus that had existed on foreign affairs in all regions of the country began to break down as the maritime section of the United States, represented by the Federalists, increasingly sought accommodation with the Old World. Republican admiration for France, on the other hand, rested initially on the belief that the overthrow of the old order in that country signaled a mutual acceptance of republican principles.

The overriding significance of the dispute with the Barbary pirates is that it injected a third world into the calculations of American national interest, a barbarian world about which Americans developed general agreement. It is true that the atrocities of the Barbary states contributed to the debate over national power and

specifically over the need for a navy, a topic that triggered controversy between the mercantile and southern rural parts of the country; and some of Jefferson's most devoted supporters became the
staunchest opponents of naval power. But the more important facts
are that Jefferson himself favored the creation of a navy, that he
and Adams found themselves in agreement, and that Congress appropriated funds for a naval force prior to the undeclared war with
France. Historians have portrayed the Adams-Jefferson thinking on
this issue as ironic, given their differing ideologies and predisposi-
tions. Actually, the meeting of the minds of these two men represents in microcosm the main importance of the Barbary question: it
led to unity and a rudimentary sense of national interest in a weak
and divided country.

NOTES

1. See Gaddis Smith, "The U.S. vs. International Terrorists," *American Heri-
tage* 28, no. 5 (August 1977): 39, 43; Paul W. Bamford, *The Barbary Pirates:
Victims and the Scourge of Christendom* (Minneapolis: University of Minnesota
Press, 1972), 5–18; and Peter Earle, *Corsairs of Malta and Barbary* (London:
Sidgwick and Jackson, 1970), 6–18.

2. Bamford, *Barbary Pirates*, 5–18; Earle, *Malta and Barbary*, 6–18.

3. Albert Hourani, *A History of the Arab Peoples* (Cambridge, MA: Harvard
University Press, 1991), 250–53.

4. See Frederick W. Marks, *Independence on Trial: Foreign Affairs and the
Making of the Constitution* (1973; reprint ed., Wilmington, DE: Scholarly Re-
sources, 1986), 37–38; Raymond Bixler, *The Open Door on the Old Barbary
Coast* (New York: Pageant Press, 1959), 10; Smith, "Terrorists," 37–38; and
Gary E. Wilson, "American Hostages in Moslem Nations, 1784–1796: The Pub-
lic Response," *Journal of the Early Republic* 2, no. 2 (Summer 1982): 123–24.

5. Wilson, "American Hostages," 124–26.

6. Smith, "Terrorists," 38; Wilson, "American Hostages," 125–27.

7. Gary E. Wilson, "The First American Hostages in Moslem Nations, 1784–
1789," *American Neptune* 41 (July 1981): 214.

8. Frank E. Ross and M. A. Washington, "The Mission of John Lamb to
Algiers, 1785–1786," *Americana* 28 (July 1934): 287–94.

9. Liva Baker, "Cathcart's Travels or a Dey in the Life of an American Sailor,"
American Heritage 26, no. 4 (June 1975): 53; Wilson, "First American Hostages,"
215–16.

10. Ray W. Irwin, *The Diplomatic Relations of the United States with the
Barbary Powers, 1776–1816* (Chapel Hill: University of North Carolina Press,
1931), 44–46; Marks, *Independence on Trial*, 42; Wilson, "First American Hostages," 218–19, and "American Hostages," 127.

11. Winston B. Lewis, "The Birth of a Navy," *U.S. Naval Institute Proceedings* 101 (1975): 22–23, 63.

12. James A. Field, in *America and the Mediterranean World, 1776–1882*
(Princeton, NJ: Princeton University Press, 1969), 34–48, stresses the differences

between Adams and Jefferson but then shows how both Federalists and Republicans came to support the navy. See also Smith, "Terrorists," 39.

13. Smith, "Terrorists," 38.

14. Dumas Malone, *Jefferson and the Rights of Man* (Boston: Little, Brown and Company, 1951), 27–28, 30; Smith, "Terrorists," 39; Wilson, "First American Hostages," 217–18.

15. Quoted in Field, *America and the Mediterranean World*, 43; Smith, "Terrorists," 39.

16. Wilson, "First American Hostages," 221.

17. Wilson, "American Hostages," 134–37.

18. Smith, "Terrorists," 40; Wilson, "American Hostages," 128–38.

19. Frank E. Ross, "Mission of Joseph Donaldson to Algiers, 1795–97," *Journal of Modern History* 7, no. 4 (December 1935): 425.

20. Ibid., 424–33.

21. Wilson, "American Hostages," 138–41.

22. James A. Carr, "John Adams and the Barbary Problem: The Myth and the Record," *American Neptune* 26, no. 4 (October 1966): 240–43.

23. Ibid., 250–51.

24. Samuel F. Bemis, ed., *The American Secretaries of State and Their Diplomacy*, 10 vols. (New York: Cooper Square Publishers, 1963), 3:73–79.

25. In his report of April 26, 1806, James Cathcart advises James Madison that "our efforts . . . ought to be to effect the destruction of his [dey of Tunis] commerce; if our Squadron should be too much reduced, an offensive war will immediately take place." U.S. Department of State, Record Group 84, Records of the Foreign Service Posts of the Department of State, "Notes from the Legation of Tunis," no. 1 (Washington, DC: National Archives Microfilm Publications, 1943), 27.

26. Gary E. Wilson, "American Prisoners in Barbary Nations, 1784–1816" (Ph.D. diss., North Texas State University, 1979), 283–307.

27. Ibid.

28. Allan R. Millett and Peter Maslowski, *For the Common Defense: A Military History of the United States, 1607–1983* (New York: Free Press, 1984), 98–102, 118.

29. Wilson, "American Prisoners," 314–19; Carr, "Adams," 254.

30. Wilson, "American Prisoners," 314.

31. Wilson, "American Hostages," 133–38.

32. Paul A. Varg, *Foreign Policies of the Founding Fathers* (East Lansing: Michigan State University Press, 1963), 1–10.

Chapter 2

A Question of Character: The Mailed Fist of the Nineteenth Century

As the difficult experience with the Barbary pirates demonstrates, American policy toward those who endangered the lives and property of U.S. citizens through the nineteenth century differed substantially from the direction taken on such matters in the twentieth. In the earlier period, force became the fulcrum of the American approach: decisive, often brutal, retribution whenever the nation's military power would permit its use. Between the settlement with the Barbary states and the turn of the century, among the instances of foreign attacks on U.S. citizens were five in particular that engaged and kept the attention of officials in Washington: the killing of American seamen by a band of Malay pirates during the administration of Andrew Jackson; violence by an Argentine agent against U.S. citizens on the Falkland Islands, also during the Jackson administration; the Austrian arrest of the Hungarian national but declared citizen Martin Koszta in Turkey in 1852; Chilean violence against U.S. sailors during the *Baltimore* affair of 1891; and Chinese attacks on Americans during the Boxer Rebellion of 1900. In none of these episodes were foreign governments responsible for instigating the actions, although in all of them, governments— or in the case of the Malays, a quasi-government—eventually became involved. None of the incidents invoked vital American interests, but all of them raised questions about national honor.

In each of these cases, policymakers in Washington and military men on the scene acted in accordance with nineteenth-century notions of courage and honor as well as their perception of the pragmatic requirements of dealing with "less civilized" people. "True men" were willing to be tested by physical activity or struggle; masculine virtues counted for much and feminine ones for much less; strenuousness was an end in itself; a sense of will, firmness of purpose, resolution to endure, and capacity for action held top priority in the hierarchy of values; and the United States should never suffer indignities at the hands of those it thought to be physically, morally, intellectually, and, especially, racially inferior.

THE FIRST OF these episodes occurred along the northwestern coast of Sumatra in February 1831. Buyers from Salem and Boston had been engaging in the pepper trade with native growers in the area for several years, to the advantage of both the local growers and the American merchants. Indeed, the indigenous population on northern Sumatra had long favored U.S. interests over those of both the British and the Dutch, who had imperial designs in the region. Thus, it came as something of a surprise when, early on the morning of February 7, 1831, as the crew of the *Friendship* began taking on its load of pepper, local Malays from the village of Kuala Batu, a community of no more than five thousand inhabitants, attacked and killed several of the sailors and seized the cargo.

The events resemble those of a Hollywood movie. As the *Friendship*, a 316-ton vessel owned by a Salem, Massachusetts, company sat anchored off the coast of Kuala Batu, Captain Charles Endicott, two of the officers, and four members of the crew went ashore to oversee the weighing of the pepper. This supervision was necessary because both sides had been known to cheat in these transactions. While Endicott was ashore, his first officer, Charles Knight, allowed several armed natives to come aboard, whereupon these men attacked Knight, stabbed him and two crew members to death, and wounded three others. The remaining seamen dived overboard, swam to shore, and hid in the underbrush. The pirates proceeded to plunder the vessel of $12,000 of specie and nearly $30,000 worth of cargo, including twelve chests of opium. Whether the pirates'

main target was the opium is open to speculation; Captain Endicott concluded that they were addicts desperate for a fix. But they also took everything of value not excluding the instruments and provisions.

When Captain Endicott noticed the mayhem, he moved to save his ship and crew. He and the six men with him jumped into their small boats and began rowing frantically toward the *Friendship*. However, it quickly became apparent that other natives, who gave chase after Endicott, would prevent the rescue, and the captain and his men proceeded southward along the coast to the port community of Muckie, a town roughly twenty-five miles from Kuala Batu, where other American vessels were anchored. Crews from these ships assisted Endicott in retaking the *Friendship* on February 9. With the ship back in his possession, Endicott and his remaining crew set sail for the United States, arriving in Salem on June 16.[1]

The Jackson administration, upon learning of the attack, did not waste time in debating how to respond. Jackson and Secretary of the Navy Levi Woodbury decided that the United States must demand restitution or indemnity for the lives and property lost as well as punishment of the perpetrators of the crime. The president authorized the commissioning of Captain John Downes, commander of the frigate *Potomac*, a fifty-gun vessel carrying a crew of five hundred officers and men, for the Southeast Asian assignment. Downes's task was to gain an apology and an indemnity from the Malays, and if they did not respond favorably, to punish them severely; if they did not agree to end their violence against American shipping, he was to inform them that the president would send additional warships to complete the job.[2] Although Jackson, given the absence of any national interest in the region, had no policy toward Southeast Asia, he could not ignore the representations of congressmen from maritime districts, nor could he overcome his own prejudices. National honor required a response to the depredations of these "murderous barbarians."

Downes took his assignment seriously—too seriously, as it turned out. Leaving New York on August 26, he sailed to Rio de Janeiro and then on to the Cape of Good Hope. At Cape Town he received advice from British naval officers, who portrayed the Malays as irredeemably violent and unresponsive to persuasion and thus incapable of negotiation. He was advised to shoot first and ask questions later. Flying the Danish flag to mislead the natives, Downes arrived at Kuala Batu on February 5, 1832. During that afternoon he sent a part of his crew toward the coast, at least ostensibly to gauge the intentions of the "enemy." This party reported back that they had received hostile signs from the Batuans,

Commodore John Downes. *Courtesy National Archives*

allowing Downes to claim later that he made no demand for satisfaction because he was convinced, "from the knowledge I already
had of the character of the people, that no such demand would be
answered, except only by refusal."[3]

   At four o'clock the next morning, February 6, Downes sent
ashore a party of over 250 marines and sailors to avenge the attack
of the previous year. This force, which landed to the north of Kuala
Batu, quickly overran the town's three forts, primitive structures
built of sod and defended by small cannon and muskets, and burned

the town itself. The invading force did not recover any of the cargo from the *Friendship*, nor did it capture the raja or the perpetrators of the February 1831 attack. It did manage to kill approximately one hundred natives, including some women and children, while only two Americans were killed and seven wounded. After further bombardment of Kuala Batu and other villages along the coast by the cannon aboard the *Potomac*, the native authorities gave Downes their assurances that no further attacks against American commerce would occur, and the captain left Sumatran waters on February 18.[4]

Downes returned to a political storm in the United States. As a result of a letter written by one of the men aboard the *Potomac* and passed to another vessel, word of the U.S. attack had preceded Downes's arrival. Newspapers opposed to President Jackson, especially the *National Intelligencer*, engaged in heated editorializing in July 1832 about the illegality and immorality of the captain's actions. These reports of the bombardment and landing at Kuala Batu also coincided with the heated issue of Jackson's veto of a bill to renew the charter of the Second Bank of the United States. The president's critics argued that he had exceeded his constitutional authority in sending the mission in the first place, that he had committed an act of war without a congressional declaration. The *Washington Globe*, the proadministration and Democratic Party outlet, quickly countered by labeling Jackson's critics "learned Pufendorfs" deserving of contempt: "Shame," the *Globe* decried, "upon such unmanly and disingenuous subterfuges for party effect!"[5]

Jackson ultimately released a copy of his instructions to Downes, which proved that the latter had indeed exceeded his instructions. Then, the president and his subordinates proceeded to launch a defense of the action: Secretary of the Navy Woodbury announced that Downes had terminated the "menace" of the "sea-robbers" and extracted from them "acknowledgements of past errors" as well as promises not to repeat these errors.[6] In his message to Congress of December 1832, Jackson gave his views on the affair. "An act of atrocious piracy" had been committed against an American trading ship. He had dispatched a frigate to demand satisfaction and to "inflict chastisement." "This last was done, and the effect has been an increased respect for our own flag in those distant seas."[7]

Jackson's message reflected his perception of the value of "chastisement" in winning respect from these Southeast Asian "savages." But respect, like honor, credibility, and gratitude, is an ephemeral sentiment when applied to relations between sovereign states. It has almost no meaning at all in relationships with loosely organized villagers such as the Sumatrans against whom, in any event, the United States could not engage in any systematic, collaborative display of force as it did toward the Barbary states.

Despite Jackson's "lesson" to the natives, in 1838 another American ship in the same region was captured and pillaged, with loss of life. This time the American naval commander in the region, Commodore George C. Read, conducted a more judicious military/diplomatic action against the Sumatrans. He allowed the local rajas plenty of time to relinquish the murderers and compensate for the property loss, but when they failed to comply he, too, eventually resorted to military force; he bombarded Kuala Batu and then destroyed a local village, fortunately, in contrast to Downes's operation, causing only one Sumatran fatality.[8]

IN THE SAME MESSAGE to Congress in which he discussed the Malay pirates, Jackson cited a problem that his administration faced in the South Atlantic. An Argentine governor-proprietor in the Falkland Islands, Louis Vernet, had seized three American fishing schooners, one of which he arranged to send to Buenos Aires for adjudication, in August 1831. The president informed Congress that he was dispatching a squadron to the South Atlantic to protect American fishing rights in the region, rights that no pretender to authority over the Falklands could take away even if that individual claimed the full support of the Argentine government.[9]

Jackson thus placed the United States in the tangled web surrounding authority over the desolate islands and at the same time asserted his anger against the leadership in Buenos Aires. Alternately claimed by France, Great Britain, and Spain, the Falklands in the 1820s attracted the attention of the new government in Argentina. In 1764 the French had planted the first "colony" on the two 2,000-square-mile windswept islands, but in January 1765 the British established a settlement at Port Egmont. Spain, which had received confirmation of its ownership in the 1713 Treaty of Utrecht, took offense at the French and British and by 1774 had managed to supplant both these rivals. Spain held control until the Napoleonic Wars, at which time it began losing its American empire. In 1811, when Napoleon occupied Spain, the Spanish withdrew their garrisons, and eventually claim to the islands fell to the Argentines when a naval officer from that newly independent nation sailed out and took "possession." In 1823, Argentina appointed a governor and subsequently granted exclusive fishing and cattle-raising concessions to several individuals, including Louis Vernet, a French adventurer who had lived for some time in Germany and the United States before going to Argentina in the early 1820s. In June

1828, Vernet arrived on Soledad (or East Falkland) to take up his concession.[10]

In June 1829, Vernet became political and military governor, a position that he chose to take seriously. Because he had sole right to exploit the seal fisheries, but ships from other nations persisted in intruding, he vowed to enforce Argentine law. He moved to arrest anyone who violated his monopoly. He did not portray himself as the protector of the interests of Argentine colonists since the latter consisted of only seventy-five to one hundred hardy individuals. Acting under what he considered clear authority, Vernet seized the three American vessels, one of which quickly escaped to return to the United States to report the incident to President Jackson.[11]

Prior to Vernet's seizure, the U.S. attitude toward Argentina and the Falklands was essentially one of indifference. Since Argentine independence from Spain in 1810, Washington had conducted a perfunctory relationship with Buenos Aires while simultaneously accepting the primacy of Great Britain over the Falklands. Jackson inherited and continued the policy of protecting U.S. commercial interests while ignoring the sovereignty status of the islands.

In spite of Vernet's arbitrary action, better U.S. diplomatic representation might have averted a confrontation. The American minister in Argentina, John M. Forbes, a man of extraordinary talent and judgment, had died not long before the incident, leaving U.S. interests in the hands of a consul, George Slacum, who possessed a fiery temper, no tact, and few diplomatic skills. Slacum delivered a sharp message to Foreign Minister Don Tomás de Anchorena challenging Vernet's right to seize the American vessels and demanding Argentina's disavowal of the act. Anchorena's decision to put him off by denying that as consul he had any right to represent U.S. views only served to inflame Slacum.[12]

Simultaneous to this exchange, the USS *Lexington,* under Commander Silas Duncan, whose personality was no less aggressive than Slacum's, arrived at Buenos Aires and gave the consul an instrument of force. Duncan and Slacum agreed that the commander would sail to the Falklands to obtain "satisfaction" for the United States, an action that Duncan carried out with great efficiency. He entered Soledad harbor, took one of Vernet's assistants prisoner, seized all the guns on the island, burned the powder, destroyed the dwellings, and arrested most of the inhabitants. He declared East Falkland free and independent, then sailed away to Montevideo, Uruguay.[13] Argentine reaction was perfectly predictable: Foreign Minister Anchorena condemned the raid in the harshest terms and declared Slacum persona non grata.

Duncan's actions had not received the prior consent of President Jackson, who did not learn of them until much later. When he did become aware in April 1832, he heartily approved of the attack on the basis that Vernet was nothing but a pirate who deserved such harsh treatment. The president's position resembled that of James Monroe at the time of Jackson's own rampage through Spanish Florida in 1817. Neither the Argentines nor Vernet, Jackson believed, had any right to assert authority over international territory in which Americans had fished for over fifty years.

Through the summer of 1832 the matter devolved into a heated debate between Argentina and the United States, which came to a conclusion only after the fortuitous intervention of the British.

Slacum, anathema to the Argentines, returned home, but the political hack who assumed the diplomatic assignment in his place, a Massachusetts politician and longtime Jackson supporter named Francis Baylies, was equally volatile and tactless. His arrival in June resulted in little more than the restatement of the U.S. insistence that Vernet had no authority to interfere with American fishing. The Argentines, meanwhile, had begun demanding an indemnity for the damage that Commander Duncan had inflicted on the Falklands. In January 1833 the British vessel *Cleo* arrived at the islands, landed a contingent of marines, lowered the Argentine flag, put up the British colors, and deported the remaining Argentine subjects; Great Britain thus reasserted the claim that it had seemingly abandoned in the 1770s. The British agreed not to discriminate against American fishing vessels, thereby solving the problem for President Jackson, who remained strangely silent as Argentina then sought to invoke the Monroe Doctrine.[14] Jackson clearly allowed his concern for fishing rights and riposte to the "piratical" Argentines to take precedence over Monroe's statement of the principle of European noninterference in the Western Hemisphere.

Neither of these episodes during the Jackson administration assumed much importance in the nation's foreign policy, which simply did not represent a primary concern during the Jackson years. Indeed, if the Barbary pirates issue has become a mere footnote in most studies of diplomatic history, the Kuala Batu and Falklands affairs normally receive no mention at all. They are worthy of study principally as examples of nineteenth-century responses to violence against Americans involved in activities abroad.

NEARLY TWENTY YEARS later the United States engaged in a sharp confrontation with Austria over its treatment of a former officer in the Hungarian revolt of 1848. Martin Koszta, a subordinate to nationalist leader Louis Kossuth and a captain in the Hungarian revolutionary army, which fought valiantly for independence from the Austrian empire, became the object of this confrontation. When Austria crushed the Hungarian uprising in August 1849, Koszta, Kossuth, and many of their countrymen fled to Bulgaria and then to Turkey, where they went into exile. The Hungarians evoked the admiration of the American people, who saw the revolution as an attempt to emulate their own example; they particularly admired Kossuth, a figure who received tremendous adulation during his trip to the United States in 1851–52. Koszta remained in Turkey until May 1850 when he left for England, where he lived until emigrating to the United States in the fall of 1851. It was his stay there, and particularly his declaration on July 31, 1852, of his intention to become a citizen, that made him a significant figure in U.S. diplomacy.

Determined to become a good American, Koszta diligently studied English and sought to join the small army of upwardly mobile

immigrants in the United States. His first job was that of stevedore at the port of New York. Later he worked as a night watchman and a carpenter's apprentice. During his employment as night watchman in the lumberyard of German immigrant August Ritter, himself an 1848 revolutionary, Koszta soon impressed the firm's management with his ambitious nature and became a clerk in the enterprise. Hoping to branch out into the import-export business, Koszta's employer approached him in the summer of 1852 to propose making a trip to Turkey to explore the possibilities; with his contacts in the Greek, English, and Italian communities within Turkey and his language abilities, the young Hungarian seemed like the ideal person for such a mission. That Koszta's decision to go showed very poor judgment became evident in light of subsequent events.[15]

His troubles began in the late fall of 1852 after his arrival at the Turkish port of Smyrna on the Aegean Sea. Aware that he was treading in dangerous waters, given the fact that he had not yet achieved American citizenship, he contacted the U.S. consul to ask for protection as if he were a citizen. The consul in Smyrna apparently took pains to impress upon him that because he had not completed the naturalization process this was not possible; he could expect nothing beyond the "unofficial influence" that the consul could provide in the event he experienced difficulties. The Turks were more generous. They gave him an internal pass that afforded him privileges as a visiting foreigner, based on his declaration of intent to become a U.S. citizen. Turkish authorities were following an ancient custom of allowing Westerners to reside in the country as "subjects" of a foreign, Christian representative if they could portray themselves as coming under that representative's jurisdiction, even in an informal way.[16]

Armed with this certification, Koszta proceeded to carry out his employer's instructions in Smyrna and Constantinople, but it was in Smyrna that he chose to spend most of his time. It appears that temptations of the flesh overcame the young Hungarian, and he engaged in activities not encompassed by his assignment: he became romantically involved with two young ladies, the daughter of an Italian restaurant owner and a young French divorcée.[17] While Koszta, who thus far had made no attempt to remain inconspicuous, waited for a rendezvous with the restaurateur's daughter outside the family café, a group of thugs in the employ of the Austrian consul general at Smyrna—men who had identified him as a Hungarian exile—followed him and spied on him for several days, kidnapped him, and threw him in the bay. As he struggled to keep from drowning, additional assailants hauled him aboard a small lifeboat that transported him to the Austrian ship *Hussar* anchored nearby. He was now a prisoner, presumably ready for transport back to Austria, where he would be tried, convicted, and probably executed for his insurrectionary activity.

Koszta's friends and acquaintances immediately mobilized in his support. Both of his lady friends hurried to make contact with businessmen and public officials who could put pressure on the Austrian consul, Peter Ritter von Weckbecker, for the Hungarian's release. Meanwhile, the exile community, excited in the extreme,

Captain Duncan Ingraham. *Courtesy Library of Congress*

wanted to storm the Austrian ship and seize the prisoner from his captors. Dissuaded from that course of action, they conducted a search of Koszta's quarters in an attempt to find official papers, perhaps an American passport, to use in his defense. What they found was a copy of Koszta's declaration of intent to become a U.S. citizen. They thereupon hastened to take this document to the American consul, Edward Offley.[18]

The American navy was not known for its ubiquitousness in the mid-nineteenth century, but just as an American sloop had fortuitously appeared at Buenos Aires some twenty years before, one showed up at Smyrna just after Koszta's kidnapping. Naturally the exiles not only appealed to the consul but to the commander of the naval vessel as well. The ship was the USS *St. Louis,* and its commander, Captain Duncan Ingraham, was a veteran of the sea who at age fifty had already spent forty years in the navy. He had served during the War of 1812 on board the USS *Madison* at age ten.[19]

Ingraham had barely put into port on June 23 when a group from the foreign community called on him about the crisis at hand. In this group were some Italians, several Greeks, and a number of Hungarian exiles, all supported by the café society. Ingraham listened as they told of the kidnapping. He responded that he would study the matter and act upon his assessment of the situation. Several American and English businessmen followed soon after to see if anything could be done for Koszta.

Next came Consul Offley, who appeared on board ship not long after Ingraham wrote him a note about the matter. Offley's comments indicated the danger of delay. He could not do anything for the young Hungarian because technically Koszta was not yet a citizen, nor could the U.S. minister at Constantinople. Indeed, in the consul's opinion the whole matter would have to go to the State Department for final determination, a process that would take many months. In the meantime, the Austrians could present the United States and the world with a fait accompli in regard to Mr. Koszta; they could try and execute him before any word came out of Washington. The urgency was clear to Captain Ingraham; it was time to apply a little naval justice, to take summary action in accordance with the broad latitude naval commanders enjoyed in emergency situations. Ingraham and Offley then went to visit the captain of the *Hussar* where Koszta was being held captive.

Getting no satisfaction from the commanding officer, Offley and Ingraham then called upon Weckbecker, who arranged for them to interview Koszta. The Hungarian, who had spent the previous twelve hours or so in chains, his clothes still wet from the drenching in the bay, did not give the appearance of health and serenity.

He admitted that he did not have an American passport—only the document of intent—but at the same time expressed surprise at the harshness and arbitrariness of his treatment.[20]

Later, on the evening of June 23, a mob sympathetic to Koszta rioted outside the café where he had been kidnapped. The crowd attacked a couple of Austrian sailors, stabbed one of them to death, and battered the other with sticks and a chair as he fought to defend himself, barely escaping with his life. This action added to the highly charged atmosphere already present; when Austrian Consul Weckbecker found out about this outrage and lodged a formal protest with the Turkish governor of Smyrna, he became highly abusive, verbally attacking the Turks and their sultan. This prompted an exchange with the governor, an official up to this point sympathetic and respectful of the sailors, resulting in the physical assault of Weckbecker by the governor, who literally shoved the Austrian consul out the door. The Austrians now had further reason to be uncompromising.[21]

During the next two days, Offley and Ingraham wrote reports about the Koszta case to John Porter Brown, the American chargé d'affaires in Constantinople. Offley took the position that his government should not permit the Austrians to get away with the abduction. Ingraham expressed his continuing confusion and exasperation that Koszta had left the United States before getting his citizenship but said that he, too, wanted to see his release. Moreover, he was struck by the human side of the affair—that the young Hungarian had done nothing wrong, and that he had been abducted in a neutral country and might well be executed for earlier "crimes" that Ingraham did not interpret as such.[22]

When Offley received his reply from Brown on June 27, the affair took a decided turn. The American chargé informed Offley of his support for Koszta and his own intercession with the Austrian minister for the Hungarian's release. That Koszta technically had not become a citizen was less important to Brown than the intention he had expressed and the atrocity committed by the Austrian consul. The chargé urged Offley to continue seeking the Hungarian's release. When Offley's appeal to the consul proved unavailing, he conferred again with Ingraham about the next step. Before Ingraham could decide what to do, he received two pieces of information: the *Hussar* was loading its guns, and the Austrians would place Koszta aboard one of their steamers the next day to take him off to Trieste. Unwilling to wait for further Austrian initiative, Ingraham maneuvered his vessel between the *Hussar* and the steamer, an action that would allow the Americans to observe any Austrian transfer of Koszta.[23]

Having acted to prevent the surreptitious transporting of Koszta out of Smyrna, Ingraham thereafter played a major role in the settle-ment of the case. On July 2 he received a message from Brown in which the latter strongly implied that Ingraham should "demand" the Hungarian's release and, if the Austrians refused, "take him out of the vessel." Ingraham needed no further encouragement. He promptly drafted an ultimatum to the Austrian commander: "I have been directed by the American chargé at Constantinople to demand the person of Martin Koszta, a citizen of the United States, taken by force on Turkish soil and now confined on board the brig *Hussar*, and if a refusal is given to take him by force."[24] The note was deliv-ered at about 9:00 A.M. He demanded a reply by 4:00 P.M. Ingraham then proceeded to train his guns, at very short range, on the *Hussar*, even though the combined guns of the various Austrian ships in port exceeded the number on the *St. Louis* by twelve and even though the Austrians could have executed Koszta in retaliation. Cognizant of the possibility of bloodshed and of the probable disapproval of his government, at 3:00 that afternoon the Austrian consul ordered the young Hungarian released to the custody of the French consul general, where he remained for several months until his departure for the United States in October 1853.

Koszta's release did not come until after a lengthy and heated exchange between the Austrian and American governments. The Austrian chargé d'affaires in Washington submitted a bitter protest against Ingraham's action and demanded that the U.S. government give Koszta over to the Austrians and disavow all of its officials party to the affair. Secretary of State William Marcy responded with a ringing defense of Offley and Ingraham in which he advanced the argument that while Koszta had not become an American citizen, the fact of his domicile in the United States and his statement of intent to become a citizen gave him the right to Washington's protection.[25]

ALTHOUGH, AS PREVIOUSLY noted, most of the episodes of victimiza-tion of Americans through the nineteenth century resulted in some measure of bitterness between the United States and other govern-ments, the incidents themselves originated in the activity of indi-viduals or groups not initially encouraged by a national government. The *Baltimore* affair was no exception. This incident did not in-volve private citizens engaged in commerce or adventure but Ameri-can sailors in a foreign port. It is important for the same reason that the other episodes are notable: as an indication of the far-flung ac-tivities of Americans in the nineteenth century and as a case study of the U.S. responses to violence against its nationals.

USS *Baltimore. Courtesy Library of Congress*

Crew of the USS *Baltimore. Courtesy Library of Congress*

On October 16, 1891, sailors from the warship *Baltimore* went ashore in Valparaiso, Chile, after more than nine months of continuous duty. The ship, along with several other U.S. vessels, had been in Chilean waters since April to show a naval presence protecting American interests, minor though they were, as well as the lives of Americans in Chile during a civil war. As over one hundred sailors made their way into the city, each with his own purpose—to get a haircut, have dental work done, get a meal, find female companionship, get drunk—they met with harassment from the local people, military personnel, and police. Eventually, violence resulted in the deaths of two sailors and serious injury to many more.

The trouble occurred because it was widely accepted in Chile that the United States had taken sides in its recent civil war. During the conflict the regime of José Manuel Balmaceda, once a popular figure who had made a commitment to use the lucrative revenues from the abundant nitrate fields for a variety of social programs, had come under attack from a rebel force consisting of leaders of the Chilean congress supported by the navy. Balmaceda triggered the action when he issued a decree in 1890 calling for the bypassing of the congress and the implementation of the previous budget. Congressional forces eventually gained sufficient popular and military support to win the war in the summer of 1891.[26]

Several factors led the Chileans to believe the United States guilty of intervention. Its minister was a militant, volatile, extremely Anglophobic Irishman, Patrick Egan, a recently naturalized American citizen whom Secretary of State James G. Blaine had sent to Chile to counter British influence in the country. Over the years the British had gained the largest percentage of Chilean trade and eventually came to dominate the nitrate fields. As the revolt spread, Egan made no secret of his support for the Balmaceda regime, which in any event was the de jure government of the country. Egan was disposed, both out of hatred for the British, who backed the rebels, and out of his conception of proper international behavior, to support the existing government. Especially considering that the rebels went on to win the civil war, Egan's position does not appear to have been particularly farsighted; a more circumspect approach on his part would have resulted in better short-term Chilean-American relations.[27]

American reaction to a rebel attempt to purchase arms in California also invited antagonism in Chile. The steamer *Itata* came to San Diego in the summer of 1891, took on a load of "supplies," and eventually brought them back to Chile where, as a result of Washington's protests of the violation of U.S. neutrality, the rebels finally surrendered them to American vessels. Courts in the United

States subsequently issued a verdict in favor of the rebels, but not before its image had been badly besmirched in rebel eyes. This and other incidents contributed to putting Americans in bad odor in Chile.[28]

The sailors, 117 of them, thus went ashore in a hostile environment. Captain Winfield Scott Schley, commander of the *Baltimore*, had kept them aboard ship for a considerable period of time, well beyond the end of the conflict in late August. Schley, who had probably stayed on longer than warranted in Chilean waters, had postponed the men's liberty until he assumed that the atmosphere in Valparaiso was sufficiently hospitable. However, as they made their way into town, the sailors received warnings from numerous Chileans with whom they came in contact; they were urged to find accommodations before dark and to be exceedingly careful.[29]

They were not careful enough. Several incidents occurred, but the one that occasioned the most U.S. outrage and ultimately resulted in the death of an American sailor took place outside the True Blue Saloon, a two-storey, balconied structure located in the western sector of Valparaiso. Two seamen, Charles Riggin and John Talbot, had been barhopping across the city, consuming indeterminate amounts of whiskey and carousing with other sailors from the *Baltimore* and various Chileans. They happened into the True Blue Saloon where they spent thirty minutes or so visiting with a couple of friends who had previously wandered into this den of iniquity. Riggin then left, while Talbot stayed to pay his respects to the barmaid.

A commotion in the street outside diverted Talbot's attention from the young lady. Riggin was engaged in a shouting match with a Chilean sailor, a ruckus that apparently required the friend's intervention. Before the altercation ended, the disputants had attracted a rather large crowd and Talbot had knocked the Chilean to the pavement—by the American's account, after the Chilean had spat in his face. The two men then fled in front of the mob by jumping on board a streetcar, which the crowd, using bricks and cobblestones, quickly stopped and smashed into pieces. Talbot, although wounded, got away, while Riggin was stabbed and finally shot in the throat either by one of the mob or by a member of the police force that arrived to quell the disturbance. He died soon afterward.[30]

Other attacks occurred in different parts of the city, with some resulting in injury and one leading to the death of William Turnbull, a coal heaver from the *Baltimore*. Altogether, seventeen men had been wounded, two killed, and forty-eight arrested in less than twenty-four hours. Descriptions of the attacks varied depending on their source, with local officials contradicting the sailors' accounts, but the crowds seemed largely to blame for the violence; and the Chilean government, therefore, was culpable to some degree.[31]

In the aftermath of the affair, Captain Schley conducted an investigation that, not unexpectedly, indicted the mob for its acts of violence and the police for malfeasance. His report, which formed the basis for the subsequent diplomatic position of the U.S. government, laid the blame for the murders of Riggin and Turnbull, as well as the injuries to the others, exclusively on Chile, denying that the sailors had been drunk. In fact, Schley called attention to their sobriety and suggested that the actions against them arose out of long-standing hostility toward the United States. Egan, as U.S. minister, endorsed this interpretation of events.[32]

Meanwhile, the Chilean government embarked on its own investigation but took its time in doing so. Not surprisingly, it came to dramatically different conclusions: the U.S. sailors had gotten drunk in a notoriously violent part of the city, had behaved poorly, and had incited a riot; the police, when they arrived on the scene, had performed properly. Riggin, the government concluded, had been shot not by any member of the police but by someone from the crowd. Those sailors arrested had been simply protected from their own irresponsibility.[33]

This is where the matter stood when President Benjamin Harrison, for reasons that remain unclear, chose to make an issue of it in his annual message to Congress. The United States, he said, had comported itself properly during Chile's civil war, paying scrupulous attention to the risks and obligations of neutrals, and it had given no cause for grievance on the part of the new government. What happened was that the crowds and possibly the police had been guilty of unprovoked, unwarranted, and coordinated attacks on American sailors in different parts of the city that now required "prompt reparation." If the latter were not forthcoming, Harrison said, he would take the issue again to Congress, implying ominously that he would seek authority for military action. The president's tone was extremely bellicose, and it represented a departure from the measured and judicious position taken earlier by Secretary of State Blaine.[34]

Chilean reaction to Harrison's message did more to bring the matter to a head than anything else. The foreign minister, Manuel Antonio Matta, drafted a statement for the Chilean minister in Washington, attacking President Harrison's remarks as "deliberately incorrect." Unfortunately, it was widely circulated after it appeared in prominent newspapers back home and was made public in the Santiago Senate. Matta defended his government's interpretation of events in language at least as intemperate as that of Harrison. He

President Benjamin Harrison. *Courtesy Library of Congress*

then went on to impugn the integrity of the president, Secretary of the Navy Benjamin Tracy, and the U.S. minister in Chile as well.[35]

Chile followed up this verbal assault in January 1892 with its final report on the incident, a form of apology, and a demand that Egan be removed as minister. As a result of its investigation, Chile was preparing indictments not only against its own nationals implicated in the riot but, astonishing to American officials, also against at least one U.S. seaman. That Santiago was prepared to issue a semiapology did not mitigate anger in Washington. The call for Egan's removal evoked only scorn from Secretary Blaine, who implied that unless Chile apologized for the incident and paid adequate reparations the United States would sever diplomatic relations.[36] Harrison and Blaine then lost patience. The secretary of state sent a message to Egan in Valparaiso reviewing the American position and instructing him to demand an apology and reparations as well as repudiation of Matta's "insulting" circular.

When Chile failed to respond in a manner that administration officials deemed adequate or timely, President Harrison decided to act in accordance with the previous threat. On January 25 he sent all of the correspondence on the *Baltimore* incident, along with his own statement, to Congress. Among other topics, his message repeated the litany of charges against Chile: the crime against American sailors, the "cowardly" failure to acknowledge regret or to apologize, the failure to pay reparations, and the unacceptable tone of the Matta circular. Although Harrison did not ask for a declaration of war, he raised the issue to the level of war; certainly, use of military force was the next step.[37]

Fortunately for both parties, Chile gave in. Three factors informed this decision: recognition on the part of its officials that American power, particularly its naval strength, which had been growing since the 1880s, made the United States vastly superior and the guaranteed victor in a military showdown; the inability of Santiago's diplomats to evoke support from western European nations in the event of a military confrontation, as the major European powers were largely concerned with balancing their imperial competition in Asia, Africa, and the Balkans; and change in the Foreign Ministry that resulted in the replacement of Matta with Luis Pereira, who not only had no ego involved in the affair but also was actually pro-American in disposition. On January 25, the very day of Harrison's message to Congress, the United States received a message from Pereira promising that Chile would pay reparations for deaths and injuries, the amount to be determined by arbitration; would withdraw and repudiate the offensive sections of the Matta circular; and would suspend its request for Egan's recall.[38] Eventually, Chile indemnified the families, giving ten thousand dollars each for those killed, five thousand each for those seriously injured, and a few thousand or a few hundred each for others, depending on the damages they had suffered.

Interestingly, and not surprisingly, the American press and public opinion generally reinforced the administration's attitude throughout the affair and, in the process, celebrated qualities that are revealing about the nation's values in the nineteenth century.[39]

Secretary of State James G. Blaine. *Courtesy Library of Congress*

The *New York Daily Tribune* contended that the United States must boldly assert its claims if it were to satisfy the convictions "of every person who is capable of reasoning as a man and not as a woman."[40] Harrison and Blaine, as well as several members of Congress, spoke of what would constitute the "manly" thing to do, either on the part of the United States or that of Chile. Words such as "honor," "glory," "pride," and "honesty" are sprinkled freely throughout comments about the incident. Theodore Roosevelt, then a member of the recently created Civil Service Commission, and Brooks Adams, historian and grandson of President John Quincy Adams, both expressed deep "disgust" that Harrison did not declare war on behalf of American honor. Republican congressman Nelson Dingley of Maine remonstrated in the House of Representatives that war was the only way to uphold the "dignity and honor of this country." The *New York Daily Tribune* opined that sometimes it was "necessary to fight for the honor of the flag and safety of American citizens against outrage, violence and murder."[41]

Boxers awaiting execution. *Courtesy Library of Congress*

In July 1900 a large force of antiforeign Chinese fanatics and soldiers enjoying the backing of the moribund Manchu dynasty attacked the legation quarter in Beijing (then known as Peking), placing all foreign diplomats and support personnel as well as women and children under siege for nearly two months. Legation defenders put up a determined military resistance but relief did not come until an international army fought its way into the city in early August. Americans lost their lives in the siege, and Americans participated in the military expedition to end it.

Known as "Boxers" because of their custom of shadowboxing and their emblem of the clenched fist, adherents of this populist movement, which had its origins during China's troubles of the late 1890s, possessed a semicoherent "ideology" strangely evocative of a number of other mass movements through the ages. Boxers adorned themselves with crimson, charm-filled turbans; red arm bands with white charms on their wrists; and red leggings. Their ceremony consisted of invoking spirits, swearing oaths, receiving magical powers, incanting various kinds of mumbo-jumbo (which made them impervious to bullets), and inducing emotional frenzies similar to epileptic seizures. At the center of their beliefs was hatred of foreigners and foreign influence, but they also worried about the "polluting" power of women and "corruption" among officials. They enjoined one another to kill foreigners and corrupt Chinese officials and to avoid lusting after women. Interestingly, however, they had no one national leader and no centralizing national organization.[42] The Boxers spread across North China, especially where there were concentrations of foreigners. For a while they enjoyed nearly universal sympathy in the villages and farming areas of the North China plain. In the spring of 1900 probably the greatest numbers were centered in the province around Beijing.

Given developments in China in the decade of the 1890s, it is hardly surprising that the Boxer movement would have an antiforeign dimension. Beginning in 1895 with Japan's victory in the Sino-Japanese War, first Japan and then the European powers began a scramble in China for such prizes as mining rights, permission to build and control railroads, port privileges, authorization to conduct missionary activity, and domination within certain geographic areas. These concessions were in addition to those already gained from the Chinese dating back to the 1840s.

The effect on many of those Chinese who became aware of what rights and privileges Japan and the European countries had been granted was the development of suspicion and hatred toward foreigners. When missionaries from abroad took up residence in the interior, they built spire-topped churches, houses, and chapels that tended to disturb the spirits of wind and water, the geomancy that had dominated the minds of the peasantry over the centuries. Natural catastrophes thus became the fault of the missionaries. Moreover, Christian converts refused to contribute to their communities' idolatrous rites or even to festivals and other communal entertainments because Christians were usually not permitted to participate in these events.[43]

The Chinese experience with foreigners in the economic realm brought other grievances. That an uneducated peasantry would despise railroads that brought them insignificant economic benefit while running through ancestral burial grounds is less than surprising. That they would look with disfavor on telegraph lines with their disruption of nature's harmony, with the unsightly poles and the low humming of windswept wires, is hardly startling. Railroads also brought competition to camel drivers, chair bearers, muleteers, and innkeepers. The telegraph gave foreigners ready access to home offices and lessened the likelihood of Chinese influence over their behavior; foreign agents behaved aggressively, even boorishly. These conditions created a fertile environment for an antiforeign uprising.[44]

Boxer activity in the form of attacks on Christian converts, the burning of churches, and the killing of missionaries first occurred in Shandong province and then, during 1899, to an increasing degree in Zhili. Toward the end of 1899 the foreign community in Beijing had begun to take notice of the Boxers, especially after the *North China Daily News* referred to them by name on October 2. On December 31 a group of Chinese murdered a British missionary, S. M. Brooks, prompting a vigorous protest from the British ambassador to the Foreign Office in Beijing.

The British protest exposed the ambivalent attitude of the Chinese government toward the Boxers. At the court were advisers who desired strong repudiation and suppression of the movement while others counseled the opposite course (that is, endorsing them). As Boxer violence continued in the countryside early in 1900, and as Boxer units began filtering into Beijing, it became increasingly obvious that the government was finding them useful to its causes. They served it in several ways: as a counter to the foreign powers who had recently forced concessions from China, as a vehicle to stop the 1898 reforms, and as opposition to the spread of Christianity. As the Boxers' rallying cry became "Support the Qing, Destroy the Foreign," more and more elements at the court counseled accommodation. Thus, the ministers of the foreign nations were prompted to step up their efforts to force a repudiation; they called upon the court to issue an anti-Boxer edict and asked their home offices to approve a naval demonstration in Chinese waters.[45]

The foreign governments did not permit the naval demonstration, and by late May 1900 it became clear that Boxer activities were precipitating a crisis. Boxers committed wholesale slaughter of Chinese Christians in and around Beijing while posting placards warning ominously that foreigners were targeted for extinction. By the end of the month, they had killed a number of foreigners in the Beijing vicinity. The situation had become so serious that the ministers called up the legation guard from Tianjin—seventy-five British, seventy-five Russian, seventy-five French, fifty Americans, forty Italians, and twenty-five Japanese—followed a few days later by fifty Germans and thirty Austrians. Perhaps because of the call-up, the Boxers increased their attacks on foreigners. Meanwhile, the court vacillated in its attitude toward them, sometimes, as along the Beijing-Tianjin Railway, engaging them in battle, while at other times conciliating them.[46]

As the crisis intensified in early June and it seemed clear that all foreigners, including diplomatic personnel, were in real danger, the British ambassador precipitated a showdown with the Boxers and the Chinese government: he requested that Admiral Edward Seymour of the Royal Navy send a column of troops to Beijing to protect the legation. Seymour left Tianjin on June 10 with two thousand men of international derivation, planning to repair the railroad as he advanced. He got only part of the way, owing to unexpected damage to the rail line and attacks by the Boxers, who killed or wounded over two hundred of his men. Seymour was forced to retreat to Tianjin, where in a change of plans he decided to make his way up to Beijing in river junks.

Simultaneously, Boxer attacks in Beijing succeeded in severing the Beijing-Tianjin telegraph cable, and Boxer mob activity in Tianjin led the legation troops to capture the Dagu forts on June 17. This in turn prompted the Chinese government, which on the same day as the fort seizure had become incensed over the contents of a forged ultimatum from the foreign powers purporting to undercut its sovereignty, to declare war on all of the foreign powers. The proclamation, actually a collection of court edicts, appeared on June 21. On June 19, Chinese officials had warned the legation that they should evacuate and promised safe passage to the coast, but the diplomats, understandably, had questioned the government's ability to provide adequate protection given the fluidity of conditions in the country.[47]

What followed was an effort by the Chinese government to enlist Boxer support against the foreigners while preventing Boxer domination of northeastern China. The sieges that occurred in Beijing and Tianjin were joint campaigns in which soldiers and Boxers had varying degrees of control. In Beijing, government troops held the ascendancy, probably keeping the ordeal from becoming as bad as it might have become for the inhabitants of the legation quarter.[48]

It could have been worse, but it was bad enough. Comprised of 470 inhabitants, including 149 women and 79 children, the legation community had the protection of a guard force of only 450 men, a ragtag group representing seven countries with no natural leadership, not enough weapons, and insufficient ammunition. Against them were thousands of regular army troops and an untold number of Boxers who began the systematic shelling of and assault on the compound. The scorching heat of the Beijing summer, the stench from inadequate sanitation, the cramped living and sleeping quarters, not to mention the insufficient supply of food and water, began to take their toll. Water was barely potable; the siege required the foreigners to eat their horses and mules. Along with the physical deprivations came the psychological suffering that accompanies the imminence of death. The siege went on for fifty-five days. During this period seven Americans, including an infant, lost their lives.[49]

In Tianjin a similar situation existed, only there the Boxers played a more powerful role. The foreigners, assisted initially by some two thousand international troops, congregated in the foreign concessions until they could be rescued by an adequate force. Periodic Boxer attempts to storm these zones resulted in fierce battles in which more Boxers than foreigners lost their lives. Finally, on July 13 an international army of roughly twenty thousand men launched a concerted attack on strong points in and around Tianjin and defeated the Boxers and their government allies within twenty-four hours. After adding reinforcements this army then mounted an expedition to relieve the siege of Beijing.[50]

Led predominantly by Japanese and Russians, the allied force advanced on Beijing almost unimpeded. This offensive was marked by considerable looting and the torching of villages as the foreign forces sought revenge for Chinese violence against their nationals. On August 14 the army lifted the siege of the legation, after which the Dowager Empress Tzü Hsi fled the city.[51] The allied powers were now in control of Beijing and of the railroad lifeline to Tianjin and Dagu. However, Boxers dominated the rest of Zhili and a good part of the remainder of North China, meaning that while the

U.S. troops sent to put down the Boxers. *Courtesy Library of Congress*

immediate danger had passed, some sort of general settlement would have to follow. An agreement would prove difficult to devise in view of the weakened condition of the Chinese government.

The divisions among the powers and their inability to agree on the kind of treatment China should receive rendered the situation even more complicated. On one side stood Germany, which, despite losing only one life among the 242 missionaries and civilians killed by the Boxers, favored a punitive approach; on the other stood Russia and France, with backing from Japan and the United States, which favored a more moderate posture. Those who supported the latter approach did so because they believed that their commercial and territorial interests would be better served through moderation and not because of any affection for the Chinese. In fact, the Russians, for their part, were carrying on secret negotiations with the Chinese to gain concessions in Manchuria.[52]

After several weeks of discussions the powers finally agreed on several points that would form the basis of a settlement with Beijing.[53] On December 20 they reached a final settlement when China signed a note spelling out its obligations and responsibilities. Condemned for permitting crimes against "the laws of humanity and against civilization," China had to pay reparations to the German government for the killing of its minister and to the Japanese for the murder of the chancellor of their legation; mete out punishment to those government officials responsible for allowing or encouraging attacks on foreigners; construct monuments in foreign cemeteries; pay an equitable indemnity; refrain from importing arms and munitions; permit permanent legation guards; eliminate the forts of Dagu; permit foreign troops to occupy key points between Beijing and the coast; and ban participation in any antiforeign society. The powers, including the United States, also gave considerable thought to insisting that in the future the Chinese foreign minister speak a language other than his own but did not make this a part of the terms of agreement.[54] As for the Boxers, a combination of government suppression and prohibition, along with the foreign troops looting, pillaging, and killing in the villages, brought about their demise. In other words, joint slaughter quickly ended the movement.

The Boxer uprising occurred simultaneously with the U.S. campaign to quell the activities of Emilio Aguinaldo and his rebel forces in the Philippines. Accordingly, for the United States the trouble in China had a dual impact: it not only diverted attention from the military activity in the nation's new Pacific colony, but it also suggested to the American people the lesson that unless indigenous movements were suppressed, they could lead to the wholesale slaughter of Westerners. The McKinley administration, at least through the presidential campaign of 1900, kept the Boxer issue alive as a way of generating greater support for its Philippine policy.

It soon became clear to American officials, however, that some of the other nations involved in the relief of the legations in China were not averse to avenging brutally the atrocities that had been committed against them and that, in their own interests, were prepared to impose penalties on China that were potentially detrimental to the United States. Moreover, as policymakers in Washington eventually became aware, U.S. newspaper reports of foreign excesses in China began to turn public opinion away from the idea of severe punishment.

While there is no doubt that the United States took a more moderate posture than many of the other powers in the settlement of the Boxer affair, there is also no doubt that it never questioned the use of force to protect American lives. As prime targets of the Boxers, American missionaries spurned the ways of the gentle Galilean. Just before the siege began, the *New York World* carried a cable from a committee of missionaries in Beijing stating: "Arouse the Christian world immediately to our peril. Should this arrive too late, avenge us." Another communication suggested that punishment of the Chinese was not un-Christian, given the nature of that people as a lesser order of humans: "It is not bloodthirstiness in missionaries to desire to see further shedding of blood, but an understanding of Chinese character and conditions." The missionary W. S. Ament expressed the views of many of his colleagues when he said: "The soft hand of the Americans is not as good as the mailed fist of the Germans. If you deal with the Chinese with a soft hand, they will take advantage of it."[55] Taking this line of thought further, the *New York Tribune* stated that it was necessary for the United States to use force in China as the "duty of civilization toward barbarism, the duty of law and order toward riot and anarchy." Decrying moderation and fear of joint action with other powers as the policy of "babes, not men," the pro-missionary *Independent* urged military action.[56]

What, then, was Washington's foreign/military policy during the Boxer Rebellion? In sum, it was to secure the release of Americans held captive and to exact retribution without general war with China that would destroy the Beijing government and allow the European powers and Japan to divide the country. The McKinley administration, with Secretary of State John Hay in the predominant position, proceeded cautiously, operating under several constraints, one of which was the military. The United States had seventy-five thousand troops fighting the Filipinos, all of them needed in that campaign. If the effort to relieve the legations had become any more than a limited military action, the United States would have had to come up with more troops, not an easy proposition. It also would have been necessary in the event of a larger military operation to have had a declaration of war, which the McKinley administration, given the temper of the times, wished to avoid as it would have further intensified the political debate with the anti-imperialists.[57]

Ultimately, the United States satisfied its policy requirements through a two-dimensional approach. Diplomatically, it conveyed its political concerns about China in a circular note of July 3. Urging cooperation and restraint, Secretary Hay wrote that "the policy of the United States is to seek a solution which may bring about permanent safety and peace to China, preserve Chinese territorial and administrative entity, protect all rights guaranteed to friendly powers by treaty and international law, and safeguard for the world the principle of equal and impartial trade with all parts of the Chinese Empire."[58] Militarily, the United States acted by sending the warships *Oregon*, *Brooklyn*, and *Newark*, and the gunboat *Monocacy* to Dagu; by the end of August it had over six thousand men in China. By all accounts, the dual approach effectively involved the nation in twentieth-century China.

ON THE ASSUMPTION that how the United States conducted itself abroad, how it supported its foreign-military policies, how it perceived other peoples, and how it portrayed its actions domestically provide important information about its history, it follows that the episodes depicted in this chapter and the preceding one convey valuable insights about the United States in the nineteenth century. Accounts of American foreign affairs are certainly no less a significant source of information than many of the other topics that have received so much attention in recent years.

Historians have long acknowledged that Americans in the nineteenth century were strident nationalists, a fact confirmed by the response to attacks on U.S. citizens abroad, whether in the Mediterranean, along the coast of Sumatra, or in the South Atlantic. Policymakers also insisted that the free flow of commerce was a principle worthy of the most vigorous defense. Vigilance in protecting against every challenge to the country's trade became accepted policy, as did the insistence on safeguarding American citizens living or doing business outside the nation's borders.

Part of this nationalism was the belief, held by both the public and officials in charge of foreign policy, that the United States was special and unique. The superiority of republican institutions and their universal validity were articles of faith to nineteenth-century Americans, and thus the United States, in the words of historian Michael Hunt, became a "dynamic" republic. The existence of these institutions also led American statesmen to adopt a pose of self-righteousness and moralism, a sense of national perfection reinforced by seldom having to invoke self-interest. The absence of hostile neighbors and the geographic position of the United States brought about a condition of relatively free security that obviated the need to use the accepted language of international relations, thereby again reinforcing the sense of national superiority.

As noted previously, four other historical factors also account for the U.S. response to lives at risk through the nineteenth century: the broad latitude given naval officers to make decisions at the scene of a crisis; the absence of media attention engendering concern about the possible risk of military force to the lives of Americans in harm's way; the general assumption that "real" men enthusiastically subjected themselves to tests of physical activity or struggle, that strenuousness and courage held first rank in the lexicon of personal and national values, and that physical tests of manhood and nationhood should not be averted; and the general consensus that "inferior" or "less civilized" people could be treated as harshly as necessary.[59]

NOTES

1. See John Belohlavek, "Andrew Jackson and the Malaysian Pirates: A Question of Diplomacy and Politics," *Tennessee Historical Quarterly* 36 (Spring 1977): 19–21; David Long, "Martial Thunder: The First Official American Armed Intervention in Asia," *Pacific Historical Review* 42 (May 1973): 143–48; and U.S. Department of State, *American State Papers: Documents, Legislative and Executive, of the Congress of the United States*, 6, *Naval Affairs* (Washington, DC: Gales and Seaton, 1861), 4:154–55.

2. Levi Woodbury to John Downes, August 9, 1831, *Naval Affairs*, 4:153.

3. Downes to Woodbury, February 17, 1832, ibid., 4:157–58.

4. Ibid.; Long, "Martial Thunder," 152–53; Belohlavek, "Andrew Jackson," 22–23.

5. Long, "Martial Thunder," 156–57; *National Intelligencer*, July 10, 13, 1832; *Washington Globe*, July 11, 1832.

6. Report of secretary of the navy, *Naval Affairs*, 4:158.

7. Quoted in Long, "Martial Thunder," 158.

8. Ibid., 160.

9. William Hatcher, *Edward Livingston: Jeffersonian Republican and Jacksonian Democrat* (Baton Rouge: Louisiana State University Press, 1940), 408–9; John M. Belohlavek, *Let the Eagle Soar: The Foreign Policy of Andrew Jackson* (Lincoln: University of Nebraska Press, 1985), 184–85.

10. Fritz L. Hoffman and Olga M. Hoffman, *Sovereignty in Dispute: The Falklands/Malvinas, 1493–1982* (Boulder, CO: Westview Press, 1984), 17–18, 64–78; Max Hastings and Simon Jenkins, *The Battle for the Falklands* (New York: W. W. Norton and Company, 1984), 1–5.

11. Belohlavek, *Let the Eagle Soar*, 182.

12. Hoffman and Hoffman, *Sovereignty in Dispute*, 72–75.

13. Belohlavek, *Let the Eagle Soar*, 183–84.

14. Ibid., 189–90. For two useful translations of much of the diplomatic communications between Buenos Aires and Washington during the crisis, see William R. Manning, *Diplomatic Correspondence of the United States: Inter-American Affairs, 1831–1860*, vol. 1, *Argentina* (Washington, DC: Carnegie Endowment, 1932), 65–179; and Paul D. Dickens, "The Falkland Islands Dispute between the United States and Argentina," *Hispanic American Historical Review* 9 (1929): 485–86. See also Secretary of State Edward Livingston's detailed in-

structions of January 6, 1832, and background material to Baylies in U.S. Department of State, Record Group 84, Records of the Foreign Service Posts of the Department of State, "Diplomatic Instructions—American States," no. 9 (Washington, DC: National Archives Microfilm Publications [hereafter NAMP], 1946), 14:231–49.

15. See Andor Klay, *Daring Diplomacy: The Case of the First American Ultimatum* (Minneapolis: University of Minnesota Press, 1957), 9–36.

16. Ibid., 34–35; Samuel F. Bemis, *The American Secretaries of State and Their Diplomacy*, 10 vols. (New York: Cooper Square Publishers, 1963), 6:269–71.

17. Klay, *Daring Diplomacy*, 35.

18. Ibid.

19. Ibid., 48–58.

20. Ibid., 59–62; *New York Weekly Tribune*, December 17, 1853.

21. Klay, *Daring Diplomacy*, 66–67.

22. Ibid., 7.

23. Ibid., 81.

24. Quoted in Klay, *Daring Diplomacy*, 92.

25. Bemis, *Secretaries of State*, 6:271–72; John Bassett Moore, *A Digest of International Law*, 8 vols. (Washington, DC: Government Printing Office, 1906), 3:820–54; Ivor D. Spencer, *The Victor and the Spoils: A Life of William L. Marcy* (Providence, RI: Brown University Press, 1959), 264–73. See also Secretary of State William Marcy's note of August 26, 1853, in U.S. Department of State, Record Group 84, Records of the Foreign Service Posts of the Department of State, "Diplomatic Instructions—Turkey," no. 162 (NAMP, 1946), 1:371–75.

26. U.S. Department of State, *Papers Relating to the Foreign Relations of the United States, 1891* (Washington, DC: Government Printing Office, 1892), 163 (hereafter cited as *FRUS*, followed by the appropriate year). Nine months before the incident, Secretary Blaine acknowledged a note from Chilean Foreign Minister Don Prudencio Lazcano of a revolt by a Chilean naval division at Valparaiso. In this note his government informed Washington that it had "outlawed the revolting squadron" and that "it is not responsible for the acts of the rebels in respect to foreigners or citizens." U.S. Department of State, Record Group 84, Records of the Foreign Service Posts of the Department of State, "Notes to Foreign Legations—Chile," no. 12 (NAMP, 1949), 6:377–78.

27. *FRUS, 1891*, 92–163; Joyce Goldberg, *The Baltimore Affair* (Lincoln: University of Nebraska Press, 1986), 20–32.

28. *FRUS, 1891*, vii, 141, 163. In late November, Acting Secretary of State William Wharton acknowledged the Chilean request to cancel the commission of its consul general in San Francisco. U.S. Department of State, "Notes to Foreign Legations—Chile," no. 12, 6:389–90.

29. *FRUS, 1891*, 194–95.

30. Ibid., 204.

31. Ibid., 204–5. See also Goldberg, *Baltimore Affair*, 1–19.

32. *FRUS, 1891*, 206–7, 208.

33. Ibid., 214.

34. Ibid., vi, x.

35. Ibid., 267–68, 271.

36. Ibid., 287, 289–303. See also Secretary Blaine's comments to President Harrison on the offensive nature of the circular and his instructions to Egan for its immediate withdrawal. U.S. Department of State, Record Group 84, Records of the Foreign Service Posts of the Department of State, "Diplomatic Instructions—Chile," no. 37 (NAMP, 1946), 17:391–95.

37. Goldberg, *Baltimore Affair*, 104–5, 175. See also Benjamin Harrison, *Public Papers and Addresses of Benjamin Harrison, Twenty-third President of the United States, March 4, 1889–March 4, 1893* (Washington, DC: Government Printing Office, 1893), 174–86.

38. *FRUS, 1891*, 309–12.

39. Goldberg, *Baltimore Affair*, 109.

40. Edward Nelson Dingley, *The Life and Times of Nelson Dingley, Jr.* (Kalamazoo, MI: Ihling Brothers and Everand, 1902), 343; John Hay, *Letters of John Hay and Extracts from His Diary*, 2 vols. (Staten Island, NY: Gordian Press, 1969), 2:235–36.

41. *New York Daily Tribune*, January 20, 27, 1892.

42. Joseph W. Esherick, *The Origins of the Boxer Uprising* (Berkeley: University of California Press, 1987), 293–95.

43. Peter Fleming, *The Siege of Peking* (New York: Harper and Brothers, 1959), 37–38.

44. Ibid., 43–44.

45. William J. Duiker, *Cultures in Collision: The Boxer Rebellion* (San Rafael, CA: Presidio Press, 1978), 48–56.

46. Esherick, *Boxer Uprising*, 287–88.

47. Ibid., 302–3.

48. Ibid., 306–7.

49. Duiker, *Cultures in Collision*, 107; Fleming, *Siege of Peking*, 141–46.

50. Esherick, *Boxer Uprising*, 308–9.

51. Ibid., 309–10.

52. George Nye Steiger, *China and the Occident: The Origin and Development of the Boxer Rebellion* (New York: Russell and Russell, 1966), 257–61. See also Delbert McKee, "The Boxer Indemnity Remission," *Society for Historians of American Foreign Relations Newsletter* 23 (March 1992): 1–19.

53. Steiger, *China and the Occident*, 258.

54. Ibid., 267; *FRUS, 1900* (Washington, DC: Government Printing Office, 1902), 244–45, 228. See also Secretary Hay, "The President approves seven proposed conditions." U.S. Department of State, Record Group 84, Records of the Foreign Service Posts of the Department of State, "Diplomatic Instructions—China," no. 43 (NAMP, 1946), 6:128–29.

55. Quoted in Stuart C. Miller, "Ends and Means: Missionary Justification of Force in Nineteenth Century China," in John K. Fairbank, ed., *The Missionary Enterprise in China and America* (Cambridge, MA: Harvard University Press, 1974), 273, 274, 276.

56. Quoted in Marilyn Young, *The Rhetoric of Empire: American China Policy, 1895–1901* (Cambridge, MA: Harvard University Press, 1968), 153, 154.

57. Ibid., 149–54.

58. *FRUS, 1900*, 299.

59. Thus, when historian John Fiske and Congregationalist minister Josiah Strong extolled the superiority of the Anglo-Saxon "race" and predicted colonization of the world by English-speaking people, or when political scientist John Burgess stated that there was "no human right to the status of barbarism," they gave coherent voice to the convictions of many of their countrymen as demonstrated in the responses to violence or indignities visited upon Americans. John W. Burgess, *Reconstruction and the Constitution, 1866–1876* (New York: Charles Scribner's and Sons, 1901), 133; John W. Burgess, *Political Science and Comparative Constitutional Law*, 2d ed. (Boston: Ginn and Company, 1890), 30–40; Josiah Strong, *Our Country: Its Possible Future and Its Present Crisis*, rev. ed. (New York: Baker and Taylor, 1891), 207–28; John Fiske, *The Destiny of Man* (Boston: Houghton Mifflin Company, 1881), 96–107 (themes of racial hierarchy later expanded in his "Manifest Destiny," *Harper's Magazine*, March 1885); George Fredrickson, *The Inner Civil War: Northern Intellectuals and the Crisis of the Union* (New York: Harper and Row, 1965), 130–50; R. Jackson Wilson, *In Quest of Community: Social Philosophy in the United States, 1860–1920* (New York: John Wiley and Sons, 1968), 26–84; Henry F. May, *The End of American Innocence: A Study of the First Years of Our Time, 1912–1917* (New York: Alfred A. Knopf, 1959), 9–106.

Chapter 3

A Study in Contradiction: Theodore Roosevelt's Responses to Hostage Crises

On September 3, 1901, Ellen Stone, a portly, fifty-five-year-old, unmarried missionary on assignment in European Turkey, was kidnapped by a band of Macedonian rebels and held for a ransom of twenty-five thousand Turkish pounds, an amount equal to roughly one million late twentieth-century dollars. She remained in captivity for six months as Theodore Roosevelt, who succeeded to the presidency eleven days after the abduction, struggled to find a way to free her consistent with the requirements of national honor and his personal predilections. The affair is significant in any account of American lives at risk because the motive for violence came from a qualitatively different source than in any previous case and because U.S. responses were constrained in much the same manner as in the hostage episodes of the later twentieth century. It is also meaningful because in large measure it determined President Roosevelt's behavior in the Perdicaris incident later in his administration.

Owing to a complicated set of circumstances peculiar to Macedonian history, these were "friendly" kidnappers. Known as the Internal Macedonian Revolutionary Organization (IMRO), the band that seized Stone in 1901 was engaged in a struggle to free their homeland from Turkish rule. Macedonia, located just south of the Balkan Mountains and situated in a strategically important area between Central Europe and the Mediterranean (see map on p. 30), had been the object of Great Power rivalry for years. In 1878, Russia defeated Turkey in a war that the czar hoped would establish an independent but pro-Russian Bulgarian state that would take its place alongside other pro-Russian, Slavic Christian states in the Balkans. Indeed, the Treaty of San Stefano of 1878 established a Greater Bulgaria covering much of the area from the Danube River to the Aegean Sea to the Black Sea, including Macedonia. This new Bulgarian state was so large that the European powers, at the Treaty of Berlin (Reinsurance Treaty of 1887), stepped in to force the Bulgarians to divest themselves of Macedonia and give it back to Turkey.[1]

Unfortunately, neither the Bulgarians nor the Macedonians desired a continuation of Turkish rule. Accordingly, two organizations committed to the expulsion of the hated Turk soon came into existence: the IMRO, a group of Macedonian rebels desiring complete autonomy, organized in 1893; and the Supreme Macedonian-

President Theodore Roosevelt. *Courtesy Library of Congress*

Adrianopolitan Committee (SMAC), an organization of Bulgarians formed in 1895, whose objectives were flexible enough to permit either Macedonian independence or annexation by Bulgaria. For several years these two groups cooperated with one another as the SMAC bestowed its blessing on the IMRO, while the latter created a revolutionary militia and stashed away arms for the final showdown with the Turks. IMRO units collected taxes from peasants and set themselves up as a pretender government. All went well until the Turks found out about the organization in 1897, after which Constantinople waged a vigorous military campaign to destroy it. This Turkish-IMRO struggle went on until 1903.

By 1901 the IMRO had concluded that it could not win independence without intervention by one or more foreign powers. Since none of the European nations came forward to provide aid and assistance, the group began trying to win sympathy in the United States through propaganda and misinformation about Turkish rule in Macedonia. This propaganda generally found a sympathetic audience among Americans, who had never been very favorably disposed toward the Ottoman Empire, but it did little to win material support. In keeping with John Quincy Adams's dictum of seventy-eight years before, the United States was willing to extend its prayers and benedictions to Turkish victims but nothing else.

Two developments forced the IMRO into more direct action. In 1901 the cooperation that had existed with the SMAC ended upon the demotion and arrest of its head, Boris Saraffof, a Bulgarian officer who was favorably disposed toward the Macedonian revolutionaries. Saraffof's rival, determined to purge both organizations of all elements not supportive of annexation, became president of Bulgaria. This forced the autonomists, particularly those in the IMRO, into a desperate struggle for survival against both the Turks and the new Bulgarian regime. Primary leaders of the Macedonian independence movement were Yani Sandansky, a socialist who had once been a schoolteacher, and Khristo Chernopeef, a revolutionary chieftain and implacable opponent of the Bulgarian annexationists. In early fall of 1901, Sandansky and Chernopeef came to the realization that they had to move quickly in pursuit of independence or risk losing their following. Thus, they came up with the idea of a kidnapping, the seizure of an American missionary whose capture would serve two purposes—it would impel the United States to apply pressure on Turkey to relinquish Macedonia, and it would raise money for use against the new tormentors in Bulgaria.[2]

In pursuit of money to fund their activities the revolutionaries had undertaken a number of robberies, extortions, and kidnappings in the past, but nothing quite as grandiose or with a possible payoff quite as large as that envisioned in the seizure of Stone. In 1896 one of their members made off with $80,000 from a postal box in a daring escapade that turned out badly because he dropped the satchel and its contents into a river as he fled from his Turkish pursuers. In 1898 the group offered through an agent in St. Petersburg to send a contingent of troops to fight in the Spanish-American War in return for money from the United States. They once kidnapped the son of a rich Turk and demanded $24,000 for his release only to have the victim escape after grabbing a revolver and shooting a guard who had fallen asleep on the job. A similar effort against a Greek moneylender resulted in another hostage escape and no ransom. Just prior to making the decision to seize an American missionary, the organization developed an elaborate plan to kidnap another wealthy Turk, but to the great disadvantage of the missionary community, and not least to Stone herself, the poor fellow suffered an incapacitating stroke before he could be taken.[3]

Having miserably failed in most of their previous fund-raising efforts, the IMRO logically turned to an inviting target: the American missionary community. These missionaries had begun residing in European Turkey as early as 1810 when the American Board of Commissioners for Foreign Missions was founded. They increased their numbers to well over a hundred clergy scattered throughout Bulgaria and Macedonia by 1900, and their influence became increasingly pervasive because Robert College in Constantinople trained a high percentage of Bulgarian government bureaucrats and teachers as well as educators in positions throughout Macedonia. Not surprisingly, a close relationship developed between these missionaries and educators and those rebelling against the Turk. Graduates of missionary schools became leaders of revolutionary units; the Protestant churches along Bulgaria's side of its border with Macedonia shielded and encouraged nationalist activity. That the Turks would see these Christian missionaries as purveyors of a hostile theology and as spokespersons of a threatening political ideology seems obvious. That Turkey would seek to limit the activity of missionaries and that missionaries on their part would oppose its control of Macedonia also seems obvious. For the United States to free Macedonia, wrote J. F. Clarke, head of the Theological Seminary in Bulgaria, would be "like the act of freeing Cuba and the Philippine Islands."[4] It was precisely because of sentiment like Clarke's that the IMRO assumed that seizing a missionary, especially if the act could be portrayed as one perpetrated by Turks, would trigger anti-Turkish sentiment in the United States.

Why Ellen Stone became the choice had less to do with her background than with her availability. Stone was in Bansko, a town

Ellen Stone, Congregational missionary. *Courtesy Houghton Library, Harvard University (originally published in* American Heritage)

in the northeastern sector of Macedonia and near an active IMRO chapter just across the Bulgarian border, to train teachers in the elementary schools sponsored by her church and to conduct Bible classes for local Christian women. Nothing in her background had prepared her for the rigors of life as the hostage of a group of rag-tag revolutionaries. Originally from Roxbury, Massachusetts, where she was born in 1846, Stone had been in turn a schoolteacher and an editor with the *Boston Congregationalist* before volunteering for missionary work. The American Board of Commissioners for Foreign Missions sent her to Samokov, Bulgaria, in 1878 to teach in a girls' school, an assignment that soon soured because she could not get along with her supervisor. After that she settled in Plodiv where she spent ten years saving souls, teaching English and basic hygiene, as well as conducting Bible studies to help the local women spread the Word. By the late 1890s she had been assigned to a mission station at Salonika, which required extensive travel throughout Macedonia. It was in conjunction with her duties in this position that she found herself in Bansko in September 1901.

Her duties completed, Stone and her party of nine, including Katerina Tsilka, who would join her in captivity, had just departed Bansko on September 3 when they were seized by a group of twenty IMRO militiamen, called *chetniks*. These "brigands," as they were known thereafter by the American press and public officials, waited in ambush beside a mountain pathway next to a sharp cliff to capture their prey. Five of the brigands were dressed in Turkish uniforms; all wore black makeup and tattered cloth on their faces and necks; all, according to Stone, were "rugged and athletic," as well as "wild and fierce." With great fanfare, yelling, screaming—all in a crude, not very believable Turkish—and waving weapons, the kidnappers led their hostages to the top of the mountain where they held them through the night. To lend verisimilitude to their fierceness, the brigands mercilessly beat an unfortunate Turk who happened on the scene minutes after the abduction took place. Disdaining all valuables including money, watches, and gold chains, the kidnappers took only the food of their victims, plus a Bible. Then, on September 4, they released everyone but Ellen Stone and Katerina Tsilka. Given turn-of-the-century morality, taking a woman hostage required a chaperone, so they took Tsilka, then five months pregnant, because she was the only available married woman. Born in Bulgaria, trained as a nurse at New York Presbyterian Hospital and a companion to her husband in missionary work, Tsilka had traveled to Bansko to visit her parents. While there she had suffered through the sudden illness and death of a young son, her only child. Her grief could not have been made easier by her sudden captivity.[5]

Under the circumstances (the rugged, mountainous terrain over which they were spirited from place to place), Stone and Tsilka were not badly treated. The brigands helped them on and off their horses, often carried them in areas where their mounts could not go, made certain that they had plenty of food, took care that they had adequate covering at night, and even occasionally gave them flowers. At the same time, the captors did not disguise their menacing nature. Adorned with pistols, daggers, and cartridge belts and dressed in shabby, unwashed clothing, neither their appearance nor their language hid their intent: unless they received ransom in the amount desired, they would kill their hostages.[6]

The world learned slowly of the abduction and the ransom demands—and even more slowly the identity of the kidnappers. The latter took pains to convince both the group they released as well as Stone and Tsilka that they were Turks. This seemed implausible from the start, at least to those close to the scene. On September 9 the kidnappers forced Stone to draft a ransom note addressed to a friend in Bansko, who, as fate would have it, refused to retrieve the note from his doorstep out of fear that the Turks would connect him to the rebels. Having gotten no results after two weeks, the brigands pressed Stone to write a second note (filled with lamentations about what would happen to her and Tsilka should the money not be paid), which they delivered via carrier to H. C. Haskell, the missionary station chief at Samokov, on September 24. Meanwhile, notice of the capture of Stone and Tsilka, though not the motive for it, came to Dr. John House, senior missionary in Macedonia, on September 5.[7] He relayed the message to the U.S. consul in Bulgaria, P. H. Lazzaro, who in turn sent it to Charles Dickinson, the consul general in Constantinople. Word reached the State Department via two routes nearly simultaneously: from official channels in Constantinople and through missionaries in the United States reporting to Secretary of State John Hay.[8]

The news caused a paroxysm of worry among missionaries and Washington's policymakers. No American missionary had ever been kidnapped before in the Balkans, and as a result no one knew how to proceed. Since the activity had taken place in Turkish territory, the first impulse was to invoke Turkish responsibility and ask Constantinople to help secure the release of the hostages. But Lazzaro urged caution in a message to Dickinson out of concern that if Turkish troops pursued the kidnappers too closely, they would kill the women, a fear that Stone herself had expressed in a note to a representative of the Missions Board in Constantinople on September 20.[9]

Responding to American pressure applied through Dickinson and U.S. Minister John Leishman, the Turks attempted to get to the bottom of the affair. They questioned everyone in Stone's original party, and they arrested some Bulgarian Muslims whom they thought might have useful information. They also began detaining and roughing up members of the IMRO in Bansko as well as people in the Protestant community, confident that there had been close co-operation between the two groups. Their activity became so intense that the missionaries protested to the Missions Board office in Boston, which in turn asked the State Department to call off the Turks.

For its part the Bulgarian government took action as soon as it learned of the kidnapping on September 5. Worried that it would be blamed by both Turkey and the United States, it set up tight border patrols to keep the brigands from crossing into Bulgaria, and it too began interrogating people who had connections with the IMRO. Officially, Bulgaria took the position that Turkish soldiers had been responsible for the kidnapping.[10]

Given the fear of physical harm to Stone, the Missions Board quickly began considering the payment of ransom. The assumption was that as a woman she was more vulnerable and less able to bear up under the rigors of life in the Macedonian wilds than a male counterpart might have been. Letters poured into the Missions Board office from friends, relatives, and sympathizers. On the belief that if it somehow raised the large sum of money required the Turks could eventually be pressured into compensating the contributors, the Missions Board decided on September 24 to pay the ransom.[11]

This decision would have met with the approval of Ellen Stone (had she known of it) but it certainly did not win acceptance among other missionaries in Bulgaria and Macedonia. Believing that rewarding terrorism would beget more terrorism, they feared for their lives if this kidnapping succeeded. To quote one of them: "What is paid will be a price on our heads." Protests from the field and, it may be assumed, knowledge of the amount of money demanded led the Missions Board at the end of September to reverse its original decision to pay the ransom.[12] Having decided that the Christian ideal of sacrificing one life would be offset by the saving of several, yet reluctant to assume the moral consequences of this position, the Missions Board turned the problem over to Theodore Roosevelt.

The Roosevelt administration soon learned that there was no easy solution despite the president's personal belief in bold behavior. Pressuring Turkey was not deemed wise because its pursuit of the brigands could result in Stone's death, either at the hands of the brigands themselves or through action on the part of the Turks, who on similar occasions had been less than respectful of the lives of either the kidnappers or captives. That the Turks would be unwilling to pay the ransom and thus contribute to their own eviction from Macedonia seemed axiomatic to officials in Washington, who by the end of September knew that the brigands were representatives of the IMRO out to gain control of the territory. Pressure on Bulgaria seemed equally problematic, even though U.S. officials assumed a close connection between the brigands and that country, because the kidnapping had occurred in Macedonia where the Bulgarian government could legitimately claim it had no responsibility.

Consul General Dickinson, who on October 4 became the U.S. agent in Sofia, assumed otherwise and set about forcing the Bulgarians to secure Stone's release. Directed by the State Department "to exercise discretion" and "reticence" and to "abstain from discussing any question of responsibility," Dickinson did exactly the opposite. His first action on his arrival in Sofia was to invade the foreign minister's private domicile and insist on an audience; when put off, he managed to arrange a Sunday morning meeting at which he demanded that the Bulgarian government use its influence with the SMAC to force an end to the kidnapping. He then insisted that Bulgaria detain all officers of the IMRO living in the border region. Dickinson's behavior became altogether so offensive that the minister of internal affairs finally informed him to put up or shut up: either turn over any evidence he had of Bulgarians' complicity or acknowledge that they were telling the truth when they said they had no connection to the kidnapping.[13]

Although the Roosevelt administration was not willing to endorse Dickinson's imperious behavior, it did feel constrained to register its desire for Bulgarian assistance in ending the affair. This was especially true once it became clear that help from Turkey would not be forthcoming. Roosevelt himself implied Bulgarian involvement in one note conveyed through the U.S. agent, and said that if Stone were harmed "the American people will be satisfied with nothing less than unhesitating ascertainment of responsibility and due redress."[14] Meanwhile, the State Department, through its minister in St. Petersburg, Charlemagne Tower, asked the Russian foreign minister to pressure the Bulgarian government to help arrange for Stone's release. The Russians quickly complied with the request, informing the Bulgarians that they would lose favor in Europe unless they cooperated. As events transpired, such cooperation did not constitute a problem; indeed, there is no evidence that the Bulgarian government was anything but honest and aboveboard throughout the affair.

But goodwill and cooperation did little to secure Stone's release, the main concern of Roosevelt and his advisors in the fall of 1901. As he pondered the proper course for the United States to take, the president considered several options including simply announcing that Stone, like all missionaries, operated without the official sanction or approval of the U.S. government and thus could not expect protection in the wild and godforsaken part of the world into which she had gone. As Roosevelt noted to Assistant Secretary of State Alvey Adee: "Every missionary, every trader in wild lands should know and is inexcusable for not knowing [*sic*] that the American government had no power to pay the ransom of anyone who is captured by brigands or savages."[15] The president then went on to indicate to Adee exactly why it would not be possible for him to adopt a laissez-faire position in this particular case. "If a man goes out as a missionary," he wrote, "he has no kind of business to venture to wild lands with the expectation that somehow the government will protect him as well as if he stayed at home. If he is fit for his work he has no more right to complain of what may befall him than a soldier has in getting shot. But it is impossible to adopt this standard about women."[16]

Roosevelt's view was perfectly consistent with the prevalent opinion of his day: women required special protection. However, at the same time, he was saying obliquely that unless the United States did something to free Stone, abuse would be heaped upon him at the worst possible time—just as he was settling into the presidency and attempting to prove his mettle. Stone's family and friends, needless to say, were not bashful about applying pressure on the administration, which they did constantly either through the Missions Board or directly in a letter-writing campaign. Nor were they reluctant to involve the press to incite public concern. Roosevelt, the hero of San Juan Hill in the war with Spain, knew better than anyone the effect that the sensational press could have on American opinion.

The president's subsequent action does not fit the swashbuckling image that posterity holds of him. He knew that Stone could not be abandoned to her fate given the political realities. He also was aware, however, that he could do little to free her short of undertaking military action that would involve his administration in a war with the Ottoman Empire and bog down American marines in the mountains of Macedonia. His dilemma was compounded by his knowledge that negotiating with brigands on ransom demands was not only risky politically but also could lead to a repeat performance in the Balkans or elsewhere. Like a number of his twentieth-century successors in similar situations, Roosevelt had to construct a policy that would get Stone out alive, satisfy the requirements of international theater, and avoid further terrorist attacks.

The only answer was to turn the matter back to the missionaries—that is, to ask that they pay the ransom, after which Roosevelt would ask Congress to reimburse all who had contributed. When representatives of the Missions Board came to the president, he suggested that the way to proceed was to raise money through popular subscription. The United States could then pay back the subscribers and later collect the funds from the Turks.

This plan, however, did not take into account the impact of popular subscription on the negotiating process. Raising enough money would require publicizing the kidnapping and keeping information about Stone before the public—exactly what a president hoping to avoid political fallout would wish to avoid. Moreover, assuming that negotiations went forward, it was obviously desirable to free Stone for as little money as possible, but striking a negotiating posture on this basis when newspapers gave regular reports on the extent of the contributions would become difficult, to say the least. The kidnappers maintained sufficient contact with the outside world to gain this valuable information.[17]

Throughout the nineteenth century, U.S. envoys abroad had enjoyed considerable latitude for independent action, owing to inadequate communication facilities and, often, to lack of interest on the part of policymakers in Washington. That this had begun to change by the early twentieth century does not mean that old habits had been broken; they die hard. American representatives continued to assume the right to make on-the-spot decisions that a later generation would never consider making. Dickinson in Sofia assumed that he had free rein to determine policy in the Stone affair. He refused to consider the payment of ransom, despite Roosevelt's commitment to that course of action, on the belief that life in the Balkan region would be impossible for Westerners if a kidnapping succeeded. He remained resolutely determined to gain Stone's release through pressure on the Bulgarians and the Russians even though the futility of that approach should have been clear by mid-October.

Dickinson's schemes included a plan to rescue Stone and Tsilka using military force. He would convince the Bulgarian government to station troops near the Macedonian border and thus set a trap into which Turkish troops would drive the kidnappers. When it learned of the plan, the State Department hastened to put a stop to it, believing correctly that although it might lead to the punishment of the brigands, it could also lead to the death of Stone. Later, upon hearing through a contact that the hostages were being held in a Macedonian monastery where they were guarded by only four men,

Dickinson came up with the idea that if he bribed the guards and told them the brigands planned to cut them out of the ransom money, he could get them to set the women free. This plan also came to naught.[18]

By the end of November control of policy had shifted to Washington. Responding to intense publicity and to pleas from, among others, Charles Stone, Ellen's brother, the State Department moved to repudiate Dickinson and begin negotiations to pay the ransom. Secretary of State Hay thereupon brought Dr. George Washburn, head of Robert College in Constantinople, into the process. Washburn, sympathetic to the leadership in Bulgaria and personally acquainted with many of the public figures, argued that pressuring the Bulgarian and Russian governments would not work. He believed that it would be necessary to carry on discussions using negotiators who knew the people and the language in the region, and he had someone in mind.[19]

Under authorization from the State Department, Washburn met with the U.S. chargé d'affaires at the legation in Constantinople, Spencer Eddy, and they appointed two men to carry out the paying of the ransom: W. W. Peet, the Bible House treasurer in Constantinople, and Alexander Gargiulo, an interpreter at the U.S. legation. These two were to secure Turkish authorization and the proper papers for travel in Macedonia where they were to locate the brigands and seek to purchase Stone's release.[20]

Had they known what was in store for them Peet and Gargiulo might have refused the assignment. They had no trouble getting into Macedonia, but once there they had to locate and begin talks with the kidnappers, who had become skittish in the knowledge that the duo was being tracked by about two hundred Turkish troops ready to pounce on the brigands, place them under arrest, and seize the ransom money. In fact, for about a month, a kind of cat-and-mouse game went on as Peet and Gargiulo tried to make contact with the elusive brigands. They finally succeeded. On February 2, without the knowledge of the Turks, they made contact through an intermediary and arranged to turn over $66,000 in gold to them. The exchange took place near Bansko, where Peet arranged to transport the ransom out of his cottage surreptitiously, sixty pounds at a time, and replace it with lead shot. In return for the money, which was roughly $34,000 less than the original demand, the brigands agreed to release Stone and Tsilka within ten days.[21]

That the brigands could not fulfill their commitment to the ten-day time limit was in no way the result of any unwillingness to comply. They spent the better part of a week dodging Turkish patrols before determining that they could safely take Stone and Tsilka to a spot near Strumitza to set them free. There, at 4:00 A.M. on February 23, they left the two captives under a pear tree. This brought to an end an ordeal of a magnitude nearly equal for hostages and kidnappers alike. For about six months the small party had struggled through and around the rugged mountains of Macedonia, the hostages concerned that they might eventually be tortured or killed, and the kidnappers, already afflicted with various preoccupations, tormented by the harsh blandishments of Stone, who kept warning of hellfire and brimstone if they failed to change their ways and accept her one true Savior. Besides the problem of Stone, who gave voice to her message freely and regularly, Tsilka in November gave birth to a baby girl. The brigands then had charge of a sharp-tempered, sharp-tongued, independent-minded, somewhat abrasive woman and a new mother and baby. (It was not easy. One young kidnapper gave up tobacco and began reading the Bible because of Stone's sermons on temperance.) All the men took turns in entertaining the women and, after the baby arrived, in making sure it was adequately protected against the elements. Winter snows brought special hardships in the mountains. Given all of these factors, it is not difficult to understand why the men acted with such alacrity in releasing the captives just as soon as they could do so in safety.[22]

Stone returned to the United States, never thereafter to visit Macedonia. She wrote her memoirs only to have the manuscript destroyed in a fire, but she was able to reconstruct events sufficiently to publish an account of her experience in *McClure's Magazine*. Over the following decade she campaigned for compensation, either from Turkey or, failing that, from the U.S. Congress, for those who had subscribed the ransom money for her release. Given her long-standing protemperance sentiments, she found a natural cause in the prohibition movement and became a crusading member of the Women's Christian Temperance Union. Apart from her activity with this group, she spent a good deal of time railing against the perfidious Turk, interestingly but not surprisingly blaming Turkey for her prolonged captivity, and inveighing against Muslim control over Christians in the Balkans. She was never terribly critical of the Macedonian rebels actually responsible for her kidnapping.

Tsilka returned to Albania with her husband. In 1903 she made a trip to the United States, where she became a mild sensation. Taking her baby with her on the lecture circuit, she reconstructed her experiences to the delight of American audiences, who, given her youth, good looks, and sprightly personality, considered her far more interesting than Stone. She went back to Albania with considerably more wealth than she could have claimed upon her arrival in the United States.[23]

The IMRO began dividing up the ransom money and preparing for a major revolt in 1903. In addition to the purchase of a new revolver for each member of the rebel band responsible for the kidnapping, the revolutionary committee used the funds to acquire a supply of rifles for the pending showdown with Turkey. After patching up the differences between the IMRO and the SMAC and working out new leadership arrangements, over fifty thousand Bulgarians and Macedonians rose up against the Turks in August 1903. The revolt went well for a while but after a few months was crushed by Ottoman authorities.[24]

Neither the outcome nor the initial American response to the kidnapping suited Roosevelt's predilections. Known as a proponent of a vigorous, assertive foreign policy and contemptuous of "less civilized" peoples like the "dagoes" of Colombia, the Philippines, and now the Balkans, the president would have liked to have sent troops into Macedonia, seized the kidnappers, and, for good measure, run the Turks out of the place. No more than Stone and countless other Americans did he wish to see a continuation of Muslim rule over Balkan Christians. That he could not act vigorously must have pained him grievously since the kidnapping clearly represented an affront to the nation's honor and prestige. However, there were simply too many constraints. His recent ascent to the presidency meant that for some time after the kidnapping occurred, he was still grappling with the problems of transition, a minor issue compared to the difficulty of assigning blame for the hostage-taking, given the dearth of information from Macedonia. Moreover, once the administration had determined responsibility, how to free the hostages and force the punishment of the guilty parties without endangering the lives of Stone and Tsilka became major stumbling blocks. Furthermore, once he had learned the facts, Roosevelt was not unsympathetic to the objectives of the kidnappers. He disliked the Turk, and, as he put it many times, no country in the world deserved a smashing more than Turkey. Apart from the fact that they held an American hostage and were not particularly loveable, the Macedonian brigands did not act contrary to the interests of the United States in trying to promote their independence.

The president also faced a multitude of other concerns. Negotiating and approving a treaty that gave the United States the right to build, control, and fortify an interoceanic canal was among the items on his agenda. Another was the choice of either Nicaragua or Panama as the appropriate site for such a canal. Still another diplomatic dilemma was a conflict brewing with the British and the Canadians over the boundary line between Canada and the Alaskan panhandle. Domestically, Roosevelt faced the issue of taking on the power of monopolies; in February 1902 his attorney general began a suit under the Sherman Antitrust Act against a railroad combine known as the Northern Securities Company. Of far greater concern was the war in the Philippines, in which roughly sixty thousand American troops still were engaged in a struggle to defeat an independence movement led by nationalist leader Emilio Aguinaldo against U.S. rule. The Philippine campaign, which produced heated debate in the United States, represented a serious logistical and operational trial for the administration.

Whether Roosevelt would have acted differently had Ellen Stone been a man is debatable. Certainly important in his effort to ransom her was the fact that she was a female and thus, he thought, deserving of special respect and solicitude. However, the only real alternative available to Roosevelt was to ignore the kidnapping, thereby making it a nonevent requiring no American response. There is some evidence that he might have used this approach if a woman's life had not been at stake.

In a sense this crisis foreshadowed the difficulties the United States would experience with terrorist groups in the latter half of the twentieth century. World power makes a nation susceptible to terrorist acts when indigenous groups assume that a particular country can make a difference in local or regional disputes. In 1901 the United States was a world-class power economically, although not militarily, but the IMRO clearly thought (correctly as it turned out) that the American response would influence events in Macedonia. As in later cases, it would be difficult to determine responsibility and more difficult still to act once blame had been assigned. To use force—the instinctive response for Roosevelt and many of his successors—would result in the killing of the hostages. To do nothing, as the Stone kidnapping proved and as later such episodes would further demonstrate, would be impossible given the public pressure. Despite his bellicose image, Theodore Roosevelt's actual policies in the Ellen Stone affair (though not in subsequent episodes) place him closer to Jimmy Carter and Ronald Reagan than to Andrew Jackson.

Ransoming Stone became more palatable to Roosevelt by using the private subscription method of raising the money, but in the end the U.S. government fully financed the transaction. Despairing of the prospect of collecting from Turkey and under pressure from Stone, who spoke out for the reimbursement of her benefactors, the

Roosevelt administration asked Congress to appropriate the funds. After years of debate Congress finally enacted a bill providing payment on May 21, 1912.[25]

IF THE KIDNAPPING of Ellen Stone occasioned a temperate and judicious response from the Roosevelt administration, the seizing a little more than two years later of Ion Perdicaris, a wealthy expatriate living in Morocco, brought precisely the opposite reaction. Indeed, the handling of the Perdicaris affair, apart from the impact it had on presidential politics in 1904, is often noted as epitomizing the aggressive, swashbuckling style of the ex-cowboy, ex-Rough Rider president who refused to knuckle under to disrespectful barbarians.

The subject (portrayed with customary Hollywood license) of the 1975 adventure film *The Wind and the Lion*, the kidnapping of Perdicaris was reported with as much bravado and excitement as any such episode in American history. On the evening of May 18, 1904, Ion Perdicaris and his family, which included his wife, her son by a previous marriage, who happened to be a British citizen, and the son's wife, were having dinner on the patio of the Perdicaris villa outside of Tangier. The pleasant gathering was suddenly and rudely interrupted by a gang of Muslim pirates directed by Mulai Ahmed el-Raisuli that broke into the mansion from the rear, knocked two of the frantic servants senseless with rifle butts, dragged another out the door, and seized Perdicaris and his stepson. Proclaiming loudly, "I am the Raisuli," the leader of the outlaw band put his captives on their horses, after stealing the finest of the steeds for himself, and then rode off with the group into the mountains.

Ion Perdicaris and his wife's son had thus become the innocent victims in a power struggle between "the Raisuli" and a powerful clique behind the sultan. One of its members, the bashaw of Tangier and Raisuli's foster brother, had arranged Raisuli's imprisonment some eight years before. Unforgiving in his attitude toward this sibling, Raisuli after his release sought to embarrass the bashaw, the rest of the clique, and the sultan himself through kidnapping and plunder. On his part, the foster brother waged war against Raisuli by burning the villages of his supporters, imposing exorbitant taxes on tribes loyal to him, and periodically attempting to trick him into concessions at the bargaining table. One campaign resulted in Raisuli's ambush of the bashaw's forces and his return of their body parts, including the head of one prominent soldier, in a basket of melons.

The sultan himself was an eccentric and weak man, head of state only by the sufferance of the Grand Vizier Ben Sliman and the French, who by virtue of the entente of April 1904 with Great

Mulai Ahmed el-Raisuli. *Courtesy Houghton Library,
Harvard University (originally published in* American
Heritage*)*

Britain had received a free hand in Morocco in return for unrestricted British suzerainty in Egypt. In lieu of more serious concerns, the sultan indulged himself with western luxuries; he owned

twenty-five grand pianos, six hundred cameras, and a gold-plated motor car—the latter unquestionably the greatest of his affectations as Morocco then had no roads suitable for automobile travel.

If the sultan was weak, his government appeared just as feeble. The army was comprised of only about two thousand ill-prepared, ill-trained troops, and the regime's finances were unsound. Thus, Raisuli had little to fear from the government. However, his forces, determined and brutal though they were, possessed insufficient power to wreak the desired revenge against the sultan and his backers. A credible solution for the rebel chieftain was to force concessions from the sultan by kidnapping a foreigner for ransom. Such an action, assuming the foreign power applied pressure on the government, would destroy the sultan's prestige, assault his treasury, and enrich Raisuli. The seizing of Perdicaris was the result.[26]

Only minutes after the abduction Samuel R. Gummere, the U.S. consul general at Tangier, received word of the outrage from the Perdicaris villa. After a quick visit to the compound where he solicitously expressed his concern to the family, he consulted British Minister Sir Arthur Nicholson, then fired off a protest to the Moroccan government and an appeal to Washington for a show of naval power: "Request man-of-war to enforce demands," he wrote. As Secretary of State Hay was in St. Louis delivering a speech at the World's Fair, subordinate officials in the Department of State, aware of Gummere's standing and the seriousness of the cable, passed the message along to the president. Roosevelt promptly dispatched a naval squadron to Morocco and, through the Department of State, a communication to Gummere directing him to hold the Moroccan government responsible for Perdicaris's safe return. The Department also informed the consul general that three or four days might elapse before the arrival of a U.S. warship.[27]

Gummere did not have an easy time dealing with the Moroccan government. Part of the problem lay in the physical location of the officials with whom he had to deal; the foreign minister, Mohammed Torres, had his offices in Tangier near the foreign legations, but the real power was in the hands of the grand vizier, the court, and marginally the sultan, based in Fez many miles in the interior. Moreover, the foreign minister had alliances with a number of Raisuli's enemies, making it impossible for him to promote vigorously the views of the United States without government capitulation to the rebel chief's demands.

A further complication was added by the rivalry among the Great Powers in North Africa. Although the French had assumed responsibility, as Admiral French E. Chadwick put it, for "the most fanatic and troublesome eight or ten million in the world," they were not entirely helpful in American dealings with the Moroccan government. Indeed, the French minister, St. René Taillandier, seemed more anxious to preserve the prestige of his government's new client in its showdown with Raisuli than in saving the lives of Perdicaris and his stepson. The French throughout seemed terribly worried that American and British naval power would undercut their influence in the region.[28]

Complications aside, Raisuli soon communicated his terms to the government through one of the *shereefs* of Wazan who, acting at the insistence of the U.S. consul, made contact with the rebel camp. Raisuli's demands were high: he wanted $70,000 in indemnity from the bashaw paid through the forced sale of his property; the immediate dismissal of the latter from his position; the ceding of the two districts around Tangier to Raisuli, who would administer them without governmental interference or taxation; the arrest

ION PERDICARIS.

Ion Perdicaris. *Courtesy New York Public Library (originally published in* American Heritage*)*

of many of his previous tormentors; and the unrestricted access for Raisuli's followers to a number of specified locations. Gummere did not see grounds for optimism, given the government's immediate rejection of the terms and the new aggressiveness of the local population arising from Raisuli's defying central authority. Given that the government had not been able to capture Raisuli despite years of trying, it did not appear that it had any chance of forcing Perdicaris's release; punishing the rebel chief as desired by Washington seemed remote.[29]

Nothing in Perdicaris's past made him a likely cause célèbre; nothing made him a probable target for kidnapping, except his very presence in Morocco. Son of a Greek immigrant father who taught for a time at Harvard before establishing a successful business in Trenton and New York and a mother from a wealthy South Carolina family, Ion Perdicaris knew the advantage of money. He studied for a year at Harvard, where he learned to appreciate art and literature, subjects in which he later dabbled in an amateurish way. Instead of serving in the Union Army during the Civil War he resolved a family conflict (his father was a Union supporter and his mother a daughter of the Confederacy) by going abroad. From then on he spent a good portion of his life outside the United States, for a time in England and after 1877 in Tangier, where he built a stately villa and indulged his many hobbies. Though he lived in the manner of a colonial overlord, he became a friend and benefactor of his Muslim hosts.[30]

At the end of May the crisis seemed to take a turn for the worse when Raisuli sent word that he not only would remain uncompromising on his terms, but he also would insist that the United States and Great Britain guarantee that the Moroccan government honor them. This sounded ominous to Gummere. It proved troubling to Roosevelt and Hay as well, who assumed the worst for Perdicaris—especially when they received notice on May 29 that the sultan's government had only two days to satisfy Raisuli's demands. Meanwhile, the American press had become restive.

President Roosevelt turned to naval power. Not long after assuming office, he had sought to impose a coherent training and exercise policy on the navy. During 1901 armored vessels were concentrated in the North Atlantic, while in the winter of 1902–03 large-scale exercises took place in the Caribbean. In the summer of 1903 one squadron conducted extensive maneuvers off the Azores while another, the European Squadron, called on a number of continental ports. Together they formed the largest American naval force ever seen in that part of the world, although not as large as the force available in 1904. In the winter of 1903–04 three fleet squadrons arrived in the Caribbean and then moved on toward European waters: the Battleship Squadron, comprised of five battleships; the European Squadron, made up of three cruisers; and the South Atlantic Squadron, consisting of two cruisers and two gunboats—an imposing array of vessels.[31]

It was this force that President Roosevelt had available during the Perdicaris affair, a degree of naval strength that surely helps account for the aggressiveness and belligerence of his approach to the crisis. The South Atlantic Squadron, sailing separately from the other two, stopped on May 26 at the port of Santa Cruz on Tenerife in the Canary Islands, where Admiral Chadwick received orders to take his fleet on to Tangier. On May 28, Roosevelt, in response to the new information from Gummere, sent orders to the European Squadron, then taking on coal in the Azores, directing that it sail for Morocco. The Battleship Squadron, also in the Azores, went on to Lisbon.[32]

When Admiral Chadwick arrived at Tangier on May 30 his assumption and that of Consul General Gummere was that the squadron's presence would calm foreigners and apply not-so-subtle pressure to the nerves of the Moroccan foreign minister. Chadwick greeted Torres, whom he invited aboard the flagship *Brooklyn*, with a proper mixture of courtesy and military threat. Torres was not impressed, not enough in any event to cave in to Raisuli. On June 1, the European Squadron arrived at Tangier, bringing to seven the number of warships in Moroccan waters.

Negotiations did not move forward rapidly between the sultan's government and Raisuli even after the two sides had made contact. Not until after the middle of June did a settlement seem possible. Partly to blame for the delay was the desire of the French and the sultan that at least a portion of the U.S. fleet be removed before they would go ahead with the discussions. Raisuli, for his part, treated one of the sultan's envoys with such cruelty that it is remarkable that negotiations did not terminate entirely. Convinced that the envoy had committed atrocities against some of his supporters, Raisuli seized him and made him a hostage. When the sultan refused to ransom him, Raisuli auctioned the man to the highest bidder among his tribesmen on the understanding that the new "owner" could avenge past wrongs however he wished. As soon as the auction ended, the highest bidder slit the envoy's throat.[33]

Meanwhile, in view of the commitment of U.S. naval power, the Department of State received news about Perdicaris that caused disquiet in policy circles. On June 1 a letter from a cotton broker, A. H. Slocumb, in Fayetteville, North Carolina, had arrived indicating that in 1863, while Slocumb himself was in Athens, Ion

Perdicaris had gone to that city for the express purpose of becoming a Greek citizen. Perdicaris had hoped that in acquiring Greek citizenship he could convince the Confederacy not to expropriate property that he owned in South Carolina because in that instance confiscation would alienate a foreign national. Regardless of his present claim, Slocumb went on, Perdicaris had become a Greek citizen in 1863 and thus, by Slocumb's presumption, had renounced his American citizenship.

Although the records are not definitive on the subject, it seems apparent that Secretary of State Hay and President Roosevelt quickly discussed Perdicaris's status—probably on June 1. Obviously concerned that they had placed American prestige on the line for an individual of doubtful citizenship, Roosevelt and Hay immediately undertook an investigation of Slocumb's information. On June 4 the Department of State wired its minister in Greece to find out the facts. His response of June 7 could not have pleased President Roosevelt: in 1862 one Ion Perdicaris, then age 22, had applied for citizenship. It had been granted on March 19, 1862 (Slocumb had been off by one year). On June 10 the U.S. minister in Greece informed Hay of his opinion that this was the same Ion Perdicaris.[34]

Apparently the president and secretary of state then pursued two courses of action: keeping Slocumb's information secret from the public and investigating further to determine whether Perdicaris had in fact renounced his American citizenship. That Roosevelt would wish to keep the new information confidential is not surprising as he had already gone out on a limb in needlessly committing U.S. military power. Whether he also hoped to use the matter as a political issue at the Republican National Convention later that same month is an open question and the major contention of a distinguished popular historian.[35]

Given the information provided by the American minister in Greece it might have been possible, had he been so inclined, for the president to wash his hands of the affair as of no concern to the United States. However, the best evidence acquired by Secretary Hay shortly after the incident ended is that Perdicaris was indeed an American citizen entitled to protection; he simply held dual citizenship. Under U.S. law he was an American citizen because his parents were citizens. Because his father had been born in Greece, Ion could become a citizen of that country by expressing his desire to do so, which is what he did on March 19, 1862. Declaring his intent to become a Greek citizen did not, however, deprive him of his American citizenship unless he intended to drop the latter. Apparently, intent to become an expatriate could be registered through service in another nation's army or through a declaration, but it had to be deliberate in some way. In Perdicaris's case, what he wanted was not to reject the United States but to avoid having to register for service in the Confederate Army because his failure to do so would result in the confiscation of his South Carolina property. He made no attempt to reside in Greece long enough to gain political rights, though by his own admission he was remiss about asserting his American citizenship after living there, largely because he spent so much time outside the United States.[36] Not surprisingly, during his captivity neither he nor his kin revealed that he had ever considered himself anything but an American citizen.

While officials in Washington pondered the issues of Perdicaris's nationality, events in Morocco provided cause for optimism. Persisting in his insistence on the release of Perdicaris, President Roosevelt had informed Hay on June 15 that the United States must take the position of demanding "the death of those that harm him if he is harmed" and further that "it would be well to enter into negotiations with England and France looking to the possibility of an expedition to punish the brigands."[37] None of this seemed necessary, however, when Gummere wired that the sultan's emissaries and Raisuli had reached an agreement, to be finalized on June 19, that would result in the hostages' release on June 21.

A hitch then occurred. When the government moved slowly to guarantee a chieftain against reprisal if he allowed his village to be used for the conclusion of the deal, it seemed that everything was off and the government to blame. This prompted a message from Gummere to Hay on June 21 urging an ultimatum in which the United States would demand an indemnity and threaten to land marines if the government showed further reluctance to settle.[38] Hay and Roosevelt decided on a response, drafted by Hay, and often recited as appropriate in all hostage cases: "This Government wants Perdicaris alive or Raisuli dead."[39] The release to the press—and to the Republican National Convention—of this resounding message imprinted it indelibly on the minds of generations of Americans. Interestingly, the remainder of the telegram, a portion not made public, cautioned Gummere not to land marines or seize the Moroccan customs. After the government's promises of immunity to the chieftain but before the delivery of the U.S. ultimatum, Raisuli and the sultan's agents completed arrangements for Perdicaris's release. On June 24, in exchange for $70,000 and some government prisoners, Perdicaris and his stepson were freed. They arrived back at his villa that night.[40]

Why did President Roosevelt authorize sending the telegram? Historian Barbara Tuchman finds the timing of its release on June 22 and the beginning of the Republican National Convention just the day before more than mere coincidence. Certain facts support her thesis. Party leaders, while generally unfriendly toward Roosevelt, found themselves powerless to prevent his nomination, given his enormous popular support and the careful orchestration conducted by the president's people behind the scenes. The convention promised to be dull, so dull in fact that the momentum and excitement needed to sustain a campaign might be lacking. *Harper's Weekly* quoted a delegate from Alabama as saying: "It is not a Republican Convention, it is no kind of a convention; it is a roosevelt." But it could not be a true "roosevelt" unless something were done to electrify the delegates and dramatize the candidate himself. What better tactic than to release a white-hot telegram threatening injury to some North African potentate? When Speaker of the House Joseph Cannon read the message, the delegates went wild. Senator Chauncey Depew said it was "magnificent." Others extolled the president's "courage," his willingness "to stand by" the citizens of the United States, and his strength of character.[41] That Roosevelt began considering a military operation in Morocco some time before the convention does not undercut Tuchman's argument. He did not have to release the famous portion of the instruction to Gummere or have it read at the convention. Given his customary approach to life, it does not seem unusual that on June 22 he would see a fortuitous coincidence of political advantage and national policy.

The "Perdicaris alive or Raisuli dead" telegram aside, a larger question intrudes. Why did President Roosevelt react so aggressively in the Perdicaris affair; indeed, why did he seem to overreact in support of a man of doubtful citizenship when he had acted so cautiously and discreetly during the Ellen Stone kidnapping? There are several answers to this question. A truism of international politics is that not only does the existence of military power incline a nation toward its use, but it tends actively to expand a nation's interest as well. In 1904, Roosevelt had impressive naval power at his disposal in a region susceptible to gunboat diplomacy; it is not surprising that he would decide U.S. interests required acting as he did. That he would choose to pursue an aggressive policy and call attention to his behavior in an election year is even less surprising. That he also had in mind to send a signal of American naval capability to the major nations of Europe, particularly Germany, which had recently intervened in Venezuela and shown unusual interest in the Caribbean, seems indisputable.

There was yet another compelling political factor motivating Roosevelt in the Perdicaris incident. He had received stinging criticism that must have proved sharply injurious to his self-image for his handling of the Ellen Stone affair. A review of the editorials of leading newspapers addressing the Stone captivity reveals almost nothing favorable to the former Rough Rider. During the crisis the *New York Times* asked: "Should crimes of that character be encouraged and made profitable by the payment of the exaggerated ransom . . . even though hope is held out that the United States Government may recover the money collected in this most atrocious form of blackmail and thus permit its return to the subscribers?"[42] The *New York Tribune*, upon the release of Stone in February 1902, opined that "brigandage in Europe in the twentieth century is a hideous anachronism, and the state which tolerates it stands arraigned at the moral bar of the world. It cannot . . . forever escape arraignment at another bar than the moral one—the bar of law backed up by righteous force."[43]

Ten days earlier the *Tribune* had said that the American people deserved "the release of Miss Stone, and [the] punishment of those responsible for the cowardly and brutal outrage upon American citizenship in her person—no matter whether they be in mountain caves and cabins or in palaces at Sophia or Istanbul. American honor demands redress, and so does the welfare of civilization."[44] The *Chicago Tribune* demanded that "the repayment of the ransom money [by Turkey] should be compelled by force."[45] Of all the newspapers, the *Houston Post* was the harshest: "This affair of Miss Stone has taxed the patience of the American people until it is about to be exhausted. . . . We have a president who boasts himself to be strenuous, but who has been playing the role of the fainéant, a do-nothing who lets himself and the country be made a mock of by a handful of foreign brigands." The editorial went on to say that "a few warships in the harbors of the countries at fault and a couple of regiments of American regulars would do the trick." As the affair neared its conclusion, the *Post* asked: "Why was the protection afforded to Miss Stone limited to vain protests and fruitless negotiations? . . . Is an American citizen abroad to be taken care of only by letter writing? Or are the army and navy of the United States to use only when there is a motive of gain and Mr. Roosevelt's rich tropical islands are in question?"[46]

As MUCH AS any president in American history and more than most, Theodore Roosevelt enjoyed the limelight and pursued a policy of heroic leadership. To put it in less flattering terms, he sought constantly to draw attention to himself, to show off. Henry Adams once confided to a friend that at one White House dinner party he had attended, all the guests had been "overwhelmed in a torrent of oratory, and at last I heard only the repetition of I - I - I attached to

HARPER'S WEEKLY

JOURNAL OF CIVILIZATION

VOL. L.   New York, Saturday, February 3, 1906   NO. 2964

THE BUSY SHOWMAN.—III.

Ladies and Gentlemen: I have the great pleasure this week of submitting to your favorable consideration my latest Foreign Exhibit. Certain curious side-show men at the other end of Pennsylvania Avenue criticise this Exhibit on the ground that it is without precedent. But precedents don't concern me. Besides, my predecessors, although worthy enough in a sense, were

Theodore Roosevelt's "Big Stick Diplomacy." *Courtesy Library of Congress*

indiscretions greater one than another."[47] Mark Twain referred to Roosevelt as the Tom Sawyer of the political world, "always show-ing off; always hunting for a chance to show off; in his frenzied imagination the Great Republic is a vast Barnum circus with him for a clown and the whole world for an audience; he would go to Halifax for half a chance to show off, and he would go to hell for a whole one."[48]

In the manner of one who seeks to attract attention, Roosevelt always desired that such attention be positive; criticism, whether justifiable or not, challenged his heroic reputation. Thus, when newspapers chided him for his failure to shoot a bear during a hunting trip to Mississippi in 1902, he responded angrily, and he decided that in the future his hunts must be unmistakably and unquestionably successful. His remarks to one of his hunting partners after the election of 1904 are revealing: "We must be dead sure that there is no slip up and that I get the game. I think the thing to do is to say we are after mountain lions, and we could make sure of killing one or two of them; but I should most want to get a bear. Have you a thoroughly good pack, and do you know the ground so that we could be sure of getting the bear?"[49]

Although the evidence is circumstantial and not definitive, it seems likely, in the absence of other explanatory factors, that Theodore Roosevelt concluded he would never again respond as he did during the Stone kidnapping. Indeed, in this regard, the president's note of March 1, 1902, to Secretary Hay is most revealing: "Will you bring up the matter at the next Cabinet meeting of making a proclamation anent Miss Stone, to the effect that never again will we sanction the payment of a ransom?"[50] Other challenges to the nation's honor, even those involving dubious claims to support, like Perdicaris's, would be met by the appearance of firm and forceful resolve. American credibility in the world community and Roosevelt's ego demanded no less.

NOTES

1. Leften Stavros Stavrianos, *The Balkans since 1453* (New York: Rinehart, 1958), 517, 408–9. See also Randall B. Woods, "Terrorism in the Age of Roosevelt: The Miss Stone Affair," *American Quarterly* 31 (Fall 1979): 480.

2. Woods, "Miss Stone Affair," 480–83.

3. Laura M. Sherman, *Fires on the Mountain: The Macedonian Revolutionary Movement and the Kidnapping of Ellen Stone* (New York: Columbia University Press, 1980), 13–21. For an excellent account of Macedonian revolutionary movements and some attention to the Stone affair see Duncan Perry, *The Politics of Terror: The Macedonian Revolutionary Movements, 1893–1903* (Durham, NC: Duke University Press, 1988), 103–5, 171, 180.

4. Woods, "Miss Stone Affair," 484.

5. Sherman, *Fires on the Mountain*, 22–26.

6. Ibid., 28–33.

7. Sherman, *Fires on the Mountain*, 33; P. H. Lazzaro to Charles Dickinson, September 5, 1901, U.S. Department of State, *Papers Relating to the Foreign Relations of the United States, 1902* (Washington, DC: Government Printing Office, 1903), 998 (hereafter cited as *FRUS*, followed by appropriate year).

8. J. W. Baird to Dickinson, September 7, 1901; John G. A. Leishman to John Hay, September 20, 1901; Leishman to Hay, September 20, 1901; Leishman to Hay, September 24, 1901, *FRUS, 1902*, 998–1001.

9. Lazzaro to Dickinson, September 5, 1901, ibid., 998. See also Woods, "Miss Stone Affair," 485.

10. James McGregor to Leishman, September 16, 1901, *FRUS, 1902*, 1001–2.

11. Alvey Adee to Spencer Eddy, October 6, 1901, ibid., 1008–9; *Christian Herald* 24 (October 16, 1901): 910; Woods, "Miss Stone Affair," 486.

12. Judson Smith to Hay, September 28, 1901, Miscellaneous Letters, U.S. Department of State, Record Group 59, General Records of the Department of State, Consular Dispatches, Sofia, Bulgarian Series, 1901–1904 (Washington, DC: National Archives Microfilm Publications [hereafter NAMP], 1946) (hereafter cited as T682). See also Adee's October 6 letter of instruction that allows for "no possibility of U.S. government paying or guaranteeing ransom," U.S. Department of State, Record Group 84, Records of the Foreign Service Posts of the Department of State, "Diplomatic Instructions—Turkey," no. 168 (NAMP, 1946), 7:580–81.

13. Adee to Dickinson, September 29, 1901, and Dickinson to Adee, October 12, 1901, Bulgarian Series 5, T682; Eddy to Hay, October 5, 1901, NAMP, 1946; Hay to Dickinson, October 5 and 6, 1901, NAMP, 1946; Dickinson to Hay, October 12, 1901, Bulgarian Series 5, T682. See also Sherman, *Fires on the Mountain*, 43.

14. Dickinson to Hay, October 12, 1901, Bulgarian Series 5, T682. On October 3, 1901, Adee had relayed the advice of Charles Stone, Ellen's brother, that Russian influence be pursued to gain her release. He also had suggested that Eddy consult informally with the Russian ambassador in Constantinople. U.S. Department of State, "Diplomatic Instructions—Turkey," no. 168, 7:577.

15. Theodore Roosevelt to Adee, October 2, 1901, in Elting E. Morison, ed., *The Letters of Theodore Roosevelt*, 8 vols. (Cambridge, MA: Harvard University Press, 1951–1954), 1:156. This presidential note probably prompted Adee's October 8 instruction to Eddy to furnish a list of all American missionary societies doing work in Turkey. U.S. Department of State, "Diplomatic Instructions—Turkey," no. 168, 7:583.

16. Morison, *The Letters of Theodore Roosevelt*, 1:157.

17. Woods, "Miss Stone Affair," 489–90.

18. Sherman, *Fires on the Mountain*, 47–48.

19. Eddy to Hay, December 15, 1901, *FRUS, 1902*, 1015–16.

20. Eddy to Hay, December 13, 1901, ibid., 1013–14.

21. Alexander Gargiulo to Leishman, January 18, 1902, ibid.; Leishman to Hay, January 20, 1902, ibid., 1018–19; Leishman to Hay, February 12, 18, 23, 1902, ibid., 1021.

22. Sherman, *Fires on the Mountain*, 58; Woods, "Miss Stone Affair," 492–93.

23. Sherman, *Fires on the Mountain*, 87–88, 97–98; Ellen Stone, "Six Months among Brigands," *McClure's Magazine* 19, no. 5 (September 1902): 464–71; Katerina Tsilka, "Born among Brigands," ibid. 19, no. 4 (August 1902): 291–300.

24. Woods, "Miss Stone Affair," 493.

25. Sherman, *Fires on the Mountain*, 96–97; U.S. Congress, House, Committee on Claims, *Repayment of Ransom of Ellen Stone*, H. Rept. 807, 62d Cong., 2d sess., May 31, 1912. Interestingly, none of the major books on Theodore Roosevelt's career deals with the Stone kidnapping or its resolution.

26. For the best accounts of the kidnapping and its background see Barbara W. Tuchman, "Perdicaris Alive or Raisuli Dead," *American Heritage* 10 (August 1959): 18–21, 98–101; Thomas Etzold, "Protection or Politics? 'Perdicaris Alive or Raisuli Dead,' " *The Historian* 37 (February 1975): 297–304; and William J. Hourihan, "Marlinspike Diplomacy: The Navy in the Mediterranean, 1904," *U.S. Naval Institute Proceedings* 105 (January 1979): 42–49.

27. Samuel René Gummere to Hay, May 19 and May 22, 1904, *FRUS, 1904* (Washington, DC: Government Printing Office, 1905), 496–97. See also Joseph Choate to Hay, May 27, 1904, ibid., 338.

28. See Tuchman, "Perdicaris Alive," 20; and Etzold, "Protection or Politics?" 299–300.

29. Choate to Hay, May 27, 1904, *FRUS, 1904*, 338; Tuchman, "Perdicaris Alive," 21; Etzold, "Protection or Politics?" 299.

30. Tuchman, "Perdicaris Alive," 21.

31. Hourihan, "Marlinspike Diplomacy," 43–45.

32. Ibid.

33. Etzold, "Protection or Politics?" 301.

34. Harold E. Davis, "The Citizenship of Ion Perdicaris," *Journal of Modern History* 13 (December 1941): 517–26; Etzold, "Protection or Politics?" 301; Tuchman, "Perdicaris Alive," 99.

35. Tuchman, "Perdicaris Alive," 99–101.

36. Etzold, "Protection or Politics?" 303.

37. Roosevelt to Hay, June 15, 1904, in Theodore Roosevelt, *Theodore Roosevelt Papers*, Series 4B: Roosevelt-Hay Letters, 1897–1905 (Washington, DC: Library of Congress, 1967), Reel 414.

38. Gummere to Hay, June 17, 1904, *FRUS, 1904*, 501–2; Gummere to Hay, June 20, 1904, ibid., 502; Gummere to Hay, June 21, 1904, ibid., 502–3.

39. Hay to Gummere, June 22, 1904, ibid., 503. A survey of the literature on Theodore Roosevelt shows that only three of the major books dealing with his career address the Perdicaris affair, and none gives it more than a page. See Frederick W. Marks, *Velvet on Iron: The Diplomacy of Theodore Roosevelt* (Lincoln: University of Nebraska Press, 1979), 145–46; Henry Pringle, *Theodore Roosevelt: A Biography* (New York: Harcourt, Brace and Company, 1931), 388–89; and Nathan Miller, *Theodore Roosevelt: A Life* (New York: William Morrow and Company, 1992), 438–39.

40. Gummere to Hay, June 23, 1904, *FRUS, 1904*, 503–4.

41. This telegram is consistent with the view expressed by Hay on May 31 when he informed the U.S. ambassador in London, Joseph Choate, that "the Moroccan Government must understand that Raisuli's life will be demanded if

Perdicaris is murdered." Hay to Choate, May 31, 1904, ibid., 338. On June 9, Hay told Gummere that "it should be clearly understood that if Mr. Perdicaris should be murdered, the life of the murderer will be demanded." Hay to Gummere, June 9, 1904, ibid., 498–99. The *Harper's Weekly* quote is taken from Tuchman, "Perdicaris Alive," 100. John Hay noted in his diary on June 23, 1904, that "it is curious how a concise impropriety hits the public." Quoted in Pringle, *Theodore Roosevelt: A Biography*, 389.

    42. *New York Times*, October 8, 1901.

    43. *New York Tribune*, February 24, 1902.

    44. Ibid., February 14, 1902.

    45. *Chicago Tribune*, October 6, 1901.

    46. *Houston Post*, November 13, 1901, February 2, 1902.

    47. Henry Adams, *The Education of Henry Adams* (Boston: Houghton Mifflin Company, 1961), 417.

    48. Bernard DeVoto, ed., *Mark Twain in Eruption* (New York: Harper and Brothers, 1940), 49.

    49. Morison, *Letters of Theodore Roosevelt*, 4:1029. See also Bruce Miroff, *Icons of Democracy: American Leaders as Heroes, Aristocrats, Dissenters, and Democrats* (New York: Basic Books, 1993), 173.

    50. Theodore Roosevelt to Hay, March 1, 1902, *Theodore Roosevelt Papers*, Reel 414.

Chapter 4

At Risk in War and Revolution: Bargaining with the Soviet Union

Two twentieth-century phenomena, world war and revolution, exposed America's citizens to increased risk abroad and created serious problems for its policymakers. Both world wars placed Americans in distant locations removed from U.S. jurisdiction, while revolution in Russia increased possibilities for mutual distrust. In the years immediately following World War I and again at the end of World War II, officials in Washington had to address the maddening dilemma of how to serve long-range foreign policy interests while successfully repatriating Americans held by the Soviet Union. For the first time since the Barbary kidnappings, a foreign government was responsible for initiating the use of pawns and hostages.

Owing to serious differences between the United States and the new Communist government of Russia, several Americans were held hostage within the Soviet Union between 1918 and 1922. The Soviet-American discord arose out of confused conditions immediately following the Bolshevik Revolution, during which time the Bolsheviks did much to antagonize Western leaders, and the West, in turn, took military, economic, and diplomatic action directly contrary to the interests of the Soviets. Comparatively weak and insecure militarily and inspired by their ideologically informed perception of the nature of their capitalist enemies, the Soviets did not shrink from dealing in human flesh when the need for diplomatic leverage arose.

Soviet-American relations during the first five years after the Russian Revolution of 1917 were defined by World War I, by virulently hostile Soviet behavior toward the country's former Western allies, by Soviet rejection of many of the accepted norms of international behavior, and by Japanese and Western, including American, intervention in the internal affairs of the USSR. The war brought conflicting preoccupations, out of which came great misunderstanding and tragedy. To the Russian Communist leaders the central issues of the period were political reform and control of the means of production; they did not care very much about the war or who won it, and immediately after the revolution they moved to withdraw from the conflict. To the Western allies the defeat of Germany was the primary focus because, they believed, its control of the European continent, if combined with the power Germany would attain by acquiring Allied colonies, would make it invincible—and perpetually dangerous. Allied leaders could not understand the lack of enthusiasm in the Soviet Union for the war effort, and they particularly deplored the separate peace eventually negotiated by the Communists.

Nothing could have been designed to give greater offense than the Soviets' Decree on Peace, issued on the day of their ascendance to power. The Decree called for social revolution in Germany, France, and England, where, it said, the class-conscious proletariat should rise up and defeat the enemies of the toiling masses. It also called for a democratic peace, one without indemnities and annexations and one in which not only would no one profit through the acquisition of territory but after which all colonial possessions would be relinquished as well. Thus, the Soviets not only signaled their withdrawal from the war—a move that would allow the transfer of nearly one million German troops to the western front—but they also appealed over the heads of governments directly to the people in Western nations.

Over the course of four months (from December 1917 until March 1918) the Soviets proceeded to negotiate with the Germans, a one-sided effort in which all the Soviet delegates could do was decide how best to surrender—and apparently how best to offend the Germans. For instance, Soviet "diplomat" Karl Radek took special pleasure in blowing his pipe smoke in the face of his German counterpart after handing out inflammatory propaganda tracts to German guards along the route into Brest-Litovsk. The Soviet Union's involvement in the war officially ended with the signing of the Treaty of Brest-Litovsk on March 3, 1918.[1]

Given the importance attached to the defeat of Germany, it is not surprising that the Allies would seek to redress the Soviet withdrawal from the war. Their first goals were to reopen the eastern front and protect military supplies previously shipped to the Soviet Union; a related objective was to empower a suitable alternative to the Communists, who, it was widely believed, in this disturbed period could claim little moral authority to govern and who, in fact, controlled only a small portion of the Russian Empire. To achieve these aims the Allies intervened in two areas: in the north at Murmansk on the north edge of the Kola Peninsula as well as at

Archangel on the White Sea; and at Vladivostok in eastern Siberia. The United States participated in both of these ventures.

During the time of the provisional government, from March through November 1917, the Allies had shipped huge quantities of war supplies to the Archangel area, a total of about 170 thousand tons of material ranging from ammunition to metals of various sorts. The purpose of these shipments, which were financed by credits from the United States and Great Britain, had been to keep Russia in the war.[2] The Soviets' seizure of these supplies and their simultaneous rejection of any obligation to repay the credits infuriated Allied leaders who had great need for the supplies in the West, particularly after the diversion of vast numbers of German forces from the eastern front to the western. Following extensive deliberations and repeated recommendations from military planners, the Allied Supreme War Council agreed in June 1918 to occupy Archangel and Murmansk out of a desire to regain control of these war supplies and concern that the Germans might occupy the two cities. In July, President Woodrow Wilson made a decision to send a force of three battalions to the northern ports while at the same time agreeing to contribute troops to an intervention in Siberia. By early August these Allied forces had taken control of Murmansk and Archangel (the greater number of the Americans at Archangel) but had not secured the war material, which the Soviets already had shipped into the interior. Archangel was handed over without bloodshed because Russian forces opposed to the Bolsheviks staged an uprising and seized the city just before the Allies arrived.

With the conclusion of the war on November 11, 1918, the main reasons for the northern intervention were no longer valid. There is no denying the fact that Allied leaders hoped that their action would also lead to the overthrow of the Communists throughout the country, but it soon became apparent that the control of Murmansk and Archangel was serving no useful purpose toward that goal. President Wilson, who had become preoccupied with his peace program in early 1919, decided that American forces should be withdrawn, and they left in June and July. The British, who remained determined to influence the Soviet Union's political future, stayed on in the north until late in September of 1919.

Meanwhile, the Allies also had undertaken a military intervention in Siberia. Many of the same factors that influenced action in northern Russia motivated Allied leaders to move into the region. At the time of the Bolshevik Revolution there were at least 800 thousand tons of war supplies scattered about the port city of Vladivostok, nearly five times the quantity held at Archangel. The Allies did not want these supplies to fall into the possession of either the Russian Communists or the Germans, about whom fear remained intense. As the Bolsheviks moved toward the conclusion of their separate peace, Allied officials became increasingly intrigued by thoughts of reopening the eastern front, and military planners spoke enthusiastically about using non-Communist Russians to establish a coordinated military effort linking up northern Russia, southern Russia, and Siberia. That this was an important motivating factor became more evident as a military crisis loomed in the West in the spring of 1918.

The existence of a large force of former Austro-Hungarian prisoners of war and the so-called Czech Legion were also factors in this decision. The 1.5 million former prisoners of war, released upon the Bolshevik withdrawal from the fighting, represented to Allied leaders a potential German resource for the seizing of Siberia, even though only a small percentage of them had come from the German-speaking sector of the Hapsburg Empire and in retrospect the whole idea seems farfetched. The Czech Legion was another matter. This force, consisting of Czech units that had defected from the Austro-Hungarian army while fighting on the eastern front as well as other Czech nationals from within the Russian Empire, had fought in the Russian army under the provisional government and soon after the signing of the Treaty of Brest-Litovsk (on March 3) became one of the strongest and best-disciplined military units in Russia. The Allies were anxious to transfer this force to the western front. The Bolsheviks agreed to allow this to occur because the presence of the armed Czech force on their territory could have been dangerous to their position if it had chosen to ally with other non-Communist forces within the country. As the only way out of the Soviet Union in the spring of 1918, given German control of the West, was through the port of Vladivostok, thousands of Czechs began making their way eastward via the Trans-Siberian Railway during the period from March through May. As events transpired, fighting broke out between the Czechs and the Bolsheviks, which resulted in the Czech seizure of three thousand miles of the western end of the railway, the part running from the Volga River to Irkutsk. Of the roughly fifty-five thousand Czechs, fifteen thousand were in Vladivostok by the summer of 1918; the other forty thousand or so were blocked to the west of Irkutsk and soon began cooperating with anti-Bolshevik groups to overthrow Soviet authority in a large area of western Siberia. On June 29 the Czech force in Vladivostok managed to end Bolshevik control of that city as well.

The appeal of the Czechs for the Allies' support immediately after their seizure of Vladivostok gave the latter an excuse to move

Machine Gun Company of the 31st U.S. Infantry at Vladivostok, Siberia, November 9, 1918. *Courtesy National Archives*

ahead with plans for the reopening of an eastern front and, possibly, for the delivery of a fatal blow to the Russian Communists. President Wilson's decision in early July to join in the northern intervention was coupled with one to send troops to Siberia to aid the Czechs by providing what he presumed was support for an underdog force under attack by the Communists and, potentially, by former Austro-Hungarian prisoners of war. Some seven thousand American forces arrived in Siberia in August and September 1918, only to find that the Czechs, whom they had been sent to protect, had secured control of the eastern end of the Trans-Siberian Railway and had linked up with their colleagues west of Irkutsk. Having only a murkily defined directive as his guide, General William S. Graves seems to have limited U.S. troop activity mainly to the guarding of a section of the Trans-Siberian Railway and watching nervously as his Japanese and Western allies sought to achieve their own goals in the region, the Japanese staying on for two years after all the Americans had left. The American troops had been totally withdrawn by April 1920, but not before they had engaged in a couple of skirmishes with Communist forces. The fact that foreign troops were there at all was a source of tremendous

annoyance to the Bolsheviks, who in the months after the conclusion of the war began strengthening their army and gaining the upper hand against their poorly organized Russian opponents.

President Wilson's rationale for agreeing to go along with the Allies in these ventures in Russia has been scrutinized by scholars for years.[3] His motives are actually less important here than are his anti-Bolshevik prejudices, the actions that he took predicated on them, and the very fact of U.S. intervention. Taking American hostages represented a way for the Kremlin to deal with Washington's behavior, although one must also conclude that in the fluid and confused state of Soviet internal affairs after November 1917, some Americans and other foreigners possibly would have suffered incarceration in any event.

Although Wilson was not a wholly enthusiastic partner in either the Siberian or northern interventions, he had adopted an avidly anti-Bolshevik position almost immediately after the November revolution, leading him into moves highly likely to antagonize Soviet leaders. One of the first such moves was the president's refusal to extend diplomatic recognition to the Soviet government and his continuing acceptance of Boris Bakhmetev, the ambassador sent to Washington by the provisional government, as the official Russian representative in the United States. More than that, the State and the Treasury Departments began working closely with Bakhmetev on the disbursement of funds under his control—monies made available by the U.S. Treasury as well as funds raised through the sale of Russian bonds before the fall of the czar. Some of this money went indirectly (through the British and the French) to General A. M. Kaledin, a leader of anti-Bolshevik forces in southern Russia, with President Wilson's approval; in the summer and fall of 1918 huge amounts went to other Bolshevik opponents.[4]

Once Wilson had resolved to join in the intervention he took an action to justify his decision that gave further offense to Bolshevik leaders: he released the so-called Sisson Papers for publication in the United States. These papers were a set of documents brought back from Russia in the spring of 1918 by Edgar Sisson, an American journalist in the employ of the Committee on Public Information, the U.S. wartime propaganda agency. They allegedly "demonstrated" that Vladimir Ilyich Lenin and Leon Trotsky were paid agents of the Germans. Whether or not Wilson recognized the documents as the forgeries that they were, his release of them threw down the gauntlet to the Russian Communists at a time when there were numerous U.S. diplomatic officials stuck in areas under Bolshevik control.[5]

American and other Western diplomatic personnel became the first hostages of the Soviets. At the time of the on-again, off-again negotiations leading to Brest-Litovsk, Allied ambassadors made a decision to leave Petrograd out of fear that German forces might occupy the city. The ambassadors moved to Vologda, a couple of hundred miles to the northeast of Moscow where they set up residence, and watched and waited in relative security but less than splendid isolation or comfort. By early July, as Soviet leaders became aware of Allied intentions to intervene in northern Russia, they sought to convince the ambassadors to go to Moscow where, one must assume in view of later developments, they would become human bargaining chips. The Soviets also placed guards around the Vologda embassies, prompting the U.S. ambassador, David R. Francis, to protest that the Soviet intent was to create a "virtual arrangement to place us under espionage or to make us prisoners."[6] The ambassadors refused to go to Moscow, insisting instead that a locomotive be provided to take them to Archangel, which, they were informed by British General F. C. Poole, would be occupied by Allied troops around August 1. Soon after their arrival at Archangel they sailed to Kandalaksha, a port under British control across the White Sea and out of harm's way.

Personnel of lesser rank did not escape Soviet clutches so readily. On August 2 the chief of the Central European Division of Foreign Affairs, Karl Radek, gave an ominous indication of his government's intentions in a statement to the Swedish consul general: "to detain all Allied agents at Moscow to be shot off one-by-

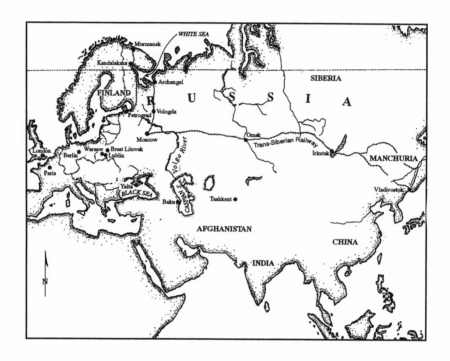

one in the measure that the advancing Anglo-French imperialists in the north dealt similarly with Soviet members."[7] By word and deed Bolshevik functionaries made it abundantly clear that they would disregard traditional diplomatic practice and take hostages to both retaliate against Allied intervention and force other nations into official negotiations with them.

The first "casualty" of this policy seems to have been the American consul at Tashkent in Turkestan, Roger C. Tredwell, who was arrested without charges on March 15, 1918. His arrest, and conceivable use as a pawn, occurred long before the United States entered the coalition of forces that landed on Soviet territory. His initial detention lasted only about five hours after which local officials released him with profuse apologies. Following the Allied intervention, however, the Soviet government, in response to the Allies' holding of a Soviet official in the Caucasus, ordered Tredwell's reincarceration on October 20. This time he remained in captivity until late April 1919, and the affair induced a lengthy and acrimonious exchange with the United States.

Meanwhile, a crisis developed in late July and early August 1918 over the detention of Allied consular officials, military missions, and some civilians. On July 29 the American consul general at Moscow, DeWitt Poole, petitioned Soviet Commissar for Foreign Affairs Georgi Chicherin to allow the departure of officers detailed to the U.S. military attaché in Russia, only to be informed that developments at Archangel made this impossible. To Chicherin's refusal, Poole replied that "the right of these persons to depart when they wished was clearly established by international law and usage and admitting of no qualification whatsoever, and that the objections raised to their departure were factitious and inadmissable."[8] Later that day Lenin made a speech in Moscow at a special session of the All-Russian Central Executive Committee in which he announced that a state of war existed between the Allies and the Soviet Union. This proclamation raised the possibility of a lengthy internment for Allied personnel, prompting further protest and requests for clarification.

Through early August, at least, the Soviets seemed to make a distinction between the British and the French on the one hand and the Americans on the other, singling out nationals of the former countries for the roughest treatment. On August 5, Soviet authorities arrested approximately two hundred French and British citizens in reprisal for the British-French invasion at Archangel, with Chicherin announcing that as long as Allied military activity continued in this area, "the Soviet Government could not be responsible for the lives of these interned prisoners."[9] Shortly thereafter, the Soviets arrested the British and French consuls general and their staffs. Commissar Chicherin then informed the Swedish consul general that Allied military missions would be allowed to leave only if the Soviet unofficial representative in Great Britain, Maxim Litvinov, and all the Russian soldiers in France were allowed to leave those countries. Chicherin stated further that in putting the nationals of the other powers into concentration camps the Soviets were thinking of them as civilian prisoners, although such procedures "apply only to members of the propertied classes who are our adversaries; no such measure is applied to our natural allies, the workers of these same countries who are now residing here."[10] At the end of August nearly one hundred previously endangered Americans were allowed to leave the country.

Action against the British took a violent turn in early September when the Soviets permitted a mass attack on the embassy in Petrograd. This aggression, triggered in part by an attempt on Lenin's life, resulted in the murder of the British naval attaché, Captain Francis N. A. Cromie, as he attempted to protect the premises, prompting a bitter response from Foreign Secretary Arthur Balfour: "His Majesty's Government will hold the members of the Soviet government individually responsible and will make every endeavor to secure that they shall be treated as outlaws by the governments of all civilized nations and that no place of refuge shall be left to them."[11] On September 4 the Soviets seized R. H. Bruce Lockhart, former British consul general in Moscow and at that time a back-channel envoy commissioned to maintain contact with the Soviet government (in effect, Litvinov's counterpart in Moscow), and held him prisoner in the Kremlin. His execution was prevented only through the "strenuous" exertions of several Dutch diplomats acting on the Allies' behalf. Lockhart, the Soviets insisted, was plotting to overthrow the government. Referring to the Soviet government as a "criminal organization" and to Chicherin as a "reptile," the Dutch minister opined that "the danger is now so great that I feel it my duty to call the attention of the British and all other Governments to the fact that if an end is not put to Bolshevism in Russia at once the civilization of the whole world will be threatened."[12]

Meanwhile, U.S. participation in the intervention at Archangel and Vladivostok led to a hardening of attitudes toward Americans in Russia as well and to increasing difficulty for them. The vice consuls in Moscow, Alfred T. Burri and Robert F. Leonard, who had gone on an "assignment" to Baku, were seized and held in Tsaritsyn for seventy-two days. There were other arrests. By the end of 1918, Burri, Leonard, and nearly all other Americans who wished to do so were permitted to leave, as were nearly all foreign nationals.[13]

Among the Americans were two exceptions. As previously noted, Tredwell, the consul at Tashkent, was arrested on October 20, 1918, and held into the spring of 1919; also in October the Bolsheviks took prisoner Xenophon Kalamatiano, an employee of the consul general in Moscow, eventually sentencing him to death as a spy. Apparently, Kalamatiano had been gathering intelligence information about political and economic conditions in various parts of Russia for Consul General Poole when he ran afoul of authori-

Crew of the USS *Albany* in the streets of Vladivostok, Siberia, 1919. *Courtesy National Archives*

ties. Both of these cases proved troublesome for Washington policymakers. Ever conscious of the "usefulness" of hostages, the Soviets on December 6 offered to release Kalamatiano if in return the United States would release Eugene V. Debs, the American socialist convicted on September 14, 1918, of violating the Espionage Act, and if Great Britain would free John MacLean, who had been convicted of obstructing recruitment for the British army.[14] Receiving no satisfaction from the United States on this proposal, the Soviets at the end of December suggested a trade in which Kalamatiano would be released in return for Soviets captured by Allied forces at Baku, Blagoveschensk, and Vladivostok. To this latter proposal the State Department responded that it would do nothing unless the Soviets released Tredwell first.[15]

As part of his mission to Russia for the American Peace Commission, William C. Bullitt pressed the Bolsheviks to release Tredwell. They complied, and on April 27 he crossed the border into Finland. The case of Kalamatiano was not as simple. Tredwell was an officially accredited representative of the American government who had not acted improperly and who, in any event, deserved prompt release in accordance with international law. Kalamatiano had been gathering intelligence. Washington, moreover, could not work a deal for him because it did not hold Soviets prisoner as was suggested, and it did not have any apparently effective leverage.[16]

Throughout 1920 the United States negotiated indirectly for the release of Kalamatiano in particular but also for the repatriation of the wife of one of its consular officers and three foreign employees of its embassy in Petrograd. One approach was a possible trade in which the Hungarian Communist Béla Kun, in custody in Austria, would be sent to the Soviet Union in return for the American hostages. This proved impossible when the Austrians decided unilaterally to send Kun to the Soviet Union after the Soviets threatened to stop the repatriation of Austrian prisoners of war in their custody. Another possible course of action was to have James O'Grady, a Labour member of the British Parliament who was negotiating an exchange of prisoners of war with the Soviets, intercede on behalf of the Americans.[17] Nothing came of this either, although O'Grady did contribute to the eventual release of the wife of the consular officer. Still another unsuccessful effort went forward through a representative of the League of Nations and the International Red Cross, Dr. Fridtjof Nansen.

In their discussions with the Red Cross representative Soviet officials revealed at least one of their motives in holding American hostages: they wished to bring about direct Soviet-American contact and a form of de facto recognition of the Soviet regime. To quote the Red Cross representative: "They [the Soviets] said they were willing to free most Americans and permit them to leave the country. They wished very much, however, to negotiate about it directly with the American Government."[18] Later, Chicherin stated that the United States should "enter into direct negotiations with M. Litvinov," at that time assistant commissar for foreign affairs.[19]

In the fall of 1920 the French government pursued a more direct approach with the Soviets, very much in accordance with nineteenth-century American initiatives in protecting its citizens, but one that Washington officials in 1920–21 did not attempt to emulate. In April 1920 the French and the Soviets concluded an agreement for the mutual repatriation of their nationals. In due course, the French returned all Soviet prisoners held in France and Algeria, but the Soviets did not comply with the bargain and offered all kinds of lame excuses for their procrastination. By the end of September the French had had enough: they informed the Soviets bluntly and unmistakably that unless all their prisoners held in Russia were repatriated by October 1, France's Black Sea fleet would take action against Soviet Russia by bombarding all the towns within its range. Chicherin immediately responded that "we bow to brute force" and quickly repatriated all of the French nationals.[20]

Despite unsettled conditions and the continued presence of U.S. hostages there, a number of Americans traveled to the Soviet Union in 1919 and 1920. Some were adventurers, some journalists, some Bolshevik sympathizers, and some Red Cross relief workers. Some, like the diplomatic personnel before them, found themselves unable to leave. A number of them landed in jail where they became useful to Soviet officials in cutting deals with the United States. Estimates vary: there may have been as many as one hundred Americans (in addition to the diplomatic personnel) held captive during 1921, with eight to ten of them, including Kalamatiano, in prison.

These hostages—the captors themselves acknowledged on several occasions that this was the proper term—were useful to achieve two high-priority Soviet objectives: to gain diplomatic recognition and along with it (or, if need be, separate from it) American medical and famine relief. Litvinov informed Dr. Nansen that recognition would have to be forthcoming before the prisoners were released.[21] On April 9, 1921, Chicherin told Nansen to relay to the United States the following message: "Our Government always glad to enjoy your cooperation but as for American Government we will wait until it enters itself into negotiations with our Government upon matter referred to in your radio[gram]. American consul has communicated with Litvinov in another matter. We cannot see why he should not enter into negotiations reciprocal repatriation."[22] To the U.S. government's argument that no formal communication would take place until the hostages were released, the Soviets revealingly replied: "Are we to understand that the detention of American citizens in Russia is the only hindrance to the resumption of trade and de facto relations between Russia and the United States of America?"[23]

Secretary of State Charles Evans Hughes believed that no formal direct communication should take place: "The Bolsheviks would make such negotiations the occasion for discussing innumerable unconnected issues involving the general relations of the United States with the Russian Soviets."[24] When this American position finally began to sink in with the Soviets and when they inferred from Dr. Nansen's comments that he was prepared to recommend both economic sanctions and use of force in the manner of the French, they changed their approach. A parallel interest began to take over—owing to crop failures and rampant epidemics, the Soviets desperately needed assistance that only the United States could provide.[25]

On July 13, Maxim Gorky sent out a telegram, authorized by the Foreign Office, to the Archbishop of New York pleading for food and medicine. Dr. Nansen immediately saw the connection between this appeal and the hostages, and less than twenty-four hours later he sent Gorky a telegram pointing out the need to free all American citizens prior to the signing of any aid agreement. This did not result in their freedom; the Soviets hung on until July 26 when they received a message from Secretary of State Hughes stating the conditions. "In the name of humanity," he wrote Litvinov, "the American Government demands of the Soviet authorities that these prisoners be at once released. It is manifestly impossible for the American authorities to countenance measures for the relief of distress in Russia while our citizens are thus detained."[26]

The Soviets responded predictably. On July 28 the Foreign Office informed both the State Department and the American Relief Administration, headed by Secretary of Commerce Herbert Hoover, that the U.S. proposal was "quite acceptable as to its basis including the release of the American prisoners."[27] Litvinov then announced their actual release on August 8.[28] Walter L. Brown, an official of the American Relief Administration, and Litvinov signed a formal agreement on August 20 under which the relief effort would go forward. This agreement, said a prominent English official, was "not far from the equivalent of de facto recognition of the Soviet Government"—something that the United States quickly took pains to deny.[29]

To state that the entire hostage episode might have been avoided in the absence of Allied intervention and incendiary Soviet activity is to suggest the obvious. Given these developments, however, it is helpful toward achieving greater understanding of the hostage issue to note the evolution of Soviet foreign policy between 1918 and 1921. An important point with which to begin is that the Soviets did not and could not pursue a conventional style of diplomacy during this period. By the end of 1918 formal diplomatic relations with the outside world were nearly totally severed: the western European nations and the United States had withdrawn their envoys from Russia and had expelled Soviet representatives ignominiously from their capitals. In the case of the United States, the Soviets set up Ludwig Martens as an unofficial envoy in New York, where he issued propaganda statements and sought to promote Soviet-American trade until his deportation in February 1921.

In order to gain information about the world, promote trade, and secure their interests, the Soviets were forced to develop a system of "para-diplomacy." As part of this para-diplomacy, they relied on contacts with Red Cross officials in a number of countries, trade representatives dispatched around the world, and officials in the Foreign Office who dealt almost exclusively with prisoners and refugees. Very much part of their "system" was to increase the number of foreign nationals they controlled as a way of promoting negotiations and, they hoped, resumption of diplomatic relations with as many nations as possible. Ties with Britain were eventually restored in this way, as were relations with Germany.[30]

With the beginning of the New Economic Policy of 1921 and the foreign policy approach of peaceful coexistence, the Soviets began to repair gradually the diplomatic damage. By early 1921 they had restored formal relations with Latvia, Lithuania, Estonia, Afghanistan, and Turkey and in March signed a trade agreement with Great Britain that signaled de facto recognition. The hostage negotiations with the United States in 1921 went forward in this context, but without the same result since Washington refused recognition until 1933.

Having eschewed the use of might in this instance—perhaps because force had achieved so little from 1918 through 1920—American policymakers ended up negotiating the release of the hostages. At the same time, they did not pay a ransom in the strict sense of the word or concede anything that they were not prepared to give up anyway. They negotiated from a position of strength, as the Soviets so desperately needed relief supplies—supplies that were furnished by an unofficial agency that collected and coordinated the dispersal of food and medicine from private sources and not by the U.S. government. Moreover, the head of the agency, Herbert Hoover, had recommended many weeks in advance of Gorky's appeal that the American Relief Administration consider aiding Russian children. A significant corollary is that no Americans lost their lives in the episode.

AMERICANS CAUGHT BY Josef Stalin's diplomatic purposes near the end of World War II were not so fortunate. In this instance the victims were prisoners of war captured by the Germans and held in camps in Eastern Europe that were overrun by Soviet military forces as these troops advanced westward toward Germany. The repatriation of the American servicemen became a way for the Soviets to gain leverage over the United States in differences between the two nations over Poland.

Various factors are customarily cited by scholars as responsible for the postwar deterioration of Soviet-American relations: the long-standing Soviet secretiveness and suspicion; the frequent rebuff of American social and cultural overtures; the difficulties encountered on Lend-Lease aid and the desire for a loan from the United States;

the revival in 1945 of Soviet propaganda and an attempt to promote international communism; the Soviet control or domination of Eastern Europe; and traditional American anti-Communist hostility. All are significant and cumulatively go a long way toward explaining the origins of the Cold War. The prisoner-of-war issue of 1945 was also a matter of considerable importance.

During the war Germany took millions of Allied prisoners who were interned in camps far removed from their home nations. Among these were over five million persons of Russian and non-Russian nationality, many of whom were taken to Germany or to other parts of Europe, and thousands of American and British troops held prisoner in Romania, Hungary, Poland, and eastern Germany. In the summer of 1944, when American and British forces advanced eastward toward Germany and the Russians pushed deeper into Eastern Europe, the liberation of prisoners began as German armies were often forced to flee too hastily to make any arrangements for their camps. Concerns for the health and safety of prisoners known to be held in Eastern Europe consequently prompted American officials to initiate negotiations with the Soviet Union in order to effect a mutual repatriation. This brought the beginning of a lengthy and difficult exchange.

In June 1944, General John R. Deane, commander of the U.S. military mission to the Soviet Union, contacted the Soviet General Staff (which had apparently given no thought to the problem), citing the camps in which Americans were known to be held in Romania and Hungary and requesting that prisoners liberated in the Soviet drive into these countries be given proper care. The General Staff responded affirmatively, but with no particular plan. Subsequently, because of the prompt action of American forces, the prisoners in Romania were flown out in U.S. aircraft. Then, on August 30, Deane and Ambassador W. Averell Harriman formally communicated with the Soviets. They urged that their respective governments agree that in areas where prison camps were expected to be liberated, a plan be made to repatriate prisoners promptly; that information be exchanged about the location of camps; that officers from each country be allowed to confer with prisoners to confirm their nationality and look after them; and that all individuals or small groups found behind their respective lines be quickly identified as to nationality.[31]

When, by November 6, Soviet officials still had not responded to the message, General Deane, now seeing the issue as one of some urgency, requested Chargé d'Affaires George F. Kennan to communicate again with Vyacheslav M. Molotov, the Soviet foreign minister. Kennan wrote Molotov asking him to press his government to come to an agreement like the one envisioned in the ambassador's message of August 30. The Soviet response, which was not proffered until November 25, consisted of two parts: a statement that the Soviet Union was prepared "to accept in principle the proposals which Mr. Harriman set forth in his letter of August 30," and a blunt protest accusing the United States of improper conduct in the treatment of its prisoners.[32] The genesis of this charge was the American internment of a particular category of Soviet nationals, the status of which caused the Kremlin leaders considerable embarrassment.

As the Soviet armies defeated German forces in the East, they came upon American officers and men almost exclusively of one status: those held prisoner by the Germans. The Allies, too, liberated great numbers of Russians whom the Germans had imprisoned, but they also captured thousands, again of both Russian and non-Russian nationality, who were wearing German uniforms and fighting in the German army. Some of these men had been forced into service; some were deserters or defectors with grievances against the Stalinist system who had gladly assisted the Nazis; and some were simply opportunists. At any rate, since many of these individuals claimed German nationality and the Soviet Union had previously made no acknowledgment of them, American officials transferred a number of them to prisoner-of-war camps in the United States. Recognizing soon that there were too many men in this group to ignore, Soviet officials, as indicated in Molotov's message, began a new tactic. Alleging that their citizens had been forced into German service and that many had defected at the first opportunity, they claimed it was gross mistreatment and an affront to the Soviet Union to place them in camps with German prisoners. The Soviets repeated their protests in two messages in January 1945.[33]

In the meantime, U.S. officials had begun screening out those soldiers captured in German uniforms who in fact claimed Soviet citizenship and had started shipping them to the USSR; in early 1945 they returned more than three thousand men in this group. However, until the war was over in Europe, the United States contended, there was good reason to accept a prisoner's word regarding nationality. Furthermore, as Acting Secretary of State Joseph C. Grew put it, the United States had "no desire . . . to hold Soviet nationals or to prevent the return to the Soviet Union of individuals who have established claims of Soviet citizenship."[34] However, it was concerned lest it violate the Geneva Convention of 1929, in which the signatory parties, including Germany, agreed that nationality of prisoners was to be determined by their uniforms unless they claimed other citizenship. It was not acting solely out of legalistic concern; there were many aliens fighting in the armed forces of the United States, some of whom had fallen captive to the Germans. American officials feared that the Nazis would take reprisals against these men if they turned over to the Soviet Union prisoners who claimed to be Germans.[35]

The Soviet Union was unwilling to accept Washington's reasoning and persisted in demanding the transfer of all prisoners while continuing to make charges about American conduct, at one point alleging that its nationals were forced to work though the Germans were not and that these men were often beaten and otherwise ill treated.[36] At the same time, Soviet officers assigned by their embassy to help sort out prisoners were, in the words of U.S. military personnel, "rude and discourteous." The Soviets were obviously annoyed and embarrassed that some of their people refused repatriation; moreover, their conduct undoubtedly sprang from a desire, based on a variety of Stalinist fears and apprehensions, to have all their citizens returned. The timing and stridency of their protests, however, indicate that they were preparing to play their hand in a related diplomatic game that was to continue over the next several months.

In the meantime, the Allies concluded an agreement at the Yalta Conference on prisoners of war that, in its essentials, stipulated that Soviet citizens liberated by the United States and American forces liberated by the Soviet Union would be promptly separated from enemy prisoners of war and held in their own camps until they could be handed over to their respective military authorities; that these authorities would inform each other about citizens found or liberated and permit repatriation representatives to go immediately to the camps or points of concentration of their citizens, where these representatives would take over administration and control of the camps; that facilities would be provided for the dispatch and transfer of officers to the camps or points of concentration; and that all citizens or prisoners found or liberated would be adequately sheltered, fed, clothed, and cared for until repatriated.[37] The British were also party to the accord and its various terms.

As was often the case in Soviet-American relations, the prisoner issue generated as much heat after agreement as before. Reports that Soviet armies were indifferent to the plight of liberated Americans soon came to the U.S. military mission in Moscow. In mid-February 1945, General Deane met three such officers who told not only of their escape from the Germans and advance eastward into the Soviet Union but also of wandering groups of American ex-prisoners in Poland needing assistance. At about the same time, the Polish minister in Moscow informed Deane of the existence of approximately three thousand Americans in Poland, while word of men who had been liberated arrived almost daily. In view of the developments, Deane contacted General K. D. Golubev, deputy administrator of the Russian Repatriation Commission, with a plan to send American contact teams of three to five men close behind the Russian lines in Poland and to fly the wounded or ill out to a hospital at Poltava. The Soviet general listened to the plea; then he stated that American contact teams could go only to Odessa and Murmansk, more than a thousand miles from the site of liberation of many prisoners. Finally, after much discussion, the Soviets did permit Deane to dispatch a group of men to Lublin but delayed their departure until the end of February and then severely restricted their movement. "Restrictions," General Deane reported, "even ran to a point-blank refusal by the Russian commandant to allow Colonel Kingsbury, the American medical officer, to visit two seriously wounded Americans known to be within a few miles of Lublin."[38]

By early March the matter was so important and the concern so acute that U.S. officials in Moscow called upon the president himself to make an appeal to Stalin, which Franklin Roosevelt did on March 3. The president "urgently" requested authorization for ten American aircraft to operate between Poltava and the advancing Red Army in Poland to help the sick and wounded. "I regard this request," the president concluded, "to be of the greatest importance not only for humanitarian reasons but also by reason of the intense interest of the American public in the welfare of our ex-prisoners of war and stranded aircraft crews."[39]

Throughout March, the American diplomatic and military team in Moscow as well as the president made frequent appeals and protests. All were to no avail; all were parried by one Soviet thrust after another. Stalin's reply to Roosevelt's first message stated that "there is no necessity to carry on flights of American planes from Poltava to the territory of Poland on the matter of American prisoners of war" because "on the territory of Poland and in other places liberated by the Red army, there are no groups of American prisoners of war."[40] Ambassador Harriman quickly pointed out to the president the falsity of this statement and informed Roosevelt that he was "outraged . . . that the Soviet Government has declined to carry out the agreement signed at Yalta."[41] He also pressed the Soviets to allow General Deane to go to Poland, which they at first had authorized and then disapproved. The Soviets also informed Harriman that they would not permit the U.S. contact team to stay in Lublin beyond mid-March.

These last developments "outraged" Harriman further. He informed the president that he felt very strongly "that we should make an issue of the matter of having our much needed contact officers in Poland which is clearly within our rights under the prisoner of war agreement signed at Yalta."[42] He urged the president to protest again to Stalin, drafting a note that he indicated Roosevelt should use as a basis for his message. The president wrote on March 17: "Frankly, I cannot understand your reluctance to permit American officers and men to assist their own people in this matter. This government has done everything to meet each of your requests."[43] This time Stalin rebuffed Roosevelt with a rude comment that his commanders could not be bothered with extra officers among them, and, at any rate, American ex-prisoners were receiving better treatment "than former Soviet prisoners of war in American camps where they have been partially placed together with German prisoners of war and where some of them were subjected to unfair treatment and unlawful inconveniences up to beating."[44]

Harriman's contempt was unconcealed. Stalin's reply was, in his words, "preposterous." "When the story of the treatment accorded our liberated prisoners by the Russians leaks out," he wrote the president, "I cannot help but feel that there will be great and lasting resentment on the part of the American people."[45] He wanted retaliation of some sort, including the consideration of placing restrictions on the movement of Soviet contact teams behind American lines or the possibility of reducing Lend-Lease support. Historian Herbert Feis, who worked closely with Harriman while writing his book on Roosevelt, Winston Churchill, and Stalin, makes the point that the Soviet position on the prisoner issue was quite important in Harriman's belief that the United States should change the basis on which it dealt with the Soviet Union.[46]

If the president, as suggested in his message of March 17 to Stalin, "could not understand" Soviet reluctance to cooperate on the prisoner-of-war issue, many policymakers, including Harriman, soon perceived the reasons. They were relating the prisoner question to the larger issue of the status of Poland, in regard to which the Kremlin had two primary objectives: to prevent American and British access to Poland until they had accomplished their mission of establishing a friendly puppet government in power; and to achieve recognition of the Polish provisional government.

The background to the inter-Allied difficulty over Poland has been told elsewhere and need not be repeated here in great detail. A brief summary will suffice. During the war a clash occurred between conflicting Allied interests and aspirations in that country. The Soviet Union, in the interest of its security, demanded Polish territory west to the borders established in the Nazi-Soviet agreement of 1939 and a "strong," friendly Polish government. On the other hand, the Western allies, who had gone to war in part because of a commitment to Poland and who were being pressured by that country's exiled government in London, hoped to secure a truly independent nation with viable boundaries. Although it was not clearly apparent in late 1944 and in 1945, the Red Army settled the dispute. As the Russians marched into Poland they set up a Committee of National Liberation, defeated the Germans and the Polish opposition to themselves, and in December 1944 established the so-called Lublin Committee as the new provisional government. On January 5, 1945, they quickly recognized the Lublin government. When the Yalta Conference convened, the Soviet Union confronted the British and the Americans, who were annoyed at its unilateral behavior and who still recognized the London Poles, with a fait accompli.

Nevertheless, Poland was a major topic at Yalta. After lengthy and at times heated discussions, which consumed the majority of the conference time, the powers arrived at a rather ambiguous accord. They agreed that, with some minor variations, the Curzon Line would comprise the eastern boundary of Poland; they put off delimiting the western boundary until the Allies could deal with a Polish government at a forthcoming peace conference. Regarding the government itself, the Allies agreed that elections would be held at an early date to determine its composition. In the meantime, the provisional, or Lublin, government was to be reorganized to include representatives of the London government in exile and democratic leaders within the country, after which the United States and Great Britain would recognize it; and, in the furtherance of this restructuring, the Polish Commission, consisting of Molotov, Harriman, and A. Clark Kerr, the British ambassador to Moscow, was established to consult with the various Polish factions.[47] Neither the British nor the Americans were fully satisfied with the accord, but they did believe that it included some safeguards; in any event, they looked upon it as the best they could do under the circumstances.

The ink was hardly dry when disagreements arose over implementation. The three members of the Polish Commission, meeting in Moscow, could not agree on the question of consultation with prospective new members of the provisional government. Molotov insisted that only those Poles who favored the Yalta solution should be involved in discussing the reorganization, which excluded most London Poles, while Harriman and Kerr maintained that certain exiled Polish leaders must be included. While the discord continued, word began reaching Harriman and the British ambassador that the Soviets and the Lublin government were arresting, deporting, or executing members of the Polish underground in the process of consolidating their power. In the midst of this, Molotov offered to allow American and British officials to go into Poland to, as Churchill put it, "see what is going on for themselves."[48]

Since Molotov was not given to fits of spontaneity, it seems apparent that Stalin had approved this offer just as he had sanctioned, at the same time, General Deane's sending of a team of officers to Lublin to look after U.S. prisoners—albeit on a severely restricted mission. As mentioned above, the Soviets, on February 26, also authorized a trip by General Deane himself relative to the prisoner matter.[49] They soon had second thoughts, however; it apparently occurred to them that the visits could be used on a quid pro quo basis, thereby facilitating official acknowledgment of the provisional government. Soviet leaders showed their concern for early recognition on March 9 in their proposal that this Polish government be invited to the San Francisco Conference. It also appeared to the Kremlin leadership that the British sought to send a high-powered commission to Poland, which they could not control. In any event, on March 1, Molotov "seemed less interested" in allowing British and American visitors into Poland; then on March 12 he revoked permission for Deane's trip.[50] There followed the aforementioned series of negative replies to U.S. proposals for aiding its liberated prisoners of war. At the same time, the Foreign Office in Moscow continued to fling charges regarding American mistreatment of Soviet prisoners.

The Soviets soon revealed their true purposes. When Harriman visited with Molotov on March 14, urging him to allow contact officers access to liberated prisoners, the foreign minister stated that his government and the Polish provisional government were fulfilling their obligations under the Yalta agreement and that both the Red Army and the Polish government objected to the presence of American officers in Poland. Harriman reported that when he "pressed him (Molotov) on what valid objection the Red Army could possibly have, he pointed out that we had no agreement with the Polish provisional government. In spite of my contention that this was a Soviet responsibility he kept reverting to the above fact. I then directly asked him if he was implying that we should make such arrangement with the Poles and if so, whether the Red Army would remove its objections. He did not answer this question directly but left me with the impression that he wished me to draw that deduction."[51] The American ambassador then reported to the secretary of state: "I feel that the Soviet Government is trying to use our liberated prisoners of war as a club to induce us to give increased prestige to the Provisional Polish Government by dealing with it in this connection."[52] Upon receiving this message from Harriman, the secretary quickly transmitted it to the president along with a covering memo: "It would appear that the Soviet authorities may be endeavoring to use our desire to assist our prisoners as a means of obliging us to deal with the Warsaw Government."[53] President Roosevelt was deeply irritated by this news and responded with his message to Stalin of March 17.[54]

The British, who had proposed sending a high-level team of observers to Poland on behalf of the Polish Commission, also realized the purpose behind preventing any further contact with liberated prisoners unless the Soviets first received compensation in the form of recognition of the provisional government: "The Soviet Government suspects that the contact officers would, under cover of dealings with prisoners of war, proceed to contact Polish leaders, and, in fact convert themselves into the proposed observation mission."[55]

In April the United States decided it was useless to press for contact teams in Poland. Thereafter, the Soviets repatriated Americans in their own way and at their own pace, while many of the ex-prisoners suffered—and some died—from the lack of food, housing, or adequate medical care.[56] Meanwhile, the Soviets strengthened the position of the provisional government and signed a mutual assistance agreement with it; and the Western allies, after presidential adviser Harry Hopkins's mission to Moscow in late May, concluded a kind of face-saving accord with the Soviets that left control of Poland in the hands of the provisional Government of National Unity, the composition of which was mainly Communist.

The end of the war in Europe speeded the repatriation process, for many ex-prisoners and large numbers of civilians could then be exchanged directly across the lines, but it also brought a new dimension to the problem. When Germany surrendered, the argument that the Nazis would take reprisals against American prisoners if the United States returned to the Soviet Union all Russians found in German uniform no longer had validity. Yet, American officials were sincerely reluctant, now for humanitarian reasons, to just turn over all prisoners, including those who did not wish to go back to the Soviet Union; the obvious collaborationists posed no problem but many prisoners claimed, legitimately, that they had been forced into German units, while many of those held in Europe who refused repatriation had not cooperated with the Nazis at all. On May 23 the State-War-Navy Coordinating Committee agreed to turn over a special group of 118 prisoners held in Europe, who had fought as German soldiers and considered themselves "political refugees" but who were identified by the Soviet embassy as Soviet citizens.[57]

However, it refused to grant blanket approval for transfers and deferred a final decision on the matter. In August, seeking a way out, the State Department requested information from its embassy in Moscow as to whether Russians taken prisoner were divested of their citizenship; the response dashed American hopes.[58]

Of the German prisoners of war of Soviet nationality held in the United States, American officials returned 3,800 to Soviet jurisdiction, leaving 154 who refused to be repatriated. Because these men so violently objected to returning to their homeland and because an investigation proved that one of the men was not, in fact, a Soviet citizen, authorities screened and rescreened them to determine their true status while working toward a final decision. The question was acute because, in addition to the prisoners of war, there were millions of interned civilians in Western Europe who had been freed by the Allies and over whom the Soviets claimed authority. Many of them, particularly Latvians, Lithuanians, Estonians, Poles, and Ukrainians, did not wish to be repatriated, yet the Yalta agreement specified the return of all Soviet citizens—without defining a Soviet citizen. At length, U.S. policymakers opted to return to the USSR all of its citizens who had lived within the 1939 frontiers; this number included most of the 154 men still held in the United States and many hundreds of thousands, both soldiers and civilians, held in Europe. This decision was reached reluctantly, mainly because the State Department was anxious "to avoid giving Soviet authorities any pretext for delaying return of American POW's of Japanese now in Soviet occupied zone, particularly in Manchuria."[59] The State-War-Navy Coordinating Committee, after three months of consideration, arrived at a more definitive decision in December 1945. It declared that the United States would repatriate, by force if necessary, persons who were citizens of and lived within the Soviet Union's boundaries of 1939 if they were "traitors, deserters, renegades or quislings."[60] Other Soviet citizens did not have to be returned against their will.

As evidenced by the amount of time spent in arriving at this solution, the problem was an agonizing one for American policymakers. The Soviet Union viewed contemptuously those soldiers who were taken prisoner, and during the war it refused any agreement with the enemy regarding mutual treatment of prisoners. As historian Alexander Dallin expresses it, "Any soldier who fell into enemy hands was ipso facto a traitor and deserved no protection from his government." Moreover, when Soviet prisoners were liberated and returned to their homeland, police met them at the ports of entry and either shipped them off to labor camps in Siberia or Central Asia or executed them. Those who had served in the German ranks or who supported General Andrei Vlasov, the captured Soviet general who in 1942 became head of a German-sponsored movement to "liberate" the USSR, obviously received particularly summary treatment. Harriman reported on June 11 that although repatriation had been under way for months, "embassy knows of only a single instance in which a repatriated prisoner has returned to his home and family in Moscow."[61] When the soldiers held in the United States (at Fort Dix, New Jersey) were informed that they would be returned to the USSR, they rioted, hoping to commit suicide by provoking the use of force against them. Three did in fact commit suicide.[62] This scene was repeated numerous times among concentrations of Soviet ex-prisoners held in Western Europe and was not limited to those who had served in Nazi uniform, making it necessary for the United States actually to use force, an exigency especially repugnant to American officials.

The dilemma was real, for not to return the prisoners was to violate the letter of the Yalta agreement; yet to do so using force was, as Acting Secretary of State Dean Acheson put it, "going against our traditional policy of political asylum."[63] The matter was further complicated by the fact that the Kremlin, furious over the delay, continued to press for repatriation of all Soviet citizens while hurling crude accusations about Allied mistreatment of prisoners. *Pravda* published an interview article alleging British and American atrocities against Soviet prisoners and contrasting this treatment to that accorded American and British prisoners by the Soviet Union, which portrayed the riot of the 154 prisoners at Fort Dix as an example of unlawful violence against its nationals.[64] Meanwhile, the United States always feared Soviet retaliation.

These allegations and, indeed, Soviet conduct on the entire prisoner question provided further proof to American policymakers of the extent to which the Kremlin would pursue its aims. Throughout, the Soviets seemed indifferent to not only the plight of American prisoners but to that of their own as well and attempted to turn U.S. consideration for the physical well-being of its liberated men in Poland to strengthen the position of the Polish provisional government. These facts annoyed and deeply troubled American officials, including President Roosevelt. It may be argued that the United States could have conceded earlier the Soviet point on Poland and thus perhaps secured approval of contact with its liberated prisoners. In retrospect such a course appears to have been appropriate because, as George Kennan quickly recognized, very little could be done about Poland anyway; but to proceed on the assumption that the repudiation of an agreement, a part of which granted the United States certain concessions, was the quickest way to achieve these concessions was not, understandably, considered particularly wise or prudent at the time.

While it may not have been a direct cause of the Cold War, the prisoner issue assumes importance because of the impression it left on American policymakers, particularly Harriman and General Deane, and because, in a broader sense, it dramatized a basic difference between the Soviet Union and the United States. On this issue all the inhumanity of the Stalinist system, in which the interest of the state took precedence over that of the individual, rose to the surface. It has been suggested that one of the fundamental causes of the breakdown of wartime unity was Washington's foolish insistence that Moscow apply liberal-democratic principles to Eastern Europe. However that may be, the prisoner question demonstrates that there were other matters that only remotely involved the Soviet rejection of liberal-democratic precepts and dealt much more with their rejection, on the eve of the destruction of Adolf Hitler's tyranny, of elemental human values. Herein lies an important element in the beginning of the Cold War.

AMERICAN IMAGES AND perceptions of the Soviet Union in the Cold War era no less than in the period after World War I assumed importance in the shaping of U.S. foreign policy. Justification and apology for Soviet behavior aside, the cruelties and abuses of that system, not least the holding of hostages to achieve political and economic objectives, provoked profound loathing and deep distrust among American officials. That Soviet rejection of the norms of international conduct and their cavalier disregard for basic human values played a part in President Wilson's decision to refrain from extending diplomatic recognition seems beyond dispute. That Stalin's ruthless brutality in expanding the post-World War II Soviet empire induced worry and concern in the hearts of both European and American officials also seems clear. Students of the Cold War who discount Stalinist cruelty miss a critical part of the story. The harshness reflected in the use of U.S. servicemen as pawns may not have led directly to the strategy of containment, to the merging of the Western zones of Germany, or the Truman Doctrine, or the Marshall Plan, or to other manifestations of American toughness toward the Soviet Union, but it helped to create the mood that made these things possible.

If it may be assumed that images and perceptions directly affected U.S. policy, it follows that American history writ large would reflect this phenomenon. It does, most decidedly. Attitudes toward the Soviet Union played no small part in provoking the "Red scare" immediately after World War I and the hysteria and intolerance of the 1920s. The Cold War, in turn, became the defining historical development in the lives of several generations of Americans after 1945.

NOTES

1. George F. Kennan, *Russia and the West under Lenin and Stalin* (New York: New American Library, 1962), 9–116; idem, *Russia Leaves the War* (Princeton, NJ: Princeton University Press, 1956), 219–41, 364–77, and 459–84.

2. From March through November 1917 the United States had guaranteed the provisional government $325 million in credits, of which it had spent $188 million. See Robert J. Maddox, *The Unknown War with Russia: Wilson's Siberian Intervention* (San Rafael, CA: Presidio Press, 1977), 33; and George F. Kennan, *The Decision to Intervene* (Princeton, NJ: Princeton University Press, 1958), 17–20.

3. Students of the Allied intervention may draw upon a vast literature. Among the works used here are Betty M. Unterberger, *The United States, Revolutionary Russia, and the Rise of Czechoslovakia* (Chapel Hill: University of North Carolina Press, 1989), 216–65; Benjamin D. Rhodes, *The Anglo-American Winter War with Russia, 1918–1919* (New York: Greenwood Press, 1988), 2–20; John Bradley, *Allied Intervention in Russia* (New York: Basic Books, 1968), 106–31; John W. Long, "American Intervention in Russia: The North Russian Expedition, 1918–1919," *Diplomatic History* 6 (Winter 1982): 45–67; and Betty M. Unterberger, "Woodrow Wilson and the Bolsheviks: The 'Acid Test' of Soviet-American Relations," *Diplomatic History* 11 (Spring 1987): 71–91.

4. Maddox, *The Unknown War*, 36–37.

5. Ibid., 78–79.

6. Consul General DeWitt C. Poole at Moscow to secretary of state, July 19, 1918, U.S. Department of State, *Papers Relating to the Foreign Relations of the United States, 1918, Russia*, 3 vols. (Washington, DC: Government Printing Office, 1931), 1:621 (hereafter cited as *FRUS*, followed by appropriate year).

7. Ibid., 650.

8. Ibid., 649.

9. Ibid., 651–52. See also Consul General Poole's August 5 telegram in which Chicherin asserted that civil persons arrested would be treated "as prisoners in accordance with the usual custom in case of war." U.S. Department of State, Record Group 84, Records of the Foreign Service Posts of the Department of State, "Russia and the Soviet Union, 1910–1929," no. 3 (Washington, DC: National Archives Microfilm Publications, 1960), 1297.

10. *FRUS, 1918, Russia*, 1:653, 660; chargé in Sweden to secretary of state, August 29, 1918, ibid., 661.

11. R. H. Bruce Lockhart, *British Agent* (Garden City, NY: Doubleday, 1933), 197–346; British chargé to secretary of state, September 6, 1918, *FRUS, 1918, Russia*, 1:665.

12. Chargé in Great Britain to secretary of state, October 5, 1918, *FRUS, 1918, Russia*, 1:677–78.

13. Acting secretary of state to commission to negotiate peace, January 28, 1919, *FRUS, 1919, Russia* (Washington, DC: Government Printing Office, 1937), 168.

14. Ibid.

15. Acting secretary of state to minister in Norway, February 18, 1919, ibid., 172.

16. Acting secretary of state to chargé in Denmark, May 27, 1919, ibid., 185.

17. Secretary of state to ambassador in Great Britain, January 10, 1920, *FRUS, 1920*, 3 vols. (Washington, DC: Government Printing Office, 1936), 3:669; memorandum by minister in Poland, May 13, 1920, ibid., 671; commissioner at Vienna to secretary of state, July 15, 1920, ibid., 676.

18. Chargé in Sweden to secretary of state, July 19, 1920, ibid., 677.

19. Ambassador in Great Britain to secretary of state, August 10, 1920, ibid., 680; secretary of state to chargé in Norway, September 24, 1920, ibid., 682–83.

20. Ambassador in France to secretary of state, October 5, 1920, ibid., 684–85.

21. Minister in Czechoslovakia to secretary of state, March 30, 1921, *FRUS, 1921*, 2 vols. (Washington, DC: Government Printing Office, 1936), 2:792–93.

22. Minister in Norway to secretary of state, April 12, 1921, ibid., 793.

23. Minister in Norway to secretary of state, May 19, 1921, ibid., 795.

24. Secretary of state to ambassador in Great Britain, June 23, 1921, ibid., 797.

25. Minister in Norway to secretary of state, July 1, 1921, ibid., 798.

26. Minister in Norway to secretary of state, July 15, 1921, ibid., 798–99; secretary of state to consul at Reval, July 25, 1921, ibid., 800.

27. London office of American Relief Administration to chairman, July 31, 1921, ibid., 809.

28. Vice consul in Reval to secretary of state, August 8, 1921, ibid., 800–801.

29. Agreement between American Relief Administration and Soviet authorities, August 20, 1921, ibid., 813–17; *New York Times*, August 9 and 21, 1921.

30. See Teddy Uldricks, *Diplomacy and Ideology: The Origins of Soviet Foreign Relations, 1917–1930* (London: Sage Publications, 1979), 28–75.

31. *FRUS, 1945, Conferences at Malta and Yalta* (Washington, DC: Government Printing Office, 1955), 413n; John R. Deane, *The Strange Alliance: The Story of Our Efforts at Wartime Cooperation with Russia* (New York: Viking Press, 1947), 182–86.

32. Chargé in Soviet Union to secretary of state, November 27, 1944, *FRUS, 1945, Conferences at Malta and Yalta*, 414.

33. Acting secretary of state to chargé of Soviet Union, February 1, 1945, *FRUS, 1945*, 9 vols., *Europe* (Washington, DC: Government Printing Office, 1967), 5:1067–72; aide-mémoires by Soviet embassy, January 4, 18, 1945, Record Group 59, Records of the Department of State, Department of State File 711.62114/1–445 and 1–1845 (hereafter cited as Record Group 59, followed by the appropriate file number). For an excellent account of the issue of Soviet citizens, military and civilian, held in the West and their repatriation see Mark R. Elliot, *Pawns*

of Yalta: Soviet Refugees and America's Role in Their Repatriation (Urbana: University of Illinois Press, 1982).

34. Acting secretary of state to chargé of Soviet Union, February 1, 1945, *FRUS, 1945, Europe*, 5:1068.

35. Ibid., 1068–69.

36. Ibid., 1070; Stalin to Roosevelt, March 22, 1945, ibid., 1083. See also ambassador of Soviet Union to secretary of state, April 10, 18, 1945, ibid., 1090–91.

37. *FRUS, 1945, Conferences at Malta and Yalta*, 754–56. See also Russell D. Buhite, *Decisions at Yalta: An Appraisal of Summit Diplomacy* (Wilmington, DE: Scholarly Resources, 1986), 60–65.

38. Deane, *Strange Alliance*, 196. The *New York Times*, February 20 and 23, 1945, reported the arrival of the three officers in Moscow and subsequently that of several more.

39. Roosevelt to Stalin, March 3, 1945, *FRUS, 1945, Europe*, 5:1072.

40. Stalin to Roosevelt, March 5, 1945, ibid., 1073.

41. Ambassador Harriman to Roosevelt, March 8, 1945, ibid., 1075.

42. Ambassador Harriman to Roosevelt, March 12, 1945, ibid., 1078.

43. Roosevelt to Stalin, March 17, 1945, ibid., 1082.

44. Stalin to Roosevelt, March 22, 1945, ibid., 1083.

45. Ambassador Harriman to Roosevelt, March 24, 1945, ibid., 1086.

46. Ambassador Harriman to secretary of state, March 14, 1945, ibid., 1081. See Herbert Feis, *Churchill, Roosevelt, Stalin: The War They Waged and the Peace They Sought* (Princeton, NJ: Princeton University Press, 1957), 598n.

47. *FRUS, 1945, Conferences at Malta and Yalta*, 869–71, 898–99, and 973–74.

48. Churchill to Roosevelt, February 28, 1945, *FRUS, 1945, Europe*, 5:132.

49. Ambassador Harriman to Roosevelt, March 8, 1945, ibid., 1075.

50. Ibid., 134–44; Ambassador Harriman to Roosevelt, March 12, 1945, ibid., 1078.

51. Ambassador Harriman to secretary of state, March 14, 1945, ibid., 1080.

52. Ibid.

53. *FRUS, 1945, Europe*, 5:1079n.

54. Roosevelt to Stalin, March 17, 1945, ibid., 1082.

55. British ambassador to secretary of state, April 7, 1945, ibid., 1090. See also Churchill to Roosevelt, March 16, 1945, ibid., 171–72. If there was any thought on the part of Harriman, Deane, or Kennan to convert the prisoner contact groups into representatives of the commission, they never communicated this plan to Washington. Because of the specific duties of prospective contact teams and the fact that the United States had long been pressing the Soviets on the prisoner issue, there seems little reason to believe that American officials saw the two groups as anything but separate, although they obviously would not have been averse to acquiring some information about Poland from whatever source. For further background on the prisoner repatriation problem and on the American initiative see Russell D. Buhite, "Soviet-American Relations and the Repatriation of Prisoners of War, 1945," *The Historian* 35, no. 3 (May 1973): 384–97.

56. Ambassador Harriman to secretary of state, April 2, 1945, *FRUS, 1945, Europe*, 5:1087.

57. Acting secretary of state to secretary of the navy, May 12, 1945, ibid., 1095–96. See also memorandum by State-War-Navy Coordinating Committee to secretary of state, May 23, 1945, Record Group 59, Department of State File 740.00114 EW/5-2345; and *FRUS, 1945, Europe*, 5:1095n.

58. *FRUS, 1945, Europe*, 5:1098n.

59. Secretary to political adviser for Germany, August 29, 1945, ibid., 1105. It is interesting that Russian expatriates in the United States urged American officials to form a Free Russian Squadron from among the Soviets held at Fort Dix. See *New York Times*, August 1, 1945.

60. Memorandum by State-War-Navy Coordinating Committee to secretary of state, December 21, 1945, and memorandum of conversation by chief of East European Affairs, December 27, 1945, *FRUS, 1945, Europe*, 5:1108–10.

61. Ambassador in Soviet Union to secretary of state, June 11, 1945, ibid., 1097. Harriman's account is corroborated most poignantly by Stalin's daughter, Svetlana Alliluyeva, who tells of a friend who was imprisoned for twelve years in a labor camp after being repatriated. See Svetlana Alliluyeva, *Only One Year* (New York: Harper and Row, 1969), 268; and Alexander Dallin, *German Rule in Russia* (New York: St. Martin's Press, 1957), 420.

62. Acting secretary of state to chargé in Soviet Union, July 27, 1945, *FRUS, 1945, Europe*, 5:1100–1102. See also *New York Times*, June 30, 1945.

63. Acting secretary to secretary, September 29, 1945, *FRUS, 1945, Europe*, 5:1107.

64. Ibid., 1093n. See also acting secretary to chargé in Soviet Union, July 27, 1945, ibid., 1100; and *New York Times*, May 1 and 4, 1945. In the meantime, some 108 Soviet citizens held in Great Britain by the U.S. Army publicly denied that they were being abused. See ibid., May 2, 1945.

Chapter 5

Trial in Mukden:
Hostages of the Chinese Communists

America's intervention in the Russian civil war pales in significance to its involvement in the struggle between the Nationalists and Communists in China after World War II, and, as might be expected given its support of the government of Jiang Jieshi (Chiang Kai-shek), U.S. officials and citizens experienced harsh, sometimes inhumane, treatment at the hands of the new regime. Communist accession to power occasioned one of the most difficult and complicated hostage incidents that the United States had ever experienced—difficult because it occurred amid the confusion of civil conflict in an area of the world inaccessible to Washington's power and influence, and complicated because responsibility for the incident lay as much in the Sino-Soviet as in the Sino-American relationship. An examination of American China policy during World War II and the early Cold War is therefore essential to an adequate explication of this affair.

American policy toward China during the mid- and late 1940s tends to prove the validity of the cliché: "the road to Hell is paved with good intentions." During World War II the United States held important military and political goals for China. Optimally, American officials sought to revitalize Jiang's armies so they might inflict heavy casualties on the Japanese, thus facilitating an Allied invasion of Japan; minimally, the United States hoped to help China remain in the war so as to tie down large numbers of Japanese troops. Moreover, the Americans desired a strong, stable, democratic, and unified China, capable of supplanting Japan as the dominant power in Asia, and also one over which they would have a measure of influence.

Both the political and military objectives required that China resolve the many internal problems it faced: runaway inflation, ill-trained armies, political corruption, famine, disease, and, most important, the debilitating civil conflict between the government and the Chinese Communists. The United States chose to assist in dealing with these problems—with the military one by urging Jiang to work with General Joseph Stilwell, commander of U.S. forces in China, to modernize the country's armies and maximize their potential; and with the political problem by trying, through the mediation efforts of the American envoy, Patrick J. Hurley, to forge a Communist-Guomindang (Kuomintang) agreement favorable to Jiang's government. Neither of these efforts proved successful through the war years.

After 1945, worry about the Soviet Union and fear that a Communist China would become a dependable Soviet client contributed to a concentrated American effort to achieve a non-Communist resolution of China's civil conflict. The United States tried hard to save Jiang's government—until the multiple paralyses of that regime became so obvious and the chances of Communist success so great that it had to give up the effort. By the time the struggle ended, American support had included the granting of aid to Jiang in the amount of hundreds of millions of dollars, the stationing for a time of fifty thousand marines in China, and the outright gift of large amounts of military equipment. What occurred was a large-scale American intervention in China's civil war, on the losing side, that lasted from 1945 until Chinese Communist armies swept to victory and forced the government to flee to Taiwan in 1949.

Although at one time or another several Americans were held against their will in Communist China, particularly in areas recently overrun by armies of the Chinese Communist Party (CCP), the most prominent hostage incident and the one with the greatest international significance was the Angus Ward affair of 1948–49. Consul general at the U.S. consulate in Mukden (currently known as Shenyang), Ward, his wife, and his staff were held prisoner from November 20, 1948, until November 21, 1949, for a good part of the time totally incommunicado. The incident, instigated by a Chinese Communist leadership concerned about its ties with the Soviet Union, seriously complicated Washington's consideration of the recognition of the Communist government; and it raised broader questions as well about Soviet influence with the CCP and, especially significant for the purposes of this study, about the options available to U.S. policymakers in hostage situations.

Ward had been in Mukden since 1946 after a long career in the Foreign Service, much of it in East Asia. Born in 1894 in Alvinston, Ontario, Canada, he was raised in Chassel, Michigan, where he became a naturalized U.S. citizen. He attended college at Valparaiso University in Indiana, then served as an officer in the U.S. Army during World War I. After the war he worked with the American relief mission in Finland and Russia before beginning a brief

career with the Internal Revenue Service. In 1925 he began his tenure with the State Department, which lasted until 1956 when he retired after serving his final four years as U.S. ambassador to Afghanistan. From 1925 to 1934 he was vice consul and consul in Tianjin (Tientsin). Ward then served as consul in Moscow and as secretary of the U.S. embassy in the Soviet Union until 1940. Between 1940 and 1944 he served as consul general in Vladivostok and also for a year in Tehran, Iran, before going to Mukden. Tall and distinguished in appearance with a Vandyke beard, Ward was known for his sharp temper and for some pronounced eccentricities, among them a love of cats that extended to carrying the ashes of several of his long-departed pets from assignment to assignment.[1]

Chinese Communist forces captured Mukden on November 1, 1948, but displayed, at least in the short term, a reasonable attitude toward foreign officials living there. Consul General Ward had several verbal and written exchanges with the new Communist mayor of the city, all of which were, during the first two weeks, decidedly satisfactory. The mayor referred to Ward as the "American Consul General" and issued identity cards for him, his personnel, and his vehicles; indeed, Ward believed that "it was obviously the intention of the Communist authorities at the time to recognize us and permit us to function as an official United States Government establishment."[2]

Suddenly, the situation changed. Ward received a note from the garrison commander addressed to "the former American Consul" and demanding the surrender of the consulate's radio transmitter within forty-eight hours. All other consuls and foreigners in Mukden were to do the same. When Ward informed the commander that forty-eight hours might not give him time to check with the U.S. government as the owner of the radio, he received a peremptory response, and, after the two days had elapsed, Communist troops surrounded the consulate, shut off the water and electricity, and placed Ward and his staff under house arrest.[3]

In making this move, Chinese Communist forces were challenging diplomatic practices that had evolved over several centuries. Consuls are not granted diplomatic immunity, but it had become universal practice to permit their free movement and to give them effective immunity. In cases in which consuls were charged with a crime (as Ward later was), it was customary to allow them freedom on bail and to permit them, during the disposition of their cases, to carry on with their duties. The Communist regimes in both the Soviet Union and China now rejected such "bourgeois" concepts of international relations.[4]

As might be expected, the American reaction was characterized by bewilderment and frustration. Ambassador John Leighton
Stuart in Nanjing (Nanking) expressed his belief that any CCP linking of the isolation of the consulate to the larger issue of the U.S.
attitude toward the Guomindang and the incipient Communist government would constitute "blackmail" about which the world needed
to know. He favored the release of the story to the press. Meanwhile, Consul General Edmund Clubb at Beijing (Peking) speculated on CCP motives while urging that the United States rely on a
Chinese messenger to find out what was going on.[5] The State Department held back out of concern that making an issue of the affair or creating international publicity might only make the situation
more difficult for Ward and his staff while complicating efforts to
free them.

The State Department swung into action on March 2, 1949. Increasingly apprehensive about the absence of any word from
Mukden, it sent messages to Ambassador Stuart and to Consuls General George Hopper in Hong Kong and Clubb in Beijing directing
them to confront the highest-ranking Communist they could find
with American concerns about the consulate. They were also to
explain international practice in regard to consuls: "Long experience has shown desirability of and international custom has sanctioned continued exercise by resident foreign consuls of their
legitimate and proper functions within their consular districts even
during periods of non-recognition between governments." Furthermore, they were to state that the United States was "reluctant" to
believe that Communist authorities would impose arbitrary restrictions "in total disregard of international comity and practices."[6] Both
Clubb and Hopper failed in their efforts to force the issue, Clubb in
particular being given the runaround by minor officials at the CCP
Foreign Nationals Office in Beijing who strongly implied that their
policy was to permit only strictly limited contact on the issue.[7]

Given the failure of this approach, U.S. policymakers began to
consider closing the Mukden consulate. On February 28, Ambassador Stuart had recommended the withdrawal of all or part of the
U.S. staff there, stating that "our patience must have some limit."[8]
Viewing Manchuria as a strategically valuable area in the Cold War
struggle with the Soviet Union and Mukden as a particularly
important observation post, Clubb recommended caution with
respect to withdrawal; in his view, to close the Mukden consulate
would play into the hands of the Soviets.[9] When officials in
Washington received reports that Ward and his staff were indeed
being held prisoner, they inclined toward Stuart's point of view.
On March 30 the British consul general in Mukden informed his

country's ambassador in Nanjing, who notified his American counterpart, that the U.S. consulate had "ceased to exist," prompting the opinion in the Foreign Office in London that the Communist action had been "more disgraceful than we had known."[10] Other such reports convinced policymakers that it was time for a showdown. On April 15 the State Department sent instructions to Clubb that he should convey to the CCP by a channel of his choosing that unless the Communists corrected the situation in Mukden and allowed consular officers to perform their duties, the American government would "have no alternative but to withdraw them."[11] A little over a month later—when still no response had been received—U.S. officials in fact made the decision to close the consulate. On May 24, Ambassador Stuart delivered a note to Huang Hua, chief of the Alien Affairs Office in Nanjing and a former student of the ambassador at Yenching University, informing him that the United States had decided to withdraw Ward and his staff.[12]

If the CCP was holding Ward incommunicado to prevent his use of the consulate as an observation post or as a way station for passing information to the Guomindang, the American decision to shut down operations should have brought an end to the crisis. It was not that simple. On June 19 the *New China News Agency* published spy charges against the consulate: "Evidence at hand shows that so-called American Consulate in Mukden and U.S. Army liaison group in Mukden are American espionage organs. American espionage service in Mukden made use of former Japanese secret service agents and Chinese and Mongolian traitors to conspire against the Chinese people and world peace."[13] The reference to espionage activity in Inner Mongolia is revealing: the concerns expressed in the news article, the details themselves, and the manner of presenting them suggest Soviet influence, as does the fact that to whatever extent the American consulates in Manchuria were observation posts, they were patently used to keep an eye on the Soviets rather than on the CCP.[14] These charges were then followed by delay upon delay in allowing Ward and his staff to depart. Thus, it is necessary to see the Ward case in the context of Soviet-Chinese-American relations, a fact that U.S. diplomats in China were beginning by June 1949 to recognize. And it is necessary for proper understanding to examine this case against the background of possible CCP approaches to the United States in early 1949.

On May 31, CCP Central Committee member Zhou Enlai (Chou En-lai) passed along a message to Michael Keon, an Australian newspaperman working in China for the United Press, who sent it on to Assistant Military Attaché David Barrett, saying that he desired improved relations with the United States. Among his points,

Zhou contended that he did not agree with Moscow's attitude toward Washington, that he and other "liberals" in the CCP regarded Soviet international policy as "crazy," and that he believed the Chinese Communists should seek American economic assistance. Admitting that he spoke for only one group within the party, Zhou said that a radical faction, including Liu Shaoqi (Liu Shao-ch'i), desired a close alliance with the Soviet Union. Unfortunately, the radicals had embarrassed the party through their access to the propaganda machinery that Zhou never had been able to control. Apparently nervous about the possible exposure of his initiative, Zhou was tense and worried as he spoke, saying that if word of the demarche leaked out he would disavow any connection to it. Barrett conveyed the message to Consul General Clubb at Beijing, who then reported it to the State Department.[15]

In his dispatch to Washington, Clubb recommended that the United States remind Zhou that it desired friendly relations with China but that those relations should be based on mutual respect and understanding.[16] The State Department agreed and drafted a reply, which Under Secretary of State James Webb took to President Harry S. Truman for his approval. Truman pronounced himself satisfied but stressed that it was important "not to indicate any softening toward the Communists but to insist on judging their intentions by their actions."[17] The reply itself, of little relevance because it was never delivered, expressed hopes for friendly Sino-American relations on the basis of mutual understanding. It also entered a complaint about CCP propaganda and, pointedly, about the treatment of American diplomatic personnel.[18] When Clubb and Barrett tried to arrange transmittal of the reply by having Keon approach his Chinese contact, this individual, after consulting with Zhou, cut off the conversations in a "Gestapo-like" manner on June 23 and said that Zhou would not accept the American response.[19] Although Zhou in his demarche had not requested a direct reply, it seems unlikely that he would not expect one if he truly desired improved CCP-American relations. That something had forced Zhou to reconsider his move seems obvious.[20]

On June 18, after Zhou's initiative but before his refusal to accept the American reply, Ambassador Stuart was invited to visit Beijing. Whether the prospect of Stuart's visit influenced Zhou's decision to cut off further contact through Keon cannot be determined. At any rate, Huang Hua, acting with the approval of both Mao Zedong (Mao Tse-tung) and Zhou, urged Stuart to go to Beijing for talks while ostensibly visiting Yenching University.[21]

Although Stuart favored accepting the invitation, officials in Washington were highly skeptical. In discussions within the State

Department and with the president, policymakers stressed the negative consequences of such a visit: it would enhance the prestige of
the Communists and be a step toward recognition; it would suggest
that the United States was breaking the united-front policy toward
the CCP; it would constitute a final blow to the Nationalist regime
unless some gesture was made to Nationalist officials, a step that
hardly seemed possible; and, in view of the political climate in which
many Republicans and Democrats were courting anti-Communist
opinion, it would create a tremendous outcry in the United States.
After careful consideration at the highest levels, Secretary of State
Dean Acheson on July 1 informed the ambassador that "under no
circumstances" was he to go to Beijing.[22]

With the rejection of the invitation, which Stuart believed caused
some disappointment and loss of face to Zhou and Mao, who had
"counted on entertaining" the U.S. envoy, the State Department
seems to have missed an opportunity to explore the possibility of
positive relations with the Communists.[23] The date of Acheson's
reply to Stuart (July 1) and developments in China related to Zhou's
earlier demarche make such a conclusion too facile, however. Internal and external pressures on both American and CCP
policymakers complicated relations between the two in the summer of 1949. American officials were highly suspicious of Communist leaders and skeptical of the motives of Zhou and other
"liberals." "The Communists," Clubb cabled in reference to Zhou
Enlai's initiative, "desire continue diet Soviet political bread but
eke out diet with American economic cake." He believed that "it
would be premature to accept the development of Titoism at this
juncture before the party rank and file have really appreciated the
gravity of their economic and political predicament."[24] Clubb expressed the view of most of his colleagues, both in China and in
Washington, in suggesting that the Chinese Communists were effective allies of the Soviet Union and in the short run could not be
diverted from that course. Ambassador Stuart expressed some fear
that his invitation to Beijing was in part a CCP tactic to gain recognition from Washington, and John Davies of the State Department's
Policy Planning Staff believed that "the Communists would try to
make as much capital as they could out of such a visit." If Stuart
made the trip, Davies averred, it should be to give the Communists
"a curtain lecture in even stronger terms than that presented by
Bedell Smith to Stalin."[25]

A factor in Washington's reluctance to pursue the CCP initiative through Ambassador Stuart was concern about domestic reaction in the United States to such a move. Scholars have greatly
exaggerated the effect of the so-called China lobby on American

China policy, and the documents demonstrate that U.S. officials, for the most part, acted on their own presumption that China represented one aspect of their country's relations with the Soviet Union. They pursued a tough line toward the CCP out of balance-of-power considerations, not because public opinion desired it. In the case of this "opportunity" of 1949, however, public opinion clearly influenced the policy decision. Students of Sino-American relations are familiar with public and congressional comments on the Truman administration's China policy going back to 1946: Henry Luce's campaign for more support for Jiang Jieshi; the urgings of William Randolph Hearst, Robert McCormick, Roy Howard, and other publishers for greater attention to Asia; the work of Minnesota Republican Walter Judd, Congressman John Vorys of Ohio, Senator Styles Bridges of New Hampshire, and Senator William Knowland of California on behalf of the Nationalists; and the shrill criticism by other Republican partisans of America's "failure" in China.

In the first nine months of 1949 administration officials felt additional pressure. Senator Arthur Vandenberg of Michigan took a vigorous stand against the termination of shipments of military supplies to the Nationalists, arguing that the "blood of China must not be on our hands." In February fifty-one Republican representatives demanded creation of a commission to look at China policy, and in March fifty senators, including twenty-four Democrats, requested support for a bill sponsored by a Democrat, Senator Pat McCarran of Nevada, calling for a $1.5 billion loan to the Nationalists and for American command of Chinese armed forces. In March and April, as the Chinese Communists were pushing the civil war to its denouement, Senators Bridges and Knowland began calling for a full-scale investigation of East Asia policy. Then, in June, using the issue of Walton Butterworth's appointment to the new position of assistant secretary for Far Eastern affairs, the critics launched a harsh attack on the administration, in the process delaying his confirmation until September 27. Debate on the choice of Butterworth, who at the time held the position of director of the Office of Far Eastern Affairs, began while the Mao-Zhou invitation to Stuart was being considered. In this context it is not surprising that what worried Butterworth most about Stuart's prospective trip was "the domestic reaction in this country to such a move." It also worried Acheson and Truman.[26]

External pressures, particularly the detention of Ward and his staff at Mukden, also influenced American officials. Clearly, these policymakers did not easily accept Ward's detention. During the period of Zhou's demarche and the invitation to Stuart, which, interestingly, coincided with the isolation of the Mukden consulate,

U.S. officials were struggling with ways to apply pressure on the CCP. The Ward case was uppermost in the minds of Stuart, Clubb, Butterworth, Acheson, and Truman as they considered responding to the "opportunities" of June 1949, and this fact partly accounts for their wariness in judging Chinese Communist intentions.[27]

If American policymakers operated under powerful constraints during the summer of 1949, so too did the leaders of the CCP. Concern that they align their foreign policy with the requirements of Marxist-Leninist ideology inclined them to view the United States harshly. The Americans, after all, had participated in Western imperialism in China and had provided large-scale support for the Guomindang in the civil war. That the radical faction of the Chinese Communist Party would use its control of the propaganda machinery to attack the United States or that this group would resist the advice of a "liberal" faction in favor of aligning China with the Soviet Union is not surprising. Ideological imperatives remained a powerful motivator in this period of revolution.

A far more significant pressure, however, was an external one, and it emanated from the Soviet Union itself. This is not to suggest that the Soviets directed the Chinese revolution or that Mao had become their puppet, as was so commonly feared in the United States. It is only to argue that the Kremlin influenced CCP-American relations in the summer of 1949.

The Soviets learned of Zhou's demarche almost immediately after it was made. Apparently Po Yi-po, a Communist internal-security official in Shanxi (Shansi) who, according to Zhou's secretary, was "under the control of the Soviets," became aware of the initiative first and undertook an intensive investigation. Po began putting together an elaborate case against the Australian journalist Keon, the ostensible purpose being to accuse him of spying and to expel him from the country, but the real point being to expose and embarrass Zhou, who had become suspect in the eyes of the Soviets and to the pro-Moscow faction within the CCP because of his earlier recommendation in Communist councils that the Chinese Communists should incline toward the United States. In any event, in mid-August, Zhou's secretary informed American officials that the Soviet Union had used the demarche as a "pretext" for the assumption of a "strong hand" in Chinese affairs.[28]

One expression of the strong hand was Kremlin pressure to intensify Americans' anger over the Ward case. Thus, in late June, Chinese Communist officials, apparently at the insistence of the Soviets, trumped up a long list of spy charges against the Mukden consul general. Ward, in the report that he cabled immediately after his release, stressed Soviet involvement: "Have come to believe pro-Moscow elements CCP utilized Consul General arrest to drive wedge between the United States and sympathetic elements CCP by aggravating conditions arrest to utmost." At the same time, Communist officials known to the U.S. consul general at Shanghai (Shang-hai) expressed their "personal conviction that Soviets [were] primarily responsible for Ward case."[29]

Soviet pressure also manifested itself in Mao's "Leaning to One Side" pronouncement of July 1. In light of Zhou's demarche and other CCP contacts with American officials, the evidence seems overwhelming that Mao's statement must be seen in the context of Soviet attempts to preempt the "liberal" faction of the Chinese party. Until July 1, 1949, the Chinese Communists had left little doubt, either in their official pronouncements or in their policies, that they subscribed to the two-camps thesis. In 1947, Chinese leaders aligned themselves publicly and immediately with the sentiments of Soviet theoretician Andrei Zhdanov and the Cominform. Articles in the Communist press in 1947 and 1948 rejected the middle road and extolled the virtues of alliance with the USSR as the leader of the anti-imperialist camp. Mao himself, in his report of December 25, 1947, entitled "Present Situation and Our Tasks," enunciated the bipolar thesis. Later, despite their favorable attitude toward the Yugoslavs, the Chinese Communists hastened to support the Cominform-Soviet line condemning Marshal Tito, and Mao again announced solidarity with the Soviet Union and the impossibility of a global third road.[30] In short, there was nothing new in Mao's pronouncement of July 1. It is difficult to see why he would feel the need to make this statement unless pressed to do so by the Soviets, who feared that a faction of the CCP was maneuvering for an understanding with the United States.

The Soviets, when they learned of Zhou's initiative toward the United States, decided to force the Chinese Communists into a choice. According to Communist sources in Shanghai, the Kremlin sent a "special emissary" to Beijing, who "forced Mao to adopt a strongly pro-Soviet line in his July 1st statement." Such blatant pressure infuriated him so intensely that he "sulked" and actually became ill, although he felt he had no other option than to comply.[31] In his pronouncement Mao declared that China had to ally itself "with the Soviet Union" and "with the proletariat and broad masses in all other countries"; he stated further that to consolidate victory the people would have to "lean either to the side of imperialism or to that of socialism." Mao's declaration showed the hand of the Soviets in other ways: it was "childish," he said, to think of receiving "genuine" American aid because internationally "the CCP belongs to the anti-imperialist front headed by the USSR and can only look for genuine friendly aid from that front."[32] Deliberately provocative, the message achieved the effect that the Soviets intended: it muted speculation in Washington about Titoism in China and convinced U.S. officials that "Mao is not for sale now."[33]

If it is understandable that the Kremlin would seek to influence Sino-American relations, it is less clear why the Chinese Communist leaders would succumb to its pressure. One factor undoubtedly was the aforementioned pro-Soviet element within the CCP, made up of individuals like Liu Shaoqi, that wanted no contact with the United States. This group, opposed to American diplomatic recognition, drew reinforcement from Soviet advisers sent to China in increased numbers during the summer of 1949.[34] These advisers exerted heavy influence in the Ministry of Justice and in other agencies in Beijing, as well as in the regional government in Manchuria. A disillusioned member of the CCP confided to an American intelligence contact that the Soviets exercised direct power over the CCP in three primary ways: through the Chinese Communist security police, which they dominated; by control of the flow of foreign news entering Communist China; and by the use of material and technical aid as leverage.[35] Indeed, the Soviets possessed such influence in Manchuria that in July 1949, Gao Gang (Kao Kang), chairman of the People's Government of Manchuria, traveled to Moscow without consulting Mao and concluded a trade agreement with Stalin.[36] In the meantime, the Soviets, in the spring and summer of 1949, placed China at the top of their foreign-policy agenda, with Vyacheslav M. Molotov himself in charge of China affairs. As Foy Kohler, U.S. chargé d'affaires in Moscow, expressed it, the Kremlin was using its best talent "to steer Chinese development in the way Moscow desires and to guarantee no deviation or heresy will occur."[37]

The Chinese Communists also remained wary of Washington's intentions. They assumed that the United States, which itself had leaned to one side during the civil war, could not be easily weaned away from the Nationalists, and they were aware of American public opinion. To risk the support of the Soviet Union for American economic aid made sense only if the latter were a sure thing, which it obviously was not. Yet, it is incorrect to think that Washington's rejection of the CCP invitation to Stuart constituted a failure to provide the necessary proof. Acheson's note to Stuart ordering him not to visit Beijing was dated July 1, the same day that Mao released his message.

Whatever Mao's personal thinking—and it is by no means clear that he favored the "liberals" within the party—he recognized that in 1949, Soviet domination of Manchuria hung like the sword of

Damocles over the Chinese Communist regime. Because the Soviets held Manchuria hostage, they could at any time threaten a separatist movement that the CCP would be powerless to prevent. Of all of the areas of China, Manchuria was the most important: it contained the only really advanced industrial complex and was the sole CCP source for the machinery required for further growth. Communist China could not achieve economic progress without Manchuria.[38]

In May and June of 1949, Chinese Communist radio broadcasts addressed the problem of Manchuria, emphasizing that the Soviet Union would aid in the expansion of industry there. The broadcasts also stressed that this industry would constitute the base for industrialization elsewhere in China.[39] Under these circumstances the CCP did not have latitude in its foreign relations for a liaison with the United States no matter how attractive that course seemed to certain members of the party.

Ward and his staff were thus caught in this tangled web of Soviet-CCP-American relations. Indeed, he had yet to run a weary race. Despite repeated attempts to close the consulate and depart in accordance with his instructions, Ward received no authorization or facilities from the CCP to do so. On July 19, when he requested a departure date of July 27, he got no answer; on August 12 he made a similar request and got a similar result; on September 3 he sent a letter to the mayor of Mukden again asking for rail transportation out of the city, only to have it denied.[40] Although permitted minimal contact with the outside world from early June onward, conditions of the consulate incarceration did not improve substantially. Over the entire period of captivity the group had inadequate water supplies, intermittent electricity, no telephones, no medical or dental attention (Ward's wife needed dental work and apparently had at least one attack of appendicitis), and all members of the staff were threatened at one time or another with firearms.[41]

The final blow occurred in the fall of 1949. On September 27, Ward dismissed a laborer, Ji Yuheng (Chi Yu-heng), an employee of the consulate who had refused to complete a job that the consul general had assigned him. The man's wages were to be sent to his residence. When the laborer—apparently at the instance of higher authority with Soviet connections—returned to the consulate surreptitiously and was discovered on October 11, Ward escorted him out firmly. This precipitated a scuffle in which Ji's brother attacked Ward while several other Chinese staff members joined in beating two of Ward's subordinates. Accompanied by a bombastic press announcement, on October 24 the consul general and four members of the staff were arrested on trumped-up assault charges. Ward and his men, CCP officials alleged, had beaten Ji![42] For nearly a month Ward and the others were each held in solitary confinement in poorly heated cells where they were fed six slices of bread and three ounces of water daily. Ward lost twenty-five pounds on this regimen, and all the men suffered severe physical and mental strain during the ordeal.[43]

The subsequent trial was a model of Communist jurisprudence. Ward and his four codefendants were denied legal counsel or access to other personnel at the consulate, were not permitted to present witnesses for the defense, could not cross-examine the plaintiffs' witnesses, and could not make any rebutting arguments. As Molotov expressed it in another context, "the guilty parties would be given a fair trial." Word of the trial prompted the second secretary of the U.S. embassy, Leonard Bacon, to observe that China had "retrogressed into legal barbarity which originally necessitated extra-territoriality."[44] The verdict, needless to say, was predictable; all were found guilty and sentenced to terms of imprisonment that varied from four to six months. All these sentences eventually were commuted to deportation. Ji was to receive both back pay and severance pay. The U.S. officials were released on November 21; they subsequently closed the consulate and left Mukden for Tianjin on

President Harry S. Truman, Angus Ward, and Secretary of State Dean Acheson confer on January 23, 1950, after Ward's release. *Courtesy National Archives*

December 7. On December 11 they boarded ship for the voyage home, their ordeal over after roughly thirteen months.

What U.S. policymakers did about this kidnapping and what they contemplated doing, especially after Ward's arrest, are critical issues to address. While Secretary of State Acheson tended to play down the seriousness of the incident, at least for a time, even he came to see it as a major impediment to recognition. Certainly, he accepted the argument that Ward's release must be a sine qua non for an exchange of ambassadors. The American public was outraged in a way that officials could not mistake; there was an outcry in the periodical press, and patriotic groups such as the American Legion bombarded Congress and the administration with calls for action.

Some officials, such as Truman, did not require pressure to stimulate their anger. The president confided to Under Secretary of State James Webb on November 14 that he was thinking of blockading the shipment of coal along the coast from Tianjin to Shanghai; and if any ships tried to run the blockade, U.S. vessels should sink them. After Ward's imprisonment, Consul General Clubb in Beijing recommended economic sanctions, including the cutting off of trade between China and Japan. Officials of the Far Eastern division of the State Department endorsed Clubb's idea of using economic sanctions as leverage.[45]

Neither of these proposals received a favorable reception from those whose job it was to weigh the various options. The Bureau of Economic Affairs rejected the cutting off of Sino-Japanese trade as "inappropriate" because it would be injurious to Japan and unacceptable to the Western powers. Moreover, interference with the trading activity of other Western nations with China would be provocative to these countries.

The Joint Chiefs of Staff, meanwhile, examined the possibility of using force to effect Ward's release. To secure his freedom with military power would require a large-scale effort in Manchuria, the site of the headquarters of the Chinese Communist army and an area of vital Soviet interest. Moscow's noninvolvement was judged to be "a remote possibility," while a global war was considered a distinct possibility. A blockade would not be effective unless the United States ran the risk of war with the Soviets or the Chinese Communists or both. Seizing Chinese Communists as counterhostages was not possible because there were no CCP members in American-held territory. In short, the United States had no viable military option to extricate Ward. This information Secretary Acheson hastened to pass along to President Truman, who agreed to back away from an extreme solution, military or otherwise.[46]

The one course that the United States could continue to pursue was diplomacy. On November 18, Secretary of State Acheson sent a message to the British and to other Western countries "which respect international law," calling on them to put pressure on the Chinese Communists. To what extent this affected the thinking in Beijing or Moscow is impossible to determine. Because of close relations and consultations between the British Foreign Office and the State Department, it is entirely possible that the combination of multinational protest and word that Washington was considering, out of extreme exasperation, military options may have gotten through to Moscow. It may not be insignificant that the British Foreign Office expert on Sino-Soviet relations during this period was Guy Burgess, a spy in the employ of the Kremlin, who later defected to Moscow. Whatever he knew, it must be assumed, became property of the Soviets as soon as he knew it, and there seems little doubt that they had a major hand in the Mukden affair.

WHETHER OR NOT information about America's consideration of the use of force motivated the Soviets to urge the termination of Ward's captivity, the process of weighing various military and economic options had deep significance. A study conducted during this incident by the Joint Chiefs of Staff, the Department of Defense, and the State Department was the first systematic assessment ever made of the options available—or not available—in hostage crises. As such, it foreshadowed responses in future situations and pointed up the dilemma that the nation faced throughout the twentieth century. Any time hostages were held, public pressure began to build for Washington to do something, often of a military nature, to either free the people being held or punish the kidnappers or both. There was always political capital to be made in attacking incumbent administrations for failing to uphold the honor of the United States. Indeed, a measure of this emotion is revealed in a *New York Herald Tribune* editorial in which the Chinese Communists were called "barbarians" and Washington officials were admonished to demand "apology and reparation to the mistreated American diplomatic officers."[47] However, it was increasingly risky to use force to free hostages for several reasons: in an interdependent world the interests of allies or other friendly states could be injured; military action could lead to full-scale war, unthinkable in an age of nuclear weapons; with modern communications those holding hostages could always secure information far enough in advance to either kill them or transfer them to secluded locations; and revolutionary regimes manifested such a degree of fanaticism that policymakers could not be certain of rational responses.

NOTES

1. *New York Times*, November 25, 1969.

2. Edwin W. Martin, *Divided Counsel: The Anglo-American Response to Communist Victory in China* (Lexington: University Press of Kentucky, 1986), 8; consul general at Mukden to secretary of state, November 5, 1948, U.S. Department of State, *Papers Relating to the Foreign Relations of the United States, 1948*, 9 vols., *The Far East: China* (Washington, DC: Government Printing Office, 1973), 7:829 (hereafter cited as *FRUS*, followed by appropriate year).

3. Martin, *Divided Counsel*, 8.

4. Secretary of state to certain diplomatic representatives, November 18, 1949, *FRUS, 1949*, 9 vols., *The Far East: China* (Washington, DC: Government Printing Office, 1978), 8:1009–10.

5. Ambassador in China to secretary of state, January 12, 1949, ibid., 8:934–35; consul general at Beijing to secretary of state, March 2, 1949, ibid., 936–37.

6. Secretary of state to consul general at Beijing, March 2, 1949, ibid., 943.

7. Consul general at Beijing to secretary of state, March 8, 1949, ibid., 944–45.

8. Ambassador in China to secretary of state, March 24, 1949, ibid., 948; ambassador in China to secretary of state, April 3, 1949, ibid., 950.

9. Consul general at Beijing to secretary of state, March 26, 1949, ibid., 949.

10. For discussion of this point see Martin, *Divided Counsel*, 11.

11. Secretary of state to consul general at Beijing, April 15, 1949, *FRUS, 1949*, 8:952.

12. Secretary of state to consul general at Beijing, May 17, 1949, ibid., 957; ambassador in China to secretary of state, May 25, 1949, ibid., 958.

13. Consul general at Beijing to secretary of state, June 19, 1949, ibid., 965.

14. Ambassador in China to secretary of state, June 21, 1949, ibid., 970. A Chinese historian who has utilized recently opened Communist archival sources confirms this interpretation: "We now know," he writes, that "the CCP's management of the Ward case was largely influenced by their determination to maintain solidarity with the Soviet Union." This historian quotes Mao Zedong as saying in November of 1948 that "so far as our foreign policy in the Northeast and the whole of China is concerned, we will certainly consult with the Soviet Union in order to maintain an identical stand [with the Soviets]." Yang Kuisong, "The Soviet Factor and the CCP's Policy toward the United States in the 1940s," *Chinese Historians* 5, no. 1 (Spring 1992): 30–31. For Mao's "Leaning to One Side" policy and later developments in Sino-Soviet relations see Qiang Zhai, *The Dragon, the Lion, and the Eagle: Chinese-British-American Relations, 1949–1958* (Kent, OH: Kent State University Press, 1994), 19–27.

15. Consul general at Beijing to secretary of state, June 1, 1949, *FRUS, 1949*, 8:357–60; *New York Times*, September 17, 1949. See also Robert M. Blum, "The Peiping Cable," *New York Times*, August 13, 1978. Blum discusses the Clubb cable, intelligently analyzing Zhou Enlai's demarche and the prospects it offered of improved CCP-American relations. He is skeptical of the possibility of drawing the CCP away from the Soviets with anything but the "boldest American response," although he concludes that if the United States had followed a more

consistently benign policy, it might have given the Chinese Communists less reason to "throw themselves into the arms of the Soviet Union."

16. Consul general at Beijing to secretary of state, June 2, 1949, *FRUS, 1949*, 8:364.

17. Memorandum by acting secretary of state regarding conversation with the president, June 16, 1949, ibid., 388.

18. Acting secretary of state to consul general at Beijing, June 14, 1949, ibid., 384.

19. Consul general at Beijing to secretary of state, June 24, 1949, ibid., 397. See also Russell D. Buhite, *Soviet-American Relations in Asia, 1945–1954* (Norman: University of Oklahoma Press, 1981), 75–79.

20. Consul general at Beijing to secretary of state, June 27, 1949, *FRUS, 1949*, 8:398. That Zhou reconsidered did not mean that he had changed his mind about the United States. He told a CIA source in late October 1949 that, while it "would be a dream on the part of the American Government to expect the Chinese Communist Party to split with the U.S.S.R.," the United States could "expect that the Chinese Communist Party will not always be anti-American." See memorandum by director of CIA to Truman, November 21, 1949, in Elizabeth Jones, ed., *Declassified Documents Reference System*, 7 vols. (Washington, DC: Carrollton Press, 1977), 3:261-D. Scholars are not in complete agreement on the authenticity of the Zhou demarche. In a recent study of Sino-Soviet-American relations Gordon Chang argues that although U.S. officials at the time accepted it as genuine, the demarche was probably fabricated. Chang bases his opinion on interviews he conducted in 1985 with two Chinese Communist officials who had been close to Zhou in 1949. Other Chinese, including one-time ambassador to the United States Zhang Wenjin, also denied the validity of the message. See Gordon H. Chang, *Friends and Enemies: The United States, China, and the Soviet Union, 1948–1972* (Stanford, CA: Stanford University Press, 1990), 304n; and Stephen M. Goldstein, "Chinese Communist Policy toward the United States: Opportunities and Constraints, 1944–1950," in *Uncertain Years: Chinese-American Relations, 1947–1950*, ed. Dorothy Borg and Waldo Heinrichs (New York: Columbia University Press, 1980), 274–75. On the other hand, a number of diplomatic historians accept the Zhou demarche as "probably" valid. See, for example, Robert M. Blum, *Drawing the Line: The Origins of the American Containment Policy in East Asia* (New York: W. W. Norton, 1982), 56–61; David Mayers, *Cracking the Monolith: U.S. Policy against the Sino-Soviet Alliance, 1949–1955* (Baton Rouge: Louisiana State University Press, 1986), 44–45; and Nancy B. Tucker, *Patterns in the Dust: Chinese-American Relations and the Recognition Controversy, 1949–1950* (New York: Columbia University Press, 1983), 48, 233n. The content of the note, the interpretation of it by U.S. officials (including Edmund Clubb), the nature of the rebuff when the United States tried to reply, and the Sino-Soviet context convince me of the authenticity of the demarche.

21. Seymour Topping, *Journey between Two Chinas* (New York: Harper and Row, 1974), 83. Topping says that, in 1971, Philip Fugh, Stuart's personal secretary, told him in Washington of the CCP invitation; and in the same year, Huang Hua, then serving as ambassador to Ottawa (in the 1970s, Huang served as ambassador to Canada and to the United Nations and as China's foreign minister), told him of it as well. Conversely, Topping notes (p. 89), Stanley Hornbeck, who

wrote the last three chapters of Stuart's book *Fifty Years in China*, did not include material on the invitation, and the State Department would not allow Topping to see the pertinent documents. Hornbeck told me of Huang's role in a conversation of January 16, 1965, but portrayed the offer as nothing more than a CCP "trick" to gain prestige. See John Gittings, *The World and China, 1922–1972* (New York: Harper and Row, 1974), 165. Gittings discusses the invitation, citing Topping as his source. See also ambassador in China to secretary of state, June 30, 1949, *FRUS, 1949*, 8:766–67.

22. Secretary of state to ambassador in China, July 1, 1949, *FRUS, 1949*, 8:769.

23. Ambassador in China to secretary of state, July 14, 1949, ibid., 784.

24. Consul general at Beijing to secretary of state, June 2, 1949, ibid., 363–64. Clubb's reference is to Josip Broz Tito, Communist leader of Yugoslavia, who broke with the Soviet Union in 1948 and thus became the first Communist to chart a course for his country independent of Stalin's control.

25. Memorandum by John Davies to George Kennan, June 30, 1949, ibid., 768–69.

26. Ibid. See also Tang Tsou, *America's Failure in China, 1941–1950* (Chicago: University of Chicago Press, 1963), 501–3.

27. Ambassador in China to secretary of state, June 1, 1949, *FRUS, 1949*, 8:959.

28. Consul general at Beijing to secretary of state, March 26, 1949, ibid., 949–50; consul general at Beijing to secretary of state, August 18, 1949, ibid., 497. Zhou indicated to a CIA source that he wanted the friendship of the United States but was "constrained from this course by the presence of the pro-Soviet Chinese Communist Party faction." See memorandum by director of CIA to Truman, November 21, 1949, in Jones, *Declassified Documents Reference System*, 3:261-D. See also O. B. Borisov and B. T. Koloskov, *Soviet-Chinese Relations, 1945–1970* (Bloomington: Indiana University Press, 1975), 74. The Soviet authors identify Po Yi-po as pro-Soviet.

29. Consul general at Beijing to secretary of state, May 25, 1949, *FRUS, 1949*, 8:344–45; consul at Tianjin to secretary of state, December 10, 1949, ibid., 1044–46; consul general at Shanghai to secretary of state, December 16, 1949, ibid., 634; ambassador in China to secretary of state, June 4, 1949, ibid., 366; ambassador in China to secretary of state, June 9, 1949, ibid., 375.

30. See Okabe Tatsumi, "The Cold War and China," in *The Origins of the Cold War in Asia*, ed. Yonosuke Nagai and Akira Iriye (New York: Columbia University Press, 1977), 238–41. A CCP delegate to a major Communist conference in Prague informed a U.S. intelligence contact that "there is not, will not, and can not be any Tito in China"; Office of Intelligence and Research (OIR) Report, December 22, 1949, reel 4, doc. 35, OSS/State Department Intelligence Reports, National Archives.

31. Consul general at Shanghai to secretary of state, August 10, 1949, *FRUS, 1949*, 8:1271–72; consul general at Beijing to secretary of state, July 19, 1949, ibid., 443. Mao indicated in his pronouncement that there were enemies "inside the Party and without." The text was published in *Pravda*, July 6, 1949; see also *Current Digest of the Soviet Press* 1 (August 9, 1949): 3–8. U.S. intelligence indicated that the Soviet adviser in Beijing "had a hand in the recent curbing of

the activities of Communist officials possessing contacts with both the National Government and the U.S.," OIR Report, December 22, 1949, National Archives.

32. Mao Zedong, *On People's Democratic Dictatorship* (Beijing: Foreign Language Press, 1952), 10–13. Ambassador Stuart reported that Mao's writing style in the pronouncement showed "interesting similarities" to that of Stalin. Ambassador in China to secretary of state, July 6, 1949, *FRUS, 1949*, 8:405–7.

33. *FRUS, 1949*, 8:407. See also Tang Tsou, *America's Failure in China*, 506.

34. Consul general at Shanghai to secretary of state, December 16, 1949, *FRUS, 1949*, 8:632–36; memorandum by ambassador in China to assistant secretary of state for Far Eastern affairs, November 28, 1949, ibid., 8:611–12.

35. OIR Report, March 22, 1949, reel 4, doc. 22, OSS/State Department Intelligence and Research Reports, National Archives.

36. See Nakajima Mineo, "The Sino-Soviet Confrontation in Historical Perspective," in *The Origins of the Cold War in Asia*, ed. Nagai and Iriye, 210; Edmund Clubb, *China and Russia: The "Great Game"* (New York: Columbia University Press, 1971), 10; and Borisov and Koloskov, *Soviet-Chinese Relations*, 52–62.

37. Chargé in Soviet Union to secretary of state, April 19, 1949, *FRUS, 1949*, 8:250.

38. Ambassador in China to secretary of state, June 9, 1949, ibid., 375, 366; consul general at Beijing to secretary of state, December 23, 1949, ibid., 645.

39. Ambassador in China to secretary of state, June 9, 1949, ibid., 375.

40. Consul general at Beijing to secretary of state, September 23, 1949, ibid., 979.

41. Consul general at Mukden to secretary of state, December 11, 1949, ibid., 1048.

42. Ibid.

43. Consul general at Beijing to secretary of state, November 28, 1949, ibid., 1027.

44. Secretary of embassy in China to secretary of state, December 5, 1949, ibid., 1039.

45. Memorandum by under secretary, November 14, 1949, ibid., 1008; consul general at Beijing to secretary of state, November 4, 1949, ibid., 1000.

46. Memorandum by chairman of the Joint Chiefs of Staff to secretary of defense, November 18, 1949, ibid., 1011–13; memorandum by secretary of state to the president, November 21, 1949, ibid., 1015–16; Martin, *Divided Counsel*, 81.

47. *New York Herald Tribune*, December 13, 1949.

Chapter 6

The Pueblo *Crisis: Hostages of North Korea*

During the early afternoon of January 23, 1968, two North Korean submarine chasers and four torpedo boats surrounded the USS *Pueblo*, an American intelligence ship engaged in electronic espionage roughly three miles outside North Korean territorial waters to the east of Wonsan. When the ship tried to flee and then did not obey commands to follow their vessels into Wonsan harbor, the North Koreans opened fire, killing one American and wounding three others, including the commander. As the panic-stricken men frantically attempted to burn or throw overboard sensitive files and destroy intelligence machinery, ten armed North Korean sailors boarded the hapless vessel and took its surviving eighty-two crewmen prisoner.[1] The *Pueblo* thus surrendered without resistance. Its skipper, Commander Lloyd M. Bucher, later contended that his ship was not equipped to offer resistance, and its crew would have suffered death had any been attempted. The North Korean government then proceeded to hold the men captive for eleven months, forced them to sign numerous contrived confessions, and savagely brutalized them.[2]

Originally the idea of Dr. Eugene Fubini, deputy secretary of defense in the early 1960s, and endorsed by Chief of Naval Operations Admiral David L. McDonald, the plan to equip light cargo vessels for electronic espionage took shape in 1965. The navy eventually designed three ships for this purpose: the *Banner,* to lurk in international waters off the coasts of China and the Soviet Union; the *Palm Beach,* to work in the Western Hemisphere; and the *Pueblo,* to listen in on secrets transmitted by the Soviets, Chinese, and North Koreans. The assumption was that since the Soviets had been using light, nonthreatening naval craft to trail after the U.S. fleet and to hang around strategic American bases picking up radio transmissions and other sensitive information, so, too, could the United States.

USS *Pueblo* off San Diego, CA, October 19, 1967. *Courtesy National Archives*

What troubled the North Koreans about the *Pueblo*'s mission, among other factors, was that the vessel could gather valuable information about their coastal defenses and their air force. Apparently, they had put in place surface-to-air (SAM) as well as cruise missiles near the coast. If the *Pueblo* waited long enough in this area, the North Koreans would eventually have to turn on their SAM radars and it could get a fix on the missile sites. Through radio intercepts and coastal observation the *Pueblo* might gain knowledge of North Korean air capabilities as well. Indeed, the *Pueblo*'s orders called for the ship to carry out these very tasks.[3]

Although the North Korean attack was a surprise, it probably should not have been. Two months beforehand the government had issued a vague warning of possible action against spy ships operating along its coast. Consistent with their general pattern of behavior at this time, the North Koreans in January 1968 also initiated violence against South Korean and American forces at the demilitarized zone (DMZ) of the divided country, resulting in very substantial death and injury tolls. Other harassing maneuvers occurred, including the seizure of South Korean fishermen and patrol boats. On both January 6 and 11, 1968, the North Koreans had called attention to the "intolerable" situation of American spy vessels operating in waters east of their coast. On January 19 the North Koreans sent word to Washington that such spy vessels might provoke them to action; only a few days later, on January 21 and 22, they sent patrol boats to observe the activities of the *Pueblo*.

Totally aside from the evidence of North Korean annoyance, American officials should have expected that electronic spying would give offense, especially to a regime openly hostile to the United States. Principles of maritime law codified long before the technological revolution were obviously inadequate to deal with electronic snooping, and to think that a small nation should automatically allow a larger, more advanced country to get away with such snooping was probably expecting too much. Certainly, in view of the simultaneous American preoccupation with Vietnam, the United States should have shown greater concern about the *Pueblo*'s vulnerability.[4]

The absence of adequate documentary evidence makes it extremely difficult to fully evaluate North Korean motives, but what seems certain is that they had some connection to President Kim Il Sung's desire to take control of the entire peninsula, to advance his nation's economic and military power, and to maneuver within the Sino-Soviet relationship. At the time of the *Pueblo* seizure relations between the Kim government and the Kremlin were good, owing to a number of important interests on the part of the North Koreans: the Soviet Union was the only adequate source of military equipment essential to maintaining or increasing Pyongyang's power; the Soviets continued to serve as North Korea's leading proponent in the United Nations, not an incidental benefit from a propaganda standpoint; Moscow provided much of the assistance and technology necessary for the survival of the North Korean economy; and better relations with the Soviets gave Kim greater flexibility in dealing with China, thus allowing him some freedom from the stultifying power of Mao's paternalism.

Prior to 1965, most clearly in the era of Nikita Khrushchev's ascendancy in Moscow, the North Koreans had leaned toward China. As a devoted Stalinist who owed his power to the former Soviet dictator, Kim was repelled by Khrushchev's revisionism and his commitment to "peaceful coexistence" with the West. Kim remained a firm believer in wars of national liberation just as he stayed faithful to his pledge to "liberate" South Korea. China's ideology and foreign policies seemed more compatible with Kim's own than did those of the Soviet Union. What ultimately brought the North Koreans around to a pro-Soviet posture in the mid-1960s was the removal of Khrushchev from power and the realization that aid from the USSR would ultimately be more important than Chinese ideology in the communization of the South.

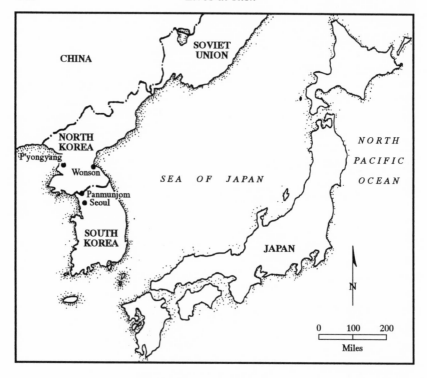

Having failed to unify the peninsula militarily in the Korean
War, the North Koreans after 1953 began a process of revolutioniz-
ing the South. They did this by infiltrating agents into South Korea
for the purpose of carrying out acts of sabotage, terrorism, and espionage, and of organizing revolutionary units on which the
Pyongyang government could depend to carry out an appropriately
timed uprising. The removal from power of Syngman Rhee's government in Seoul in April of 1960 gave the North added hope that
early communization of the South would be possible, but the absence of adequate southern Communist support and the failure of
the North's propaganda campaign prevented fulfillment of the
dream. When a military coup on May 16, 1961, brought an aggressively anti-Communist regime to power in the South, Kim's government had two motives for acting more vigorously: to communize
the entire peninsula and to head off a possible invasion of the North.

In December of 1962 and again in the fall of 1966, North Korea's
Central Committee opted for a decidedly aggressive policy. It put
the country on a military footing out of fear of a U.S.-backed invasion from the South and to set the stage for the expulsion of the
American "imperialists" from the peninsula. This meant intensifi-

cation of the plan to industrialize the North and stepped-up efforts to infiltrate the South. After the United States became engaged in the fighting in Vietnam, Kim Il Sung seems to have concluded that Korea should become a second front in the Asian struggle against imperialism. In 1967, United Nations (UN) and Republic of Korea (ROK) forces reported killing 224 North Korean infiltrators and capturing 50 others, at a cost of 124 killed on the UN-ROK side. This was a prelude to a commando raid on the South Korean president's mansion on January 21, 1968.[5]

Thirty-one North Korean commandos slipped past South Korean intelligence and attempted to carry out the assassination of President Park Chung Hee. All but one of the potential murderers were killed, but not before a frightful toll had been taken: thirty-six people, among them two American soldiers and eight South Korean civilians had been killed; and sixty-eight others, including twelve Americans, had been wounded. Whether this effort, had it succeeded, would have resulted in full-scale guerrilla warfare in the South or an open invasion cannot yet be determined. In any event, there is no gainsaying the fact of North Korean belligerency; the attack on the *Pueblo* took place two days later.

What, specifically, did the North Koreans expect to gain by taking the U.S. ship and holding its crew hostage? If Kim Il Sung's infiltration efforts were aimed at undermining the South Korean economy (which by the late 1960s had become reasonably prosperous), frightening away foreign investors, and sowing fear and trepidation among the South Korean people, it can be assumed that the

Soviet *SO-1*-class patrol boat of the type used by North Korea to seize the USS *Pueblo. Courtesy National Archives*

seizure of the *Pueblo* was a further action taken to prove that North Korea could conduct itself with relative impunity against both the South and its American protector. At one and the same time Kim could demonstrate to the world his ability to take on the Goliath of the United States, and, in parading the crew of the *Pueblo* as confessed spies, "prove" to his own people the dangerous designs of the United States, including an imminent American-sponsored invasion from the South. He could then ask for greater sacrifices in order to build up the economy and strengthen the military.

Apart from the value of the seizure in gratifying Kim's enormous ego (he seemed to relish the international attention in the weeks immediately following the kidnapping), two other factors may have impelled the North Koreans to take the U.S. ship. Assuming the inability of Washington to respond because of its involvement in Vietnam, it was entirely possible that Pyongyang believed the action would promote South Korean-American discord when the United States failed to act like a Great Power. Moreover, the ship itself, with all of its sophisticated electronic equipment, codes, and other spying paraphernalia, must have seemed extremely attractive. Despite Commander Bucher's claim that his crew destroyed most of this material before the capture, prominent naval personnel have argued that the North Koreans gained possession of an intelligence gold mine.[6]

Although no definitive evidence exists in support of this proposition, the seizure of the *Pueblo* may have been related to the Tet Offensive in Vietnam, which began some eight days later. In other words, it is possible that Kim Il Sung may have initiated the border incident, the assassination attempt, and the taking of American hostages to open a second front that would relieve pressure on Hanoi. President Lyndon B. Johnson (as he noted in his memoirs) always thought the two events were connected: "Our best estimate then . . . [was] that they were aware of the Tet Offensive in Vietnam. . . . They were trying to divert U.S. military resources from Vietnam and to pressure the South Koreans into recalling their two divisions from that area, for the seizure of the *Pueblo* was not an isolated incident."[7]

A related question is whether the Chinese or Soviets somehow played a part in the action by either gathering intelligence or helping North Vietnam. The answer, insofar as the available evidence is concerned, is "probably not." The Soviets knew that their own intelligence vessels were often vulnerable to capture, and in any case such a move did not conform to their usual modus operandi. China was at the time convulsed by the Cultural Revolution and locked in a bitter confrontation with the Soviet Union that threatened to erupt into full-scale war. This situation, and the fact that in 1968 North Korean-Chinese relations were not close, tend to rule out Beijing's participation. A further indication of the exclusively North Korean nature of this show is that no Chinese or Soviet agents appeared to interrogate Bucher or his intelligence officer, both of whom could have been forced to reveal valuable information (though the Soviets opportunistically sent personnel to check out the *Pueblo* for intelligence after its capture).[8] Presumably the Soviets would have had a better idea of what to look for than the North Koreans.

That Bucher and his men were spared torture at the hands of Soviet KGB agents does not mean that they received acceptable treatment from their captors. In fact, the North Koreans treated them most severely. The *Pueblo*'s officers and crew were held in primitive, drafty, louse-infested cells; they were periodically beaten almost to death (kidney chops with flying feet and blows to the head and shoulders with rifle butts were the most common tactics); they were given a diet insufficient to sustain most American men at a proper nutritional level, and many of them developed scurvy or other serious ailments; and those men who had been wounded in the boarding of the ship did not receive medical attention until several days after their incarceration, and as a result of this delay one of them developed gangrene.

Whenever their captors chose, the officers were forced to compose apologies and confessions to the North Korean people, which were subsequently released to the press worldwide. Bucher at first refused to comply with their insistence that he sign a confession. They beat him mercilessly, then made him kneel on the floor and put a gun to his head, telling him that he was to be executed. When given the order to fire, a soldier pulled the trigger on an empty rifle. All of these things obviously terrified the American commander, but what finally caused him to break was the sight of a South Korean prisoner hung up on a wall still alive, with one eye gouged out, a broken jaw, and half of his face torn away—a bloody, beaten mass of humanity—as well as the threat that each of his crew, starting with the youngest, would be beaten to death in the same fashion.

At one point the six officers as a group were directed to write a letter to President Johnson. Then Bucher, as commander, received instructions to draft a personal letter to his commander in chief. Especially at the beginning of their captivity, the threat of execution hung over the Americans' heads as their guards mixed warnings about instant death with blandishments about North Korean hospitality if they became "sincere." As the day of their release approached they received more and better food and regular

Commander Lloyd M. Bucher. *Courtesy National Archives*

exercise, although a new round of beatings began in early December after their captors learned that in nearly all of the internationally circulated photographs the crewmen were giving their hosts "the finger." Whether this was the reason or simply the occasion for the brutality cannot be determined; some other motive related to the negotiations for the men's release may have governed the actions. The only loss of life, miraculously, came in the initial attack on the vessel.[9]

In other times the seizure of an American ship and the incarceration of its crew would have been defined as piracy and would have evoked instantaneous and nearly unanimous outrage in the United States. However, these were not normal times, and because the mounting criticism of the nation's involvement in Vietnam had provoked general skepticism about U.S. international behavior, the result was a mixed reaction. Word of the capture of the *Pueblo* reached Washington around midnight on January 22, with President Johnson receiving the news at approximately 2:00 A.M. on the twenty-third. By 8:30 that same morning the Department of Defense had reported the incident to the American people, along with the surprising disclosure that the *Pueblo* was an intelligence-gathering vessel.

Although some jingoistic opinion surfaced immediately among congressional and opposition party leaders, what stands out is the remarkably restrained nature of the public's response. Predictably, the old Dixiecrat Democrat-turned Republican, Senator Strom Thurmond of South Carolina, counseled an aggressive course involving an "ultimatum," after which the *Pueblo* should "be taken by force if it is not delivered within a specified period of time." Ronald Reagan, then governor of California, recommended sending warships into Wonsan harbor to "get the ship back if it isn't released within twenty-four hours." Senator Richard Russell of Georgia urged the president "to take a very strong position in demanding release of the ship and return of the men." A number of other political figures spoke up in defense of national honor and the need to give the North Koreans a lesson in American military power.[10]

Out of fear that the *Pueblo* might indeed have strayed into North Korean territorial waters and concern about possible war with Pyongyang, others recommended restraint. Senator Mike Mansfield of Montana pointed out that bold action would not only doom the crew to execution, but "it could also bring about another bloody and prolonged involvement in Korea." His colleague John Stennis of Mississippi also cautioned against "rash overreaction."[11] Of all the members of the U.S. Senate, J. William Fulbright of Arkansas, chairman of the Foreign Relations Committee, expressed views that stand out as some of the most critical of the administration and, because of his position and stature, the most important. On

January 30 he wrote to a friend back in Little Rock that in his opinion sending the *Pueblo* into position off the coast of North Korea was "very imprudent" and "stupid," and that he did not know how to resolve the mess: "I certainly do not wish to start dropping bombs all over the place. . . . Surely if they have an ounce of skill and tact left they will be able to figure out a way for the exchange of prisoners, or some way to recover the men and ship without another war."[12]

A week later, in a letter to the editor of the *St. Louis Post-Dispatch*, Fulbright referred to the affair as a "non-crisis," stating that he was suspicious of the administration's version of events and did not believe the government: "It really is the most incredible and chaotic situation I have ever encountered. It is almost impossible to do business with a government which one does not believe, especially when it is one's own government."[13] Fulbright's anger and frustration came through most clearly in a set of twenty questions that he directed from the Foreign Relations Committee to Secretary of State Dean Rusk. Two of these queries were particularly pointed: Why was it "necessary to send a ship so close to the territorial waters of another state in order to collect intelligence information," and did the administration believe that the United States had "the men and the equipment to handle another ground war on the mainland of Asia without the use of tactical nuclear weapons"?[14] If the latter were not the case, Fulbright suggested, perhaps the United States should reduce its commitments around the world. Apparently the senator still remembered how he had been burned by Johnson in August 1964 during the Gulf of Tonkin incident (in which the president used alleged North Vietnamese torpedo boat attacks against two U.S. destroyers to secure a congressional resolution allowing military action against North Vietnam), and he was going to be more skeptical this time.

A complete survey of the American press is impossible, but many of the most important newspapers cautioned that one war at a time was enough. The *Wall Street Journal* noted that the United States was not prepared for a new war in Korea, while the *New York Times* voiced skepticism similar to that expressed in Senator Fulbright's letters. The major opinion polls showed that the American people were ambivalent about how to deal with the matter. The Harris Poll indicated that nearly 60 percent of those surveyed favored a peaceful resolution and that over 75 percent would go along with a negotiated return of the *Pueblo*'s crew. A Gallup Poll, conducted at about the same time, showed that nearly 40 percent of the people wanted to chastise North Korea militarily and force the release of the American prisoners. Both polls were probably correct in that people were frustrated and would have preferred to uphold the nation's honor and punish what they saw as aggression but were worried about another war.[15]

As might be expected, public pressure organized by friends and relatives began to build almost immediately for administration action to secure the safe release of the crew. Working with a "Release the *Pueblo*" group in San Diego was Rose Bucher, the commander's wife. She began a petition drive to this end, and a friend of the Bucher family distributed nearly one hundred thousand bumper stickers calling for the crew's release. The *San Diego Union* kept a running log of their captivity, while urging the Johnson administration to take whatever steps were necessary to get the men out. An East Coast organization collected over five hundred thousand signatures, and Senator Mansfield said that the United States should apologize, if that was what it took to free the crew.[16]

Meanwhile, President Johnson and his foreign policy advisers, who were also genuinely concerned about the crew's safety, struggled to deal with the crisis by somehow mitigating the acute embarrassment and yet avoiding distraction from their primary concern, the prosecution of the war in Vietnam. In the wee hours of the morning of January 23, Special Assistant for National Security Affairs Walt W. Rostow worked with his staff preparing papers for the president's later perusal. Secretary of Defense Robert S. McNamara arrived at his Pentagon office at around 7:00 A.M. to discuss with his assistants what had happened as well as possible courses of action before going on to the White House later in the morning. In the initial White House session, a meeting that the president joined after it had been in progress for some time, Secretary McNamara, Secretary of State Rusk, Under Secretary of State Nicholas Katzenbach, Assistant Secretary of State for East Asian and Pacific Affairs William P. Bundy, and Chairman of the Joint Chiefs of Staff General Earle G. Wheeler were the main participants in a discussion that brought the first critical decisions in the crisis. While agreeing to hold open the option of military force, the group decided that because the *Pueblo* was already at Wonsan and the North Koreans had SAMs around the city, along with numerous antiaircraft guns, not to mention hundreds of MiG fighter planes, a U.S. military attack could be very costly. Accordingly, the group directed General Wheeler to inform Admiral John J. Hyland in Hawaii that there would be no ultimatum to North Korea and that he was to hold all forces off the coast of South Korea until further notice.[17]

Having made this initial decision not to use force, the team began a diplomatic effort to secure the ship's release while weighing a variety of military options that might be used later. Secretary Rusk originally gave major daily managerial responsibility in the crisis to Bundy, but owing to Bundy's heavy preoccupation with Vietnam, this task soon fell to Samuel D. Berger, deputy assistant secretary for East Asian affairs and former ambassador to South Korea. Berger, a hard-driving, independent-thinking, blunt career officer, could be relied upon to organize the diplomatic effort most skillfully. One of his first moves was to send cables to over one hundred countries asking for their assistance in resolving the crisis. Illustrative of these cables is the one sent to Djakarta on January 25: "We request Government of Indonesia to support our efforts to maintain peace by instructing Indonesia Ambassador in Pyongyang to inform North Korean authorities of Indonesia's concern and belief that immediate release of *Pueblo* and crew essential to prevent further deterioration of situation."[18] Rusk, in the meantime, contacted the U.S. ambassador in Moscow, Llewellyn Thompson, asking that he urge Deputy Foreign Minister Vasily Kuznetsov to have his government intercede with the North Koreans, with the hope that because the Soviets had been using such electronic spy ships for years, they would immediately see an identity of interests with the United States.[19]

That this would amount to a vain hope became abundantly clear very soon. The Soviets not only refused to intercede with the North Koreans but also took advantage of the situation by sending technicians to Wonsan to scour the *Pueblo* for intelligence material, code machines, and other spying paraphernalia. The contact with other governments proved equally unavailing. No nation could daunt Pyongyang's resolve to embarrass the United States.[20]

During a briefing session for key members of both houses of Congress, held at the White House on the evening of January 23, embarrassment was the defining word. While General Wheeler and Secretary McNamara provided information about the crisis, President Johnson sat morosely, worrying about the politics involved, about the welfare of the crew, and about Vietnam. He could not have derived comfort from the jingoistic remarks, although these were quickly offset by expressions of contrary opinion by a number of the congressmen who already had begun to hear from their constituents.

Indeed, meetings of Johnson's advisers at the State Department and the National Security Council (NSC) at the White House on January 24 indicate the serious bind in which the administration found itself. The chief participants in the State Department brainstorming sessions were McNamara, Katzenbach, Under Secretary of Defense Paul Nitze, General Wheeler, CIA director Richard

Helms, Rostow, Berger, and Clark Clifford, former adviser to President Truman and Johnson's choice to replace McNamara as secretary of defense. All agreed with McNamara's judgment that it was a very serious crisis requiring a firm U.S. reaction, but differences emerged over why the North Koreans took the ship and over how the United States might respond. Rostow argued from the start that "this is really a Soviet job" that demanded a counteraction against Moscow, even perhaps the seizure by the South Koreans of the Soviet intelligence vessel then trailing the carrier *Enterprise* in the Sea of Japan. Others rejected this plan as too risky. McNamara and Katzenbach saw a link between the seizure and the situation in Vietnam and speculated that the campaign to capture the *Pueblo* was probably initiated by the North Koreans with Soviet foreknowledge but more than likely without much support. Wheeler proposed several possible military actions including carrying out air reconnaissance, mining Wonsan harbor, taking North Korean vessels, a U.S. air strike, attacks across the DMZ, blockading North Korean ports, and promptly replacing the *Pueblo* with the other intelligence ship, the *Banner*.[21]

All of these military measures were on the table at the NSC meeting that same afternoon and at subsequent meetings of President Johnson with his cabinet and the council. None of the measures appeared fully acceptable, and all drew comment and criticism from one or more members of the president's team, who obviously felt constrained to move cautiously. The proposal to replace the *Pueblo* with the *Banner*, for instance, while drawing support from Nitze, Rostow, and Wheeler as a move to stand tall for American rights, brought an unfavorable response from Rusk, Katzenbach, and Clifford who, in turn, pointed out that it would serve no intelligence purpose and would not help secure the crew's release. A blockade, some argued, would do little good since North Korea could be supplied overland from China and the Soviet Union, and the blockading vessels would be vulnerable to attack by Soviet-supplied North Korean vessels. Nitze, Clifford, and Katzenbach also opposed an operation, favored by the Joint Chiefs, to move ships off the North Korean coast to conduct a salvage operation, fearing that nothing in the way of intelligence material could be recovered and that the presence of so many ships in the area would be provocative. A proposal to harass North Korea by scrambling U.S. fighter planes off carriers in the Sea of Japan drew immediate opposition from Rusk, McNamara, and Clifford as futile if the objective were to rescue the crew and potentially risky because it involved the possibility of air-to-air combat with North Korean jet fighters.[22]

Concern about the risk of military action was not entirely misplaced. Although not by any means a superpower, North Korea had a substantial military capability: 500 military jet aircraft, including 350 MiG-17s, 21 MiG-21s, and 80 MiG-15 fighter planes in addition to 80 IL-28 bombers; the country, by Pentagon estimates, had as many as ten air-defense missile complexes stocked with 500 Soviet-produced missiles; its navy consisted of 4 *Komar*-class ships capable of firing guided missiles, 2 *Whiskey*-class submarines, and 40 motor torpedo boats; and its army included 350,000 to 400,000 well-trained troops equipped with Soviet tanks and weapons.[23] In addition, since 1961 the North Koreans had had a mutual defense treaty with the Soviet Union that they could invoke. Every indication pointed to a willingness on the part of Pyongyang to use its war power against the United States, South Korea, or both. On January 25 the North Koreans initiated a series of incidents along the DMZ that resulted in the wounding of several American soldiers, and they flew two squadrons of MiG fighters much closer to the border than they normally would have done.[24] Clearly, a second American front in Northeast Asia against such a force would cost lives and money, not to mention a reduction of the U.S. capability in Vietnam.

Although President Johnson and his advisers kept a number of military options open—air reconnaissance, sailing the *Banner* to the area of the *Pueblo*'s capture, blockading North Korea, and seizing a North Korean vessel—they soon decided on a mixed policy of psychological pressure and diplomatic maneuvering. This cautious approach accorded best with the degree of seriousness that the incident represented and with the hope of recovering the crew. In the final analysis, Johnson's team agreed with McNamara that "the overall political problem was far more serious than the intelligence compromise," and with Richard Helms "that in the context of the cold war, it was a nitpick."[25]

The U.S. response consisted of moving greater air and naval power into the vicinity of North Korea, calling up the reserves, taking the issue to the United Nations, and urging the Soviets to intercede with the North Koreans. Calling up the reserves, until that time avoided during the Vietnam conflict, consisted of the activation of fourteen Air National Guard, eight Air Force Reserve, and six Navy Reserve units—altogether nearly fifteen thousand men. More call-ups, the president implied, would come if needed. The reserve call-up coincided with the sending of a large naval task force into the Sea of Japan: six aircraft carriers, the *Enterprise*, the *Ranger*, the *Yorktown*, the *Kearsarge*, the *Coral Sea*, and the *Ticonderoga*; three battle cruisers, the *Canberra*, the *Chicago*, and the *Providence*; and eighteen destroyers. The captors of Bucher and his men, therefore, had some cause for concern regarding a possible attack on Wonsan or some other location in North Korea.

The United States, meanwhile, seemed to have an open-and-shut case at the United Nations. Ambassador to the UN Arthur Goldberg had in his possession intercepts of the North Korean ships' own radio messages to their headquarters just before the boarding of the *Pueblo*, in which it was clearly stated that their position was over twenty-one miles from shore. This information provided incontrovertible proof that the *Pueblo* had been in international waters. Because revelation of these intercepts, collected through U.S. listening posts, would compromise American intelligence, Goldberg had to go all the way to President Johnson to override the Pentagon's refusal to let him use the messages. In the end, however, the information made little difference. Declaring the North Korean action "deliberate" and "premeditated," Goldberg demanded Security Council intervention but to no avail. As expected, North Korea insisted that the United Nations had no right to become involved in the affair.[26]

For reasons yet unknown, but perhaps because of their desire to embarrass the United States, the Soviets, as noted, did not prove responsive to the American appeal for assistance. Secretary Rusk told congressional leaders on January 31 that "when the incident first occurred, we immediately dispatched a message to the Soviet Union. It went out within two hours of the first report of this incident that we had here in Washington. We have continued to follow up on that because we think the Soviet Union has the principal influence in North Korea and because the Soviet Union has a considerable stake in the principles that are involved in the situation . . . the freedom of the seas and the freedom of international waters." Rusk stated further that because the Soviets maintained regular contact with the North Koreans, they could, if they wished, apply pressure to secure release of the ship and the men. "But," he said, "we know that they are seriously involved in this matter with the North Koreans."[27] Whether the Kremlin was involved and to what end, neither Rusk nor anyone else at that point could prove. What they did know was that this prong of the American diplomatic initiative also had failed to work.

Having decided against an immediate military strike against North Korea and having failed in appeals both to the United Nations and the Soviets, American policymakers could, at best, hope for direct negotiations with the North Koreans themselves, assuming that the central objective was the return of the eighty-two crew members. At a meeting of the National Alliance of Businessmen on

January 27, Clifford stated that "we have enormous power. We could destroy any one of a number of their cities. But that would not get the men back alive."[28] Furthermore, President Johnson told a group of congressional leaders on February 6 that "the best thing that has happened to us was not sending U.S. aircraft in to try to rescue the *Pueblo*."[29]

Before long, the North Koreans gave a signal that they would discuss the *Pueblo* directly with the United States. In a speech at a banquet in Pyongyang honoring a visiting Romanian delegation, a high-ranking member of the party hierarchy said that while North Korea rejected military pressure and UN intrusion, it might prove willing to settle the *Pueblo* incident according to "previous practice," meaning after an American apology and demonstration of contrition in a manner consistent with the settlement of a border incident that had occurred in 1964. In that case, two American helicopter pilots had strayed across the DMZ into North Korean territory. Quickly picked up by North Korean troops, the two men were imprisoned and held in captivity for nearly a year while Washington officials attempted, through bilateral discussions with Pyongyang, to get them released. Their freedom came only after American admission of error in intruding on North Korea. Given the reference to settlement of this previous incident, American policymakers hastened to follow up the suggestion with a request for face-to-face private meetings with a North Korean representative at Panmunjom; talks began on February 2.

Owing to war fever in South Korea and to the increasingly widespread belief there that the United States, in entering into the bilateral negotiations, was acting irresponsibly toward its loyal ally (one that had sent over fifty thousand of its troops to Vietnam), President Johnson and his advisers decided to send an emissary to Seoul in early February to increase the U.S. aid commitment to the government of President Park Chung Hee. Cyrus Vance, former deputy secretary of defense (and, subsequently, secretary of state under President Jimmy Carter), spent five days in Seoul (February 10–15) negotiating an agreement in which the United States would increase its military aid by $100 million. The *Pueblo* incident, as the deal demonstrated, proved costly in ways other than loss of life and American prestige. Nearly concurrently with the conclusion of this agreement, the United States transferred over two hundred jet aircraft to its bases in South Korea and made scarce spare parts available to its two army divisions stationed there.[30]

Talks between the U.S. representative at Panmunjom and his North Korean counterpart went nowhere until almost the end of the year. To move off dead center the first American negotiator, Vice

Representatives of the North Korean and U.S. governments meet at Panmunjom, North Korea, on December 22, 1968, to sign the document that will release the crew of the USS *Pueblo. Courtesy National Archives*

Admiral John V. Smith, on April 22 had offered what he saw as a conciliatory gesture: a statement that his government would never engage in illegal activities again, if in fact it had committed any wrong act this time. The Korean negotiator would accept nothing short of an American admission of guilt, an apology, and a commitment not to allow spy ships to conduct any future missions. He presented a document to this effect to the new U.S. representative, General Gilbert Woodward, on May 8. President Johnson, in this instance acting largely on the advice of Secretary Rusk, refused to allow Woodward to sign the document, and the talks dragged on. Apart from the enormous international embarrassment associated with signing, American officials feared that the North Koreans might not return the men even after an agreement had been reached.

A breakthrough finally occurred in December. James F. Leonard, the State Department official in charge of the Korea Desk, came up with a "plan" while talking about the crisis with his wife, according to which the United States first would issue a repudiation of the document that the North Koreans presented and then sign it in return for the crew's release. After discussions among State Department personnel and with Rusk, Rostow, and President Johnson, the proposal went forward to General Woodward, with instructions to tell the North Koreans that if it were rejected, the talks would end and they would be forced to deal with the new administration of President-elect Richard M. Nixon.[31]

On December 17, Woodward met with the North Korean negotiator who, acting on instructions from a government that probably had concluded that it had already garnered maximum benefit from the hostages and did not wish to negotiate with the new administration, agreed to the American plan. The agreement, as signed on December 23, acknowledged U.S. guilt:

> The Government of the United States of America, acknowledging the validity of the confessions of the crew of the USS *Pueblo* and of the documents of evidence produced by the representative of the Government of the Democratic People's Republic of Korea to the effect that the ship, which was seized by the self-defense measures of the naval vessels of the Korean People's Army in the territorial waters of the Democratic People's Republic of Korea on January 23, 1968, had illegally intruded into the territorial waters of the Democratic People's Republic of Korea on many occasions and conducted espionage activities of spying out important military and state secrets of the Democratic People's Republic of Korea,
>
> Shoulders full responsibility and solemnly apologizes for the grave acts of espionage committed by the U.S. ship against the Democratic People's Republic of Korea after having intruded into the territorial waters of the Democratic People's Republic of Korea,
>
> And gives firm assurance that no U.S. ships will intrude again in the future into the territorial waters of the Democratic People's Republic of Korea.
>
> Meanwhile the Government of the United States of America earnestly requests the Government of the Democratic People's Republic of Korea to deal leniently with the former crew members of the USS *Pueblo* confiscated by the Democratic People's Republic of Korea side, taking into consideration the fact that these crew members have confessed honestly to their crimes and petitioned the Government of the Democratic People's Republic for leniency.
>
> Simultaneous with the signing of this document, the undersigned acknowledge receipt of 82 former crew members of the USS *Pueblo* and one corpse.[32]

Just before affixing his signature to the North Korean document, General Woodward released the U.S. statement reaffirming the position that the *Pueblo* "was not engaged in illegal activity," and the United States had consistently held to the view "that we could not apologize for actions which we did not believe took place. The document which I am going to sign was prepared by the North Koreans and is at variance with the above position, but my signa-

General Charles H. Bonesteel III, United Nations Command, and Rear Admiral Edwin M. Rosenberg, Commander Task Force 76, greet members of the crew of the USS *Pueblo* as they arrive at the United Nations' advance camp, Korean demilitarized zone, following their release by the North Koreans on December 23, 1968. *Courtesy National Archives*

ture will not and cannot alter the facts. I will sign the document to free the crew and only to free the crew."[33] "Bizarre" was the term most often used to describe the arrangements but the North Koreans did not object to the prior American contradiction of their document, and the release of the crew went forward on schedule near Panmunjom.

After their return to San Diego and a joyous Christmas reunion with their families, Commander Bucher and his crew soon settled down to the sobering prospect of a Naval Court of Inquiry review of their conduct during and after their captivity. Meeting in Coronado, California, from January 20 to March 13, 1969, the court judged Bucher's failure to defend his ship and his inability to destroy his intelligence materials, not to mention his signed confessions, as inconsistent with naval codes of conduct; in other words, the court leveled serious criticisms at the commander, recommending that he and his intelligence officer stand for general court-martial. However, as might have been expected given the publicity that the case engendered, the navy itself came under the harshest attack in the press; and public opinion, which manifested itself in hundreds of letters to congressional representatives, strongly condemned the navy for scapegoating. In the public mind the crew had received inadequate training in methods for defending the ship and destroying intelligence data; such vessels as the *Pueblo* should not be held to the same standard as combat ships; and in weathering the brutalities of imprisonment in North Korea, the crew had suffered enough. Cognizant of the explosive political nature of the case, Secretary of the Navy John H. Chafee announced on May 6 that no member of the *Pueblo*'s crew would be subjected to any disciplinary action.[34]

Chafee's announcement brought the affair to a conclusion, but for the historian two questions remain. Did the ordeal of the *Pueblo* provide a lesson applicable in subsequent crises? Furthermore, did the affair provide valuable insight into the American experience of the late 1960s? Because the Soviets had used electronic surveillance vessels like the *Pueblo* for years and because the *Pueblo* would remain in international waters, the assumption of naval officials was that its mission would incur minimal risk. Hence, they made no contingency plans for protection of the ship or for the rapid destruction of its intelligence material. One startling revelation of the special subcommittee of the House Committee on Armed Services that conducted an inquiry into the affair in the spring of 1969 (chaired by Congressman Otis Pike of New York) was the casual nature of the decisions relating to the deployment of the *Pueblo* in Korean waters—that is, the absence of planning in connection with most aspects of the vessel's mission. Assuming that the way to prevent crises is to avoid placing Americans at risk needlessly, the lesson in this episode is clear: if the intelligence mission was as important as U.S. officials claimed (and this remains in doubt), then certainly either some protection should have been afforded the *Pueblo* or the ship should have stayed farther away from the Korean coast.

Whether the *Pueblo* could have been rescued once it signaled for help is unclear. Bucher's SOS went to the commander of U.S. naval forces in Japan who then directed the request for assistance to the commander of the 5th Air Force. Because these two officers had never worked out emergency telephone or other communications and operating procedures, it took over forty minutes for the message to get through. When the air force finally launched planes from Okinawa, it had to route them to South Korea because they did not have the fuel capacity to fly to the area of Wonsan. Once they arrived, they were held on the ground out of fear that they would reach the site of the beleaguered *Pueblo* only after dark. However, a rescue operation might have come from the carrier

Enterprise, which was located to the south some 470 nautical miles from the *Pueblo*. The planes on the *Enterprise*—twenty-four F-4B Phantoms, twenty-three A-4E Skyhawks, and twelve A-6A Intruders (of which forty-one were operational)—could have gotten to the *Pueblo* in less than an hour. Precisely why they were not sent remains classified information, but General Wheeler told President Johnson in a memorandum that American officers were worried about the overcast skies and snow showers over the *Pueblo*, the presence within twenty-five miles of a North Korean base with seventy-five MiG aircraft, the need for more planes than the United States had in the area, and reasonable doubt that the planes could drive off the North Korean boats. It is difficult to avoid concluding that they might have tried and that Wheeler's memorandum was merely a rationalization of inaction.[35]

The *Pueblo* affair and reaction to it reveal a good deal about the United States in the late 1960s. Owing to government deception—at least in the initial responses after the Soviet downing of an American U-2 intelligence plane, piloted by Gary Powers, over Soviet territory during the spring of 1960 and to the Bay of Pigs fiasco (an abortive CIA-sponsored invasion of Cuba, designed to overthrow Fidel Castro, in April 1961)—a great many Americans and a sizable portion of the country's press doubted the veracity of

Rear Admiral Rosenberg, left, and Bucher leaving the mess hall of the United Nations' advance camp after the release of the USS *Pueblo* crew. *Courtesy National Archives*

official pronouncements about the *Pueblo*. Skeptics assumed that before long someone would step forward to admit that the ship had intruded into North Korean waters after all, a conclusion made more convincing once the agreement of apology was signed in December 1968. Questions about the Tonkin Gulf incident of 1964 did not help the government's credibility, nor did the continuing failure, despite promises, to bring success in Vietnam.

SELDOM IN AMERICAN history did more people hold the government in greater contempt, and seldom did any U.S. administration suffer a greater credibility gap. Johnson's failure to deliver on his domestic program goals because of the war in Vietnam and the growing questioning of the means and ends of that conflict led to an intense distrust of the military establishment, not to mention the end of the Johnson presidency. All of these factors help to explain the American response to the *Pueblo*'s seizure.

The larger significance of the *Pueblo* incident is that it symbolized a dramatic transformation in thinking about foreign policy within the United States; it became the first foreign relations crisis, apart from the continuing conflict in Vietnam, that reflected the end of what may be termed the World War II/Cold War consensus. From 1941 onward, the American people had achieved remarkable agreement. President Franklin Roosevelt had been able to lead the nation through its most popularly supported war because the overwhelming majority of his countrymen believed that they were fighting for vital territorial, economic, and political interests as well as for ideals of universal validity. The onset of the Cold War brought a continuation of the consensus. Just as Hitler, Benito Mussolini, and the Japanese military leadership had posed palpable threats to American ideals and interests so too, people thought, did Josef Stalin. Until the late 1960s the vast majority of the public considered foreign affairs in general, and communism in particular, as the most important problem that the United States faced. The historian, moreover, will search in vain for much in the way of political differences on foreign policy: reflecting public opinion, conservative and liberal leaders adopted essentially identical positions on basic matters.

That the World War II/Cold War consensus broke down in the early months of 1968 is evident in the primary concerns of Americans from that time onward. Polls have shown that far fewer people identified foreign policy issues as being of overriding importance and far fewer members of the mass public believed that the United States should maintain the range of international commitments incurred in the previous twenty years. More important, a large segment of the elite public came to regard as misguided American political, economic, and, especially, military intervention in the Third World.

NOTES

1. Prior to the attack the captain of a North Korean subchaser signaled for the *Pueblo* to "heave to." This prompted Commander Bucher, who thought he was already "hove to," to ask his executive officer, "What the hell does heave to mean?" F. Carl Schumacher, Jr., and George C. Wilson, *Bridge of No Return: The Ordeal of the U.S.S. Pueblo* (New York: Harcourt Brace Jovanovich, 1971), 85.

2. See Lloyd Bucher, with Mark Rascovich, *Bucher: My Story* (Garden City, NY: Doubleday and Company, 1970), 167–202.

3. Schumacher and Wilson, *Bridge of No Return*, 59–69.

4. Paul R. Schratz, "A Commentary on the *Pueblo* Affair," *Military Affairs* 35 (October 1971): 94–95.

5. B. C. Koh, "The *Pueblo* Incident in Perspective," *Asian Survey* 9 (April 1969): 265–73.

6. Interview with the retired chairman of the Joint Chiefs of Staff, Admiral William Crowe, in Washington, DC, July 19, 1991. In 1968, Admiral Crowe was a naval captain whose assignment was to study political and military affairs in East Asia. When the *Pueblo* incident occurred, he was put in charge of drafting a document preparing for the process of repatriation of the crew. The 100-page document was somehow leaked to the press not long after it was drafted.

7. Lyndon B. Johnson, *The Vantage Point* (New York: Popular Library, 1971), 535. See also Michael Hamm, "The Pueblo and Mayaguez Incidents: A Study of Flexible Response and Decision-Making," *Asian Survey* 17 (June 1977): 552–53.

8. Bucher, *My Story*, 311–12.

9. Ibid., 203–354; Schumacher and Wilson, *Bridge of No Return*, 200–209.

10. William A. Armbruster, "The *Pueblo* Crisis and Public Opinion," *Naval War College Review* 23, no. 7 (1971): 86–89. See also Ed Brandt, *The Last Voyage of the U.S.S. Pueblo* (New York: W. W. Norton and Company, 1969), 111; and idem, "Seizure of Vessel Scored in Capital," *New York Times*, January 24, 1968.

11. Armbruster, "The *Pueblo* Crisis and Public Opinion," 87.

12. J. William Fulbright to Huey Cochran, January 30, 1968, Papers of J. William Fulbright, University of Arkansas Library, Fayetteville, Arkansas (hereafter cited as Fulbright Papers).

13. Fulbright to Bob Lasch, February 6, 1968, Fulbright Papers.

14. Fulbright to Dean Rusk, February 2, 1968, ibid.

15. Armbruster, "The *Pueblo* Crisis and Public Opinion," 87–89.

16. Ibid., 90–91.

17. Trevor Armbrister, *A Matter of Accountability: The True Story of the Pueblo Affair* (New York: Coward-McCann, 1970), 238–39.

18. Secretary of state to embassy in Djakarta, January 25, 1968, in R. D. Vollmar, ed., *Declassified Documents Reference System*, 13 vols. (Woodbridge,

CT: Research Publications, 1987), 13, citation 777 (hereafter cited as DDRS, followed by appropriate year and volume and citation numbers).

19. Notes of National Security Council meeting of president with congressional leaders, January 31, 1968, *DDRS* (1985), 11:1405; Armbrister, *Matter of Accountability*, 247.

20. Armbrister, *Matter of Accountability*, 258.

21. Notes of State Department meeting, January 24, 1968, *DDRS* (1986), 12:475.

22. Memorandum of National Security Council meeting at the White House, January 24, 1968, ibid., 12:476; Armbrister, *Matter of Accountability*, 260–61.

23. *New York Times*, February 1, 1968.

24. Armbrister, *Matter of Accountability*, 262.

25. Memorandum of National Security Council meeting at the White House, January 24, 1968, *DDRS*, 12:476.

26. Armbrister, *Matter of Accountability*, 263, 266.

27. Memorandum of National Security Council meeting of president with congressional leaders, January 31, 1968, *DDRS*, 11:1405.

28. Memorandum of president's meeting with National Alliance of Businessmen, January 27, 1968, ibid. (1990), 16:1716.

29. Notes of president's meeting with Democratic congressional leadership, February 6, 1968, ibid., 16:569.

30. *New York Times*, February 10–18, 1968; Koh, "*Pueblo* Incident in Perspective," 278.

31. Armbrister, *Matter of Accountability*, 333–35.

32. U.S. Department of State *Bulletin* 60, no. 1541 (January 6, 1969): 1–3.

33. Ibid., 9.

34. *New York Times*, May 7, 1969.

35. U.S. House of Representatives, *Inquiry into the U.S.S. Pueblo and EC-121 Plane Incidents*, Report of the Special Subcommittee on the U.S.S. Pueblo, July 28, 1969, 91st Cong. 1st sess. (Washington, DC: Government Printing Office, 1969), 1621–22; memorandum for president by Joint Chiefs of Staff, January 30, 1968, *DDRS*, 16:164. Admiral Crowe told me that the officers aboard the *Enterprise* did not know what the *Pueblo* was and wasted a great deal of time trying to look it up in *Jane's Fighting Ships*. Crowe interview.

Chapter 7

Revolutionaries in Control:
Hostages of Iran

On November 4, 1979, a gray, drizzly, fifty-degree day in Tehran, swarms of noisy Iranian demonstrators surged into the area just outside the American embassy to voice their disapproval of President Jimmy Carter's decision of October 22 to allow the deposed shah of Iran to enter the United States for cancer treatment. At 10:30 A.M. a mob numbering about three thousand invaded the embassy and took sixty-three, later reduced to fifty-two, American employees hostage. The most fanatical segment of this mob stayed on for 444 days and nights. So did the fifty-two Americans.

Situated north of downtown on the edge of the wealthiest section of the city and within viewing distance of the Elburz Mountains, the embassy in Tehran reflected both the favor that the United States enjoyed in pre-revolutionary Iran and the importance that it assigned to that country during the Cold War. Comprising roughly twenty-seven acres with twenty-five buildings set amid rows of shade trees and carefully cultivated lawns and gardens, the compound radiated an aura of luxury unusual even for American diplomatic facilities. The embassy stood as a symbol of twenty-five years of U.S. relations with the shah.

Although for most of those years Iran held about as much interest for the average American as the Hawley-Smoot tariff holds for the typical college freshman, sustained U.S. involvement with the Peacock Throne went back to World War II. In 1941 the Soviet Union, which had signed a treaty with Tehran in 1921 that specified that if a third power threatened common borders it could send troops to Iran to neutralize the danger, began applying pressure on the Iranian government to expel German influence. In mid-August of that same year the British joined the Soviets in these representations but received little satisfaction from the shah, who had been impressed by the hitherto unchecked German successes in the war. Consequently, on August 25, 1941, the British and Soviets launched a coordinated invasion, the Soviets driving in from the north and

the British from the south. On September 9 they imposed an agreement on Iran, placing the Soviet Union in control of much of the
north and Great Britain in command of much of the south. The two
powers then deposed the shah and replaced him with his twenty-
two-year-old son Reza Pahlavi. Although not formally an occupy-
ing power, the United States, in order to ensure the continued flow
of Lend-Lease materials to the Soviets and to help protect the oil
fields, established a military mission in Iran in 1942. The next year
it created the Persian Gulf Command, a noncombatant force of about
thirty thousand men that took over and operated the country's rail-
ways and principal highways. During the war the United States also

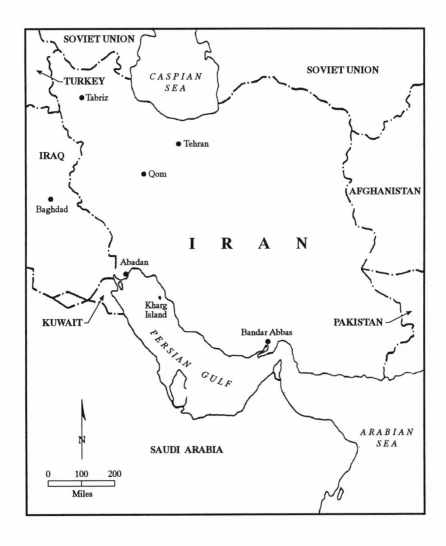

furnished Iran with Lend-Lease goods. At the conclusion of the Tehran Conference in early December 1943 the Roosevelt administration secured the agreement of the other two powers on the Declaration on Iran, which called for recognition in the postwar era of Iran's territorial integrity and independence.[1]

A central implication of the Declaration on Iran was American concern for access to oil and the prevention of British, and especially Soviet, domination of the country. Accordingly, after the end of the war the United States took the lead, through the United Nations, in applying international pressure to force the Soviets to follow the British and American example and evacuate the country, a step that the Soviets finally took reluctantly in mid-1946. As a number of historians have pointed out, this Western-Soviet clash thus represented the beginning of the Middle Eastern dimension of the Cold War because the Soviets had aspirations of turning Iran into a malleable and fully accessible client.[2]

The United States became even more directly involved in the early 1950s. When the Iranian parliament decided in April 1951 to nationalize the Anglo-Iranian Oil Company, thus precipitating a crisis in its relations with Great Britain, the United States attempted to arrange a mediated settlement. That it failed to do so and, as a consequence, did not prevent the growing pressure within the government of Mohammad Mossadegh, whom the shah had appointed as prime minister, became a matter of great concern to Washington policymakers. Mossadegh's popularity grew in direct proportion to the strength of each challenge to the British until he felt secure enough to dismiss the parliament. However, he overplayed his hand in a variety of ways and by January 1953 had been deserted by key elements in the country: the army, the clergy, and certain commercial interests. Much of his support thereafter came from the Tudeh, or Communist Party, which convinced American officials of the imminence of a Communist attempt to seize power and ally the country with the Soviet Union.

In 1953 the Central Intelligence Agency (CIA) assisted in the shah's dismissal of Mossadegh, which resulted in the reassertion of monarchical control and the widespread belief in Iran, reaffirmed so emotionally in the late 1970s, that the shah owed his power to the United States. That this was only partially true, and that the Iranian army and general public were at least equally responsible, were facts of little importance to a later generation of revolutionaries.[3] In the ten years following the 1953 U.S. intervention the shah consolidated his power, while Washington pressed for internal reform and granted large amounts of military aid to allow the monarch to address any internal or external challenge to his rule. The

United States obviously considered Iran strategically important in its ongoing Cold War struggle with the Soviet Union; during this period it provided the shah with hundreds of millions of dollars in various kinds of military assistance, including weapons technology, some of which was granted despite President Dwight D. Eisenhower's protest that Iranian requests exceeded their needs, that the major threats were not military but compelling economic and social problems. Responding to American pressure, particularly during the Kennedy administration, the shah began a process of land reform and modernization that not only brought considerable prosperity but also triggered intense reaction within the country.

To the shah's program of Westernization, which included women's suffrage, rural literacy, and the private ownership of major industries, conservative religious leaders took particular exception. They also objected strenuously to a 1963 agreement with the United States that provided for effective extraterritoriality for American military personnel living in Iran. This combination of Westernization and closer ties to the United States provoked riots in 1963 in which the fundamentalist clergy, particularly Ruholla Khomeini, played a leading role. Khomeini's arrest and banishment from the country only exacerbated the grievances of the sizeable portion of Iran's population that did not share the shah's enthusiasm for things Western.[4]

From 1963 to 1973, Westernization went hand in hand with an enormous increase in Iran's wealth. Oil revenues, for instance, reached $5 billion annually by 1973. With this tremendous increase in oil income the shah doubled and redoubled his military might, an activity that received the blessing and encouragement of President Richard Nixon and National Security Adviser Henry Kissinger. The shah also, in a remarkable display of insensitivity toward the needs of his countrymen who had not benefited from that oil wealth, hosted an extravagant party in October 1971 to celebrate the 2,500-year anniversary of the Persian Empire.[5]

If the president took offense at the shah's pretensions and expenditures, he did not betray it. Indeed, Nixon and Kissinger both moved forcefully in 1972 to incorporate Iran into their grand design. Seeking to put together a structure for peace that would allow U.S. extrication from Vietnam and serve larger American interests, Nixon had visited China in February 1972. Not long thereafter the president went to Moscow to sign the first Strategic Arms Limitation Treaty (SALT). He hoped to use Soviet suspicion of his dealings with China to secure better relations with Moscow and Chinese suspicion of his dealings with the Soviet Union to secure better relations with Beijing. That this ploy proved marginally successful seems beyond dispute, although it did not result in an immediate end to the war in Vietnam.

Because the United States was stretched so thin militarily and because it had a clear interest in regional stability in the oil-rich Middle East, President Nixon believed that the shah had a vital role to play in the American design. Nixon stopped in Tehran immediately after his visit to Moscow and agreed to open up U.S. arsenals to the shah, granting Iran access to the most sophisticated technology. The president's motive was twofold: to create a high-powered, pro-American military regime in the Middle East and to recycle the so-called petrodollars that had begun flowing out of the United States in increasing amounts to purchase Middle Eastern oil. In addition, President Nixon and the shah seemed to have entered into a special friendship that extended into their personal relations. At least this was the public notion. When addressing this point, former CIA director Richard Helms once scoffed: "I can promise you that in the case of Richard Nixon even in the United States of America he had no close friends or associates."[6]

Deferring to the shah's wishes in every request short of nuclear weapons—per the directions of Nixon and Kissinger—Washington officials over the next four years agreed to the sale of over $9 billion worth of military hardware to Iran. Much of this equipment exceeded Iran's capability to utilize it, and a good part of it was unneeded in the first place, serving largely to inflate the shah's vanity. What occurred through the mid-1970s, and eventually created the situation that Jimmy Carter inherited when he assumed the presidency, was the identification of American security interests in the region so nearly exclusively with the shah that the United States would almost certainly face difficulty if his leadership came into question.[7]

Although President Carter placed human rights and the restriction of arms sales at the center of his foreign policy agenda, his approach toward Iran under the shah did not differ substantially from that of his predecessors. Concern about the shah's use of his national secret police organization, SAVAK, to abuse and torture his political opponents, a practice that had become fairly common in the 1970s, took second place to concern for American strategic interests. At length, and after considerable debate with Congress, Carter in 1977 approved the sale of seven airborne warning and control system (better known as AWACS) planes to Iran as well as over a billion dollars worth of additional military hardware. Both he and his emissaries took pains to pledge their continuing support to the shah, whose regime was simply too valuable a source of intelligence on the Soviet Union and too important to regional stability to risk alienating.[8]

Carter also went to considerable lengths to cement a personal relationship with the shah. He entertained the monarch in Washington on November 15 and 16, 1977, despite loud protests against the shah's tyranny from Iranian students living in the United States. Indeed, tear gas used to disperse a crowd in Lafayette Park, across from the White House, irritated the eyes of both the president and his guest during the welcoming ceremonies. Less than two months later, President Carter paid a visit to Tehran while on a trip from Poland to India and engaged the shah in discussions about continuing American assistance as well as the Iranian ruler's role in helping achieve a general Middle Eastern peace. Carter became caught up in the spirit of goodwill to the point of indiscretion, as when he announced that Iran was "an island of stability in one of the more troubled areas of the world."[9]

Carter, meanwhile, did not fully understand or appreciate the deepening opposition to the shah within Iran. He and his advisers tended to rely too closely on official reports originating with the shah's lackeys and passed to Washington through Ambassador William H. Sullivan. In truth, even as President Carter concluded his visit, the revolution began gathering momentum. On January 9, 1978, the shah's police killed a number of protestors participating in a religious demonstration in the city of Qom, and about six weeks later riots broke out in Tabriz, the capital of Iranian Azerbaijan. Among the Carter administration's reactions was a move to authorize the sale to Iran of large amounts of tear gas to help in crowd control, a decision that seemed all the more sensible after a coup in Afghanistan that brought a Communist government to power; any threat to the shah's regime, even a non-Communist one from the religious right, seemed to pose a danger to regional stability.[10]

The peril increased through the remaining months of 1978. Riots occurred in Tehran, Mashhad, Khomein, and several other cities between March 30 and April 2, followed by strikes, peaceful demonstrations, and then further uproar elsewhere in the country. The bloodiest rioting took place in Tehran at the end of the summer, but other opposition action went forward in the fall as well. How many people were involved is impossible to determine; doubtless hundreds of thousands, possibly millions if those experiencing peaceful alienation from and disaffection for the shah's regime are included. Although it was not yet apparent to American officials or to some Iranians, by the fall of 1978 the country was in flames.

Historians and contemporary observers of these events have tended to describe the shah's reaction as ambivalent and indecisive, certainly as inadequate in view of the massive upheaval against his rule. What appears to be closer to the truth is that, influenced by hard-line advisers and encouraged by the United States, he tried repression, which in the end not only failed but also incited more violence, and then moved tentatively toward reform and liberalization. That the two approaches sometimes overlapped does not mean that he necessarily pursued a vacillating course, only that he did not always have adequate control over the situation.

In the early stages of the rebellion the shah gave orders to use extreme force against the opposition. His police invaded the homes and meeting places of the religious fundamentalists, in some cases murdering the clerics in cold blood, and they fired randomly on crowds of demonstrators as well. This attempt at repression was sufficiently bloody to engage the shah's conscience, if not that of some of his advisers. As many as twelve to fifteen thousand people lost their lives to the brutal behavior of both the military and SAVAK in 1978, while nearly fifty thousand more suffered serious injury. In the end the shah realized that the revolution was too widespread and that he could not condone the use of force on a scale sufficient to quell it—that he could not, as one scholar has noted, "militarily occupy his own country."[11] The British ambassador observed correctly that "it is to the eternal credit of the Shah that, right up until January 16th, he refused to contemplate a greater bloodbath which both he and I know would have availed him nothing."[12] When he realized that replacing the personnel around him with "reformers" or "moderates" would not appease the opposition and that neither repression nor liberalization would work, the shah left the country—depressed, confused, and, as the world was soon to learn, wracked with cancer. He and the empress departed for Egypt on January 16, 1979, never to return to Iran.

The shah's ultimate successor and the rallying figure of the revolution, Ayatollah Ruholla Khomeini, suffered none of the monarch's doubts about either the rectitude of his behavior or the blessings of Allah. His pursuit of power became so fanatical, his commitment to religious fundamentalism so profound, his rejection of the institutions of Western civilization so total, that he eventually came to rank among the worst tyrants of the twentieth century. Exiled since the mid-1960s, Khomeini, first from Iraq and then from Paris, rallied support for his anti-Western, anti-shah campaign through passionate appeals to the largely uneducated masses; on February 1, after the shah's departure, he returned to Iran to seize his opportunity.

A welter of confusion and bitter rivalry characterized American policy formulation toward Iran in 1978. The major players in

Zbigniew Brzezinski. *Courtesy Jimmy Carter Library*

the drama were President Carter, who had only limited time to de-
vote to the Iranian issue, at the top; Zbigniew Brzezinski, his national security adviser, who on most matters had the president's
ear; Secretary of State Cyrus Vance, a judicious, consummate professional who had the president's respect, if not always his ear;
Ambassador Sullivan, a skilled, experienced diplomat, who at first
admired the shah but by November had become skeptical of his
chances of survival; Deputy Secretary of State Warren Christopher,

who early on accepted the reality of the shah's vulnerability; Assistant Secretary of State for Near Eastern and South Asian Affairs Harold Saunders, who came to doubt the shah's chances; and the head of the Iran Desk in the State Department, Henry Precht, who had come to the same conclusion as Saunders, only earlier. In addition to these individuals a group of extragovernmental figures, most notably David Rockefeller, John J. McCloy, and Henry Kissinger, worked assiduously to influence policy. Secretary of Defense Harold Brown and CIA director Stansfield Turner also advised the president on Iran.[13]

Ultimately, a major struggle for ascendancy ensued between the State Department officials noted above and the White House-National Security Council group led by Brzezinski, a Polish émigré and hard-line anti-Soviet who favored support of the shah at whatever cost. He advised the president to cultivate the Iranian military and press it to use maximum force against the opposition. Brzezinski, Brown, and Turner were worried about a number of issues related to Middle Eastern stability and Soviet aggressiveness, but particularly motivating their support for the shah was concern about the U.S. electronic listening posts at Bihshahr and Kapkan in northern Iran. Bolstered by optimistic CIA and Defense intelligence reports, Brzezinski in particular persisted in his belief that all the shah needed was greater resolve and a willingness to use the power at his disposal. President Carter, to his disadvantage, generally accepted the advice of his national security adviser and the Rockefeller group throughout 1978 rather than that of his State Department personnel, although an attempt at cooperating with the opposition probably would not have succeeded. Moreover, Carter was unwilling to use force to sustain the shah.[14]

By mid-February 1979 the revolution, with Khomeini in substantial control, had inspired a wave of retributive violence, brutal, sometimes even creative in nature. Hundreds of thousands of armed people took to the streets, seeking out former officials and supporters of the shah and killing them on the spot; others destroyed hotels, banks, movie theaters, and any symbol of Western influence they came upon; committees dispensed summary revolutionary justice to all manner of professional people. Hundreds of executions took place in the first two months of the new regime. The pilot of the shah's plane, who had flown him from Egypt to Morocco on February 15, was forced by the arrest of his family to fly the empty 707 back to Iran, whereupon Islamic revolutionaries broke both of his hands.[15] The fundamentalists purged schools and libraries of their Western books, forced women to give up Western-style dress in favor of the *chador* (a dark cloth shawl that covers the head and

Ayatollah Ruholla Khomeini. *Courtesy Associated Press*

veils the lower half of the face), and took away most rights that had evolved for women since the 1930s.

In the months following Khomeini's return to Iran the United States struggled to develop a policy in an atmosphere of misinformation. "Ignorance here of Iran's events is massive," Precht noted from Washington to his associate in Tehran, Chargé d'Affaires Bruce Laingen.[16] No one knew what to do but to ascribe blame to others. Apparently, American officials hoped to maintain a presence, albeit reduced, in the country through the cultivation of those representatives of moderation who came to the fore. Policymakers avoided Khomeini like the plague, even though he obviously had dominated the revolution. It is not clear that this distance was a mistake in view of the ayatollah's virulent anti-Americanism. It seems unlikely that he would have acquiesced in any program of regular Iranian-American relations, moderated his internal "reforms," or eschewed his later attempt to export the Islamic revolution, but it does seem possible that the existence of a relationship might have prevented the hostage crisis of the fall of 1979. Whether the events of February 14—when a mob stormed the U.S. embassy and took over one hundred Americans hostage, only to be forced a few hours later by Khomeini's ministers to give up the hostages and leave—are an indication of what might have happened had contact been established is not certain.

In any event, this is not the place to document Iran's confused internal history during the first nine months after the revolution. More important to the hostage crisis are the shah's movements and American relations with the unfortunate former monarch. After leaving Iran the shah, the empress, their family, and a large group of attendants took refuge and relaxation on a island on the upper part of the Nile River for about a week as guests of Anwar Sadat, president of Egypt, a friend, and a fellow client of the United States. During this period the shah received encouragement from David Rockefeller and his group as well as a warm invitation from President Carter to come to the United States for an extended vacation, but he tended to favor a counterrecommendation from Sadat that he stay in the Middle East in position to return to his country and resume control at the opportune time. Accordingly, he and his entourage went on to Marrakech, Morocco, at the arranged and unenthusiastic invitation of King Hassan II. Here he spent three weeks.

By mid-March, Hassan had decided that the shah could not stay in Morocco in view of the impending Islamic summit to be held there. This triggered panic in the mind of the exiled monarch, consternation among his American friends, and serious concern among Carter administration officials, who by now desperately wished to prevent his coming to the United States. Indeed, in mid-March the State Department sent an emissary to Rockefeller asking him to tell the shah that he would be unwelcome because of the possibility of reprisals against Americans still in Iran. Rockefeller, the shah's banker who, as head of Chase Manhattan Bank, did billions of dollars of business with Iran and saw the monarch as a personal friend, refused the request. Kissinger also refused indignantly when he received a similar request. A CIA agent later gave the shah the grim news.[17]

Having learned that he could not go to the United States and knowing that his stay in Morocco would soon come to an end, the shah turned to Rockefeller to find him a place. Rockefeller, after discussions with Kissinger, approached the government of the Bahamas, which agreed to accept the monarch. On March 30 the shah flew to the Bahamas to begin what turned out to be a difficult and expensive stay in a waterfront villa on Paradise Island. Here, he and his entourage experienced security problems and costs ranging up to $24,000 per day, not to mention the eventual hostility of the Bahamian authorities, which prompted a search for a new refuge.

Once again Kissinger and Rockefeller came to the rescue. This time the choice was Mexico, where a reluctant government succumbed to Kissinger's pressures and agreed to allow the shah to lease a French-style villa at Cuernavaca. On June 10 the shah and his party took up residence in Mexico while his friends continued their efforts to convince the Carter administration to lift its objections to his coming to the United States.

Kissinger, Rockefeller, and, among others, John McCloy, former U.S. High Commissioner in Germany, whose law firm had connections to the shah's regime, went to work on Carter. Rockefeller met with the president and Kissinger with Secretary of State Vance, the most ardent opponent of admitting the shah. Meanwhile, McCloy wrote letter after letter to the secretary of state. Kissinger let it be known that he would not assist in the Senate ratification of SALT II unless the administration did right by its Iranian friend. Key congressmen began speaking out in favor of admitting the shah. Finally, in early August, as word began filtering into Washington of the former monarch's illness, Carter found it increasingly difficult to resist the pressure. In October the president learned what French intelligence knew but what his own intelligence community had not previously determined—that the shah had had lymphoma for six years and that in the absence of early treatment, best provided in the United States, he would soon die. In light of this new information, Carter announced that "the Shah is welcome as long as the medical treatment is needed." On October 22 the shah flew secretly to New York where he entered New York Hospital under the name of David D. Newsome, U.S. under secretary of state for political affairs, without the latter's permission.[18]

The shah was a very sick man, sicker than Washington officials realized. In New York, doctors removed his gallbladder as well as gallstones that were blocking his bile duct, a condition that in itself could have caused his death. They also prescribed a concentrated regimen of chemotherapy for his cancer, which presumably meant an extended stay in the United States. This latter information deeply troubled Iranian officials, who had received assurances from Chargé d'Affaires Laingen on October 21 that the United States would admit the shah temporarily as a humanitarian gesture and that President Carter desired friendly relations with the government of Prime Minister Mehdi Bazargan. A long stay for the shah meant one thing to suspicious Iranian revolutionaries: "that the Shah," in the words of Henry Precht, "had come to the United States not for medical treatment but to set up counterrevolutionary headquarters."[19]

The shah was still in New York Hospital on November 4. Although the Iranian government had assured U.S. officials of the security of the embassy in Tehran, someone had neglected to tell the students who stormed the compound that morning. Crisis came with the dawn in Washington on November 4. Elizabeth Ann Swift, political officer in the embassy in Tehran, reported the takeover while it was happening to the operations center at the State Department and to Harold Saunders, then still in bed at his home in McLean, Virginia. President Carter, Brzezinski, Vance, Brown, and others received the news in the early hours of the morning. Carter's weekend of relaxation at Camp David was interrupted by the report.

Almost from the day of the embassy seizure Carter administration officials began looking at three possible approaches: one involved military action to either mount a rescue mission or put pressure on Iran; another was diplomatic, using as many contacts around the world as seemed practicable; and the third was economic. The Joint Chiefs of Staff had military subordinates devise a rescue plan, but it was determined to be too risky and was put aside. Another early military contingency consisted of sending a carrier task force to Iranian waters; Brzezinski vetoed this plan out of fear that the Iranian "students" would kill some of the hostages. A military committee thereafter met regularly to look at a variety of options, including a rescue effort. However, given President Carter's overriding concern to avoid loss of life, military action remained on the back burner, at least until the following April. In an early diplomatic move Carter asked Soviet leader Leonid Brezhnev for his good offices but got nowhere. The CIA worked through its backchannel contacts with Yasir Arafat, head of the Palestine Liberation Organization, in the hope that Arafat, who had the goodwill of Iranian revolutionaries, could secure the hostages' freedom; this effort was also to no avail, although his intercession probably resulted in the release of thirteen women and blacks.[20]

In the weeks and months that followed, Carter's team pursued a number of diplomatic and economic approaches to end the crisis. Ramsey Clark, former attorney general in the Johnson cabinet, friend of radical causes in the United States, critic of the shah, and sympathizer with the Iranian revolutionaries, undertook a mission to Tehran on November 7 at the instance of the administration. Clark was accompanied by William Miller, a former Foreign Service officer who could speak Farsi. They got only as far as Turkey; Khomeini refused to meet with them or to allow anyone else in authority to do so, announcing that the basic precondition for negotiation was repatriation of the shah. For a while U.S. officials hoped that Khomeini would respond favorably to an overture from the pope, and the ayatollah did meet a Vatican envoy. To the latter's suggestion that he order the hostages' release, Khomeini again insisted on the shah's return, condemning in the process the Vatican's failure over all the years of the shah's repression to intervene on the side of humanity.[21]

Secretary of State Vance, meanwhile, had begun a secret demarche under the auspices of the United Nations, hoping that through the mediation efforts of Secretary-General Kurt Waldheim he could secure a softening of the revolutionaries' demands. Foreign Minister Abdolhassan Bani Sadr sent an envoy to New York in mid-November to deal with Waldheim on the matter. No longer insisting on the shah's extradition as a condition, the Iranians, at the instance of Bani Sadr, seemed for a time willing to settle for a return of the country's wealth and the holding of some sort of tribunal wherein they could attack the United States for its innumerable sins. Vance saw a chance here, but before further negotiations could proceed, Khomeini, for reasons related to his control of the revolution, sacked Bani Sadr in favor of Sadegh Ghotbzadeh. Nothing further came of these discussions.[22]

So far, despite the acute embarrassment that many Iranian leaders felt at the taking of hostages, nothing the United States had tried showed much chance of success, given the position of Khomeini. Carter and his advisers now turned to economic sanctions. On November 15 the secretary of the treasury froze Iranian assets in American banks in an attempt to gain leverage and to prevent a run on the dollar or a financial crisis in the United States. Word had come to Washington the previous day that Iran would withdraw its assets on the 15th, resources worth at least $6.5 billion. Had these funds been withdrawn, Iranian obligations would not have been covered and American officials would have looked foolish for leaving U.S. financial institutions exposed. The freeze applied only to assets of the Iranian government, but it did include funds held in U.S. branch banks overseas. The Carter administration also stopped virtually all trade with Iran, including the purchase of oil.[23]

Having pursued the carrot of negotiation and the stick of economic sanctions, Washington officials still faced the problem of what to do about the shah, whose admission to the United States had triggered the crisis. It became clear to administration policymakers that despite pressure applied by David Rockefeller and Henry Kissinger to keep him in New York, it was necessary to get the exiled monarch out of the country if negotiations were to succeed. (To the Iranian demand for the shah's extradition, an American congressman suggested that the government send Rockefeller to Tehran and keep the shah in the United States!) Out of fear that allowing his return to Mexico would constitute a flagrant disregard of Iranian public opinion, the Mexican government

Aerial view of Iranians praying in front of the American embassy in Tehran on November 13, 1979. *Courtesy Associated Press*

refused to take the shah back when he was released from New York Hospital. This refusal caused a flurry of concern within the administration and some strained discussions between President Carter's subordinates and the shah's family. The empress rejected out of hand suggestions that her husband might want to take refuge in either Paraguay or South Africa, the former out of concern for its dearth of medical facilities and the latter as the place where the shah's father had died.

Lacking a permanent location for the former monarch, Carter officials arranged to fly him to Lackland Air Force Base in Texas while they tried to find a government willing to take him in. After discussions between Presidential Assistant Hamilton Jordan and President Omar Torrijos of Panama, the latter agreed that the shah could come to his country. On December 15 he flew to Panama City and then to Contadora Island where he took up residence, his sixth stop since leaving Tehran.[24]

Before the shah left New York Hospital, word began filtering in to Washington that the Iranian militants planned to put the hostages on trial. This news was truly alarming, both to the administration and to an increasingly outraged American public. Carter responded forcefully. After considering a variety of military options with his aides, he sent a message through Swiss diplomats to the Iranian government that if trials took place or if any of the hostages were harmed, the United States would deal Iran crushing military blows. One can only speculate what these blows would have been, based on considerations at that time—the bombing of the Abadan oil refinery, the mining of harbors, the seizure of Kharg Island, or a possible naval blockade. The president's message had the desired effect in Tehran; the American hostages were neither tried nor seriously threatened with criminal proceedings thereafter.[25]

Given the response to Carter's message, it seems logical to conclude that had he chosen to avoid a high-profile response to the hostage seizure and to understate its significance and communicate through tough, no-nonsense secret statements, always ready to implement a military option, the crisis might have been resolved fairly quickly. However, the president faced a challenge from Senator Edward Kennedy of Massachusetts for the Democratic nomination for the presidency, and Carter saw a chance to make political hay with the crisis. By keeping it in the daily news, showing his compassion and stressing his presidential qualities in leading the nation, Carter overwhelmed Kennedy in the opinion polls and successfully denied him a chance at the nomination. In the process he also may have prolonged the crisis and helped guarantee his Republican rival the victory in the 1980 presidential election.

In late December 1979, at the insistence of the United States, the United Nations took up a resolution calling upon Iran to release the hostages. As part of the UN effort, Secretary-General Waldheim was to travel to Iran to see the hostages and begin discussions toward their release, failing which the organization would impose economic sanctions. Waldheim's trip proved unsuccessful and humiliating to him personally, to the United Nations, and to the United States. The Iranian students, a revolutionary power in their own right, refused to alter their stance on the hostage issue, and Khomeini, the only force within the country with the influence to make them budge, continued to capitalize on the anti-American hysteria whipped up by the hostage-holding to further his fundamentalist religious and political goals. Waldheim was harangued by a gathering of victims crippled by the shah's secret police and ridiculed by photographs in the newspapers showing him kissing the hand of the shah's sister during a previous visit to the country.[26]

Following Waldheim's trip, which commenced on January 1 and lasted a mere sixty-four hours, the United Nations met on January 13 and voted in favor of sanctions, including an embargo on all shipments of goods to Iran, except food and medicine, by whatever route and from whatever source. The Soviets, who on December 26 had invaded Afghanistan and wanted to court Tehran's favor as a makeweight against the United States, vetoed the sanctions resolution. As part of a long-range policy, the sanctions certainly would have had an impact, especially after the Iraqi invasion of Iran, but in the short run could have done little to resolve the crisis. In any event, the United States had applied sanctions of its own back in November—no purchase of oil, the cutting off of military shipments and other trade, and the freezing of assets—and after the Soviet veto, it had decided to go ahead with an effort to encourage similar behavior on the part of its allies. This latter move did not prove very fruitful, mainly because of these nations' concern for their access to Iranian oil.

Complicating the crisis for both the Iranians and the Americans, meanwhile, was the Soviet invasion of Afghanistan. Washington officials worried that this step would be the first in a Soviet expansionist effort toward the Persian Gulf. President Carter warned in his State of the Union address of January 23, 1980, that the United States could not tolerate the domination of the region by an outside hostile power. "Let our position be absolutely clear," he stated in enunciating the Carter Doctrine; "an attempt by an outside force to gain control of the Persian Gulf region will be regarded as an assault on the vital interests of the United States of America, and such an assault will be repelled by any means necessary, including military force."[27] To deal with the apparent threat in the region, the administration began discussing the creation of a "rapid deployment force," which must have led Iranian revolutionaries to ponder the possibility of U.S. military intervention. Moreover, as a massive atheistic military presence on their border, the Soviets had to give them pause as well. To some in Iran the hostages seemed incidental against the Great Power rivalry seemingly about to play itself out in the area, and these Iranians considered the hostages not only an embarrassment but also of little utilitarian value.

During the first three months of 1980, American officials attempted a diplomatic initiative with this pragmatic segment of the Tehran leadership—namely, with Bani Sadr and Ghotbzadeh, the latter as foreign minister and the former as the newly elected president. In a series of discussions with two envoys commissioned by the Iranian foreign minister (Hector Villalón, an Argentine business "operator," and Christian Bourguet, a French lawyer), American officials led by Jordan and Saunders negotiated what they thought was a satisfactory conclusion to the crisis. The "solution" included the establishment of a UN commission that would publicize Iran's grievances against the United States, the unfreezing of its assets, and the liberation of the hostages, with the timing of the

Lives at Risk

release brought into delicate balance with the airing of Iran's grievances: the hostages would be freed one hour before the UN secretary-general opened the commission's records.[28]

Accordingly, the United Nations put together a five-member commission that, following the script, traveled to Iran on February 23 as a first step toward the release of the hostages. Unfortunately, Ayatollah Khomeini refused to go along with the solution. He would not permit the commission to see the hostages, a sine qua non for its release of Iran's grievances against the United States, and insisted that the captive Americans' fate would have to be determined by the new parliament after its election. Thus, by mid-March, despite the commitment to it on the part of Bani Sadr and Ghotbzadeh, this initiative seemed defunct.[29]

The shah's departure from Panama only a couple of weeks later seemed to finish off any hope for a negotiated settlement. Under pressure from the Iranian government to extradite the monarch, Panamanian officials began indicating to the shah that they would find it necessary to restrict his movements. This restraint proved terribly troubling and led key figures in his entourage to try to find somewhere else for him to locate, possibly in the United States. Complicating the problem was the exiled monarch's physical condition, which steadily worsened during his stay on Contadora Island; he now needed an operation to remove his enlarged spleen. President Carter reluctantly agreed that he could return to Lackland Air Force Base and have the operation in Houston, but, if the shah wanted to stay in the United States, he would have to abdicate his throne. Anxious to go where he was more welcome, where his residence would create fewer international complications, and at the same time unwilling to relinquish his throne, the shah chose to accept a standing offer from President Sadat and settle in Egypt. He flew to that country on March 23, to the Iranian government's extreme annoyance.[30]

Having failed to effect a solution to the crisis through negotiation and aware of the increasing public dissatisfaction in the United States, President Carter assessed both international and domestic events with a sense of deep disquiet at the end of March 1980. His political fortunes were diminishing almost daily, and on March 25 Senator Kennedy defeated him in the New York primary. Clearly, the crisis was no longer politically useful to him. Resolved to recover by forcing the issue in Tehran, Carter on March 29 communicated a message to Bani Sadr threatening tough new sanctions unless the Iranian government took control of the hostages from the students. That the Iranian president immediately seemed willing to comply suggested the imminence of a solution and led Carter to announce Bani Sadr's move on the eve of the Wisconsin primary. Carter won the primary, but the Iranian government did not, as promised, take control of the hostages. This provoked the frustrated American president into trying one of his military options.[31]

The alternative selected, a daring attempt to rescue the hostages, had been under consideration since November 1979. When its planning and implementation are considered, the mission, in retrospect, very much resembles a combined Ian Fleming-Laurel and Hardy production. Devised by the best brains of the Pentagon, with the strong endorsement of Secretary of Defense Brown and National Security Adviser Brzezinski, the rescue operation gained approval at the highest level in a White House meeting on April 11. President Carter decided that it was time to act. So, too, did the others present at the meeting: Jody Powell, presidential adviser; Walter Mondale, vice president; General David Jones, chairman of the Joint Chiefs of Staff; Jordan, Turner, Brzezinski, and Brown. Absent from the meeting was the idea's main opponent, Secretary Vance, who was on vacation. Vance had thought that the plan would only get the hostages killed and earn the United States the enmity of other Muslim governments. The others believed that the mission promised a high probability of success and a lucrative political payoff; they should have listened to Vance.[32]

What occurred ranks among the major failures in U.S. military history. On April 24 at 7:30 in the evening, eight helicopters took off from the deck of the aircraft carrier *Nimitz* in the Arabian Sea, bound for a rendezvous and refueling stop five hours away on the Iran Salt Desert, a spot known for planning purposes as "Desert One." Simultaneously, six C-130 transports took off from another carrier. One of the helicopters experienced engine trouble after only a short penetration into Iranian airspace and made an emergency landing in the desert. The other seven flew into major desert storms, without dust filters, forcing one of the copters with failing navigational equipment to return to the *Nimitz*. When the six remaining helicopters arrived at Desert One, most of them about an hour late, they found the C-130s waiting for them. At Desert One the forces encountered an Iranian fuel truck, a pickup, and a bus containing over forty passengers. The Americans detained the bus; firing shots to stop the fuel truck, the troops caused it to catch fire, and its driver jumped out and got away with the driver of the pickup while they fired at its tires. Shortly thereafter, a third helicopter was found to have hydraulic failure and was ruled unusable. With only five helicopters remaining and six necessary to continue the mission, Colonel James Kyle sought permission to abort the American effort, which he quickly received. Then, the worst occurred. As one of the helicopters began to leave, it crashed into one of the planes causing a spectacular explosion, visible for miles, that killed five crewmen on the plane and three on the chopper. In their haste to get away, the remaining troops abandoned a cache of classified documents and the bodies of the dead servicemen.[33]

President Carter publicly announced the failed mission on April 25, and information about the plan soon began to surface. After a rendezvous in the desert, U.S. rescue teams were to assemble near Tehran, move to the embassy, cut off electricity and phones, throw gas grenades to neutralize the guards, spirit the hostages to an assembly point (either a parking lot or a soccer stadium), and then fly them out in helicopters, presumably with minimal harm to the hostages or the rescuers. It has been suggested that the second best thing that could have happened was to abort the mission in the desert. The first best would have been to scrap the idea before it was ever implemented. As noted, this was the view of Secretary Vance, who promptly resigned as he had promised President Carter he would do if the rescue operation went forward.

Meanwhile, just before the attempted rescue, Washington broke diplomatic relations with Tehran and imposed further economic sanctions. The break in relations required that all Iranian diplomatic and consular personnel leave this country and that all visas held by Iranians in the United States be invalidated. When the chargé was called in to the State Department to receive the formal note breaking relations, he and Henry Precht engaged in a heated exchange in which the Iranian official announced that the American hostages were so happy that some might not wish to leave. Precht, in reply, thundered, "Bullshit!"[34] The new economic sanctions banned financial transfers to Iran without Treasury Department license, prohibited imports from that country, and severely restricted all travel by Iranian citizens into and within the United States. They also permitted the sale to other buyers of military equipment purchased in the United States but not yet shipped to Tehran.[35]

Along with the tremendous embarrassment in Washington at the failure of the rescue attempt, the immediate results in Iran of the mission were anger, fear, and, on the part of the fundamentalist clergy, the conviction that the failure was the work of God. Khomeini announced that Carter had "lost his power of thinking." "Who has crashed down Mr. Carter's helicopters which invaded Iran?" he asked rhetorically. "The sand pebbles were acting for God. Wind is the agent of God."[36] To prevent a successful follow-up mission, the leadership promptly arranged for the transfer of the hostages to a number of different sites around the country.

U.S. hostage in Iran. *Courtesy Associated Press/Wide World Photos*

While an agitated Iranian public continued to press for an early trial for the hostages, or in any event for the "spies" among them, a number of key individuals in the leadership urged their release even after the failed raid. One member of the parliament argued that as a result of the hostage holding, "the country's image as the oppressed has become that of the oppressor."[37] President Bani Sadr, aware of President Carter's stern warning of the previous fall and of America's military capability, said that no one knew where a trial would lead. Foreign Minister Ghotbzadeh advocated their early release for three reasons: they were harmful to the nation's prestige, they were no longer useful to Iran, and their continued retention had become financially costly. Because the government's assets, totaling approximately $8.5 billion (an Iranian figure) had been frozen, the country was losing nearly $2 million per day in interest, or a total of roughly $550 million since mid-November 1979. This figure did not include the cost of the economic sanctions.[38]

As time passed, even some of the hard-liners began to moderate their statements. In September, Prime Minister Mohammad Ali Raja'i indicated a willingness to talk with the United States, while Ayatollah Mohammad Hossein Beheshti proclaimed his view that further holding of the hostages bestowed few benefits. Khomeini expressed a similar opinion, stating that if the United States met certain conditions, including the unfreezing of his government's assets and the renunciation of claims against the country, the crisis could be resolved. Not insignificant in forming the new Iranian attitude was the shah's death in Egypt on July 27.[39]

On its part the United States began a new approach after the failed rescue, one rooted in quiet diplomacy and fewer public pronouncements but including contact with Iranian clerics and initiatives through a number of other governments. Under the direction of the new secretary of state, Edmund Muskie, this course of action showed some signs of success after the new Iranian parliament sorted out its political and religious factions through July 1980. By the end of August the Islamic Republican Party seemed firmly established as the dominant force in the formation of a new government, and communications, including notes from family members of the hostages, went forward from the United States to Iranian leaders. In fact, a barrage of letters arrived in Tehran in late summer.[40]

Finally, on September 9, Iran indicated firmly that it desired a settlement. The German ambassador to Tehran informed Secretary Muskie that a prominent Iranian (Sadegh Tabolatai, brother-in-law of Khomeini's son) had told him that Iran wanted to release the hostages and wished to begin discussions to that end in Bonn. Muskie hastened to tell President Carter, who quickly placed Warren Christopher, deputy secretary of state, in charge of a task force to spearhead the negotiations. Significantly, the Iranians were no longer insisting on an American apology or a ransom of any sort, conditions that made a settlement appear all the more likely from the U.S. perspective. Two other developments made a resolution of the crisis seem possible: on September 22 border skirmishes resulted in a full-scale war as Iraq invaded Iran, an action that later received clandestine American support and material assistance; and Prime Minister Raja'i visited the Security Council in New York, where he learned the true meaning of diplomatic isolation as delegation after delegation informed him of the international disgrace that Iran had brought upon itself in taking the hostages. He learned the human meaning as well when he met with Katherine Keough, the wife of a hostage and president of the Organization of Hostage Families. According to Mrs. Keough, Raja'i gave every indication of feeling sympathy for the families as she presented their case to him.[41] It also became clear to the prime minister that any UN action in support of Iran would be difficult while the Americans remained in captivity.

Although the Iraqi invasion created a crisis in Iran and temporarily diverted the leaders' attention away from the hostages, the government soon realized that the purchase of military equipment and spare parts would be critical in pursuing the war and that such purchases would depend on access to the frozen assets under American control. It is not surprising, therefore, that much of the negotiating that took place between October 1980 and January 20, 1981, focused on money, specifically the amount that the United States was obliged to make available to Iran. Also not surprising is the fact that the negotiations proved terribly complicated and, to the disappointment of President Carter, could not be completed before the 1980 presidential election. This latter point has prompted one member of his National Security Council team, Gary Sick, to conclude that Ronald Reagan's people made secret contact with Iranian leaders, promising to sell Tehran military equipment, first through Israel and then directly, if a settlement was deferred until the election was over.[42]

Ultimately, in negotiations using Algerian officials as middlemen, Washington and Tehran were able to work out a settlement on terms that were remarkably favorable to the United States. Iran agreed to accept a sum of $7.9 billion (it had earlier claimed $14 billion) as the extent of its frozen assets and to pay off foreign, including American, banks with more than half of these funds. Iran's haste to settle in view of the war with Iraq led to an expensive conclusion of the crisis. Indeed, the settlement tends to lend credence to Sick's argument of a secret deal between Iran and Reagan's representatives.[43] Whether or not such a deal existed, however, Iran had every incentive to settle before a new administration, extremely tough in its rhetoric and already committed to dealing harshly with "barbarians" who took hostages, came into power. In any event, the Iranians released the hostages on January 20 at 12:25 P.M. Eastern Standard Time, only minutes after the inauguration of Reagan.

APART FROM THE blindfolding and the kicking around that went on in the first few days after the seizure of the embassy, the American captives had not been treated as harshly as had hostages in other such situations. However, they were denied access to world news or news from the United States except when something slipped past the guards; they were not permitted to communicate among themselves, so they left messages for each other in secret hiding places in bathrooms or other facilities; they did not get regular outdoor exercise and had to work hard at maintaining a degree of physical fitness; and they were permitted to shower or bathe only infrequently, although some, particularly the women, received better treatment than the men in this regard. The food was usually of low quality, was poorly prepared, and sometimes infested with bacteria; some of the men and women became quite ill from food poisoning. Mainly the captives suffered from boredom and worry about their families back in the United States. To deal with the boredom they played checkers, cards, or a variety of other games, sometimes with their captors, and read books and magazines from the embassy library. Some of the individuals identified as CIA employees or "spies" suffered special physical or psychological abuse. One fact that stands out about this hostage episode is that the captors seemed terribly worried about the physical condition of their charges and, in fact, were terrified that one of the hostages might die.[44] This fear suggests that the American message warning of swift, draconian retaliation in the event the Iranians harmed any of the hostages had gotten through. It also lends credence to the view that the Carter administration might have handled the crisis differently.

In evaluating Carter's response to the crisis, it is helpful to examine his objectives. His priority, despite his protestations to the contrary, was to recover the hostages alive. His second and third objectives, not necessarily in order, were to avoid compromising American interests in the region or worldwide and to preserve the nation's honor. Had the latter two objectives taken precedence over the former, the president almost certainly would have used military force. The United States had critical interests at stake in the region, as Carter made clear after the Soviet invasion of Afghanistan, and there were reasons for him to demonstrate that it could not be pushed around. However, the use of force might have driven the Iranians in the direction of the Soviets and probably would have resulted in the deaths of at least some of the hostages.

Moreover, an effective military action would not have been easy to carry out. One option considered, that of a punitive occupation of a section of Iranian territory, such as Kharg Island, would have been tactically difficult owing to the unlikely prospect of other Arab Gulf states allowing the United States to use their territory as staging areas and the consequent necessity of providing full support from a naval force. Logistically, such an occupation would have been hard to sustain and expensive. Blowing up the oil storage and loading facilities from the air would have resulted in the near elimination of Iran's foreign trade but would have caused irrevocable damage and the cutting off of oil to American allies in Europe and Asia. A blockade of shipping to and from Iranian ports was technically achievable but would have required the placing of a large number of vessels in the area of the Strait of Hormuz and the frequent stopping and boarding of ships. It also would have run some risk of a Soviet challenge. Mining Iranian ports was the most feasible form of military activity in that it could have been executed from the air quickly and fairly inexpensively, but it, too, ran the risk of alienating allies by cutting off their oil supply.[45]

As might be expected, some Americans expressed the opinion that the lives of fifty-two hostages, while precious and never to be sacrificed casually, were secondary to the larger national interest. Within the administration, this was certainly Brzezinski's view. "Yes," he said to Carter at a White House meeting on November 9, "it is important that we get our people back. But your greater responsibility is to protect the honor and dignity of our country and its foreign policy interests. At some point, that greater responsibility could be more important than the safety of our diplomats."[46] Brzezinski and others also argued that the surest way to prevent a tragic recurrence of the crisis was to punish Iran. Carter did not think that way.[47]

That the president successfully resolved the crisis does not mean that his policy is above reproach. He was not able to enlist America's allies in support of his policy. None of the North Atlantic Treaty Organization partners agreed to break off diplomatic relations with Tehran and none froze Iranian assets in its banks. Some allies, particularly Israel and France, even took advantage of the U.S. embargo to profit in arms trade deals with Iran. A more energetic, leveraged diplomatic effort toward Washington's friends would have been in order. Moreover, using the crisis for political gain against Senator Kennedy aroused public opinion and limited the administration's maneuvering room. The crisis sold a lot of advertising space on television news programs, but constant attention to Iranian behavior led to a cycle of action and reaction: television portrayed the screaming, screeching revolutionaries belching out anti-American slogans; Americans in turn either committed abuses toward Iranian and other Middle Eastern nationals living in the United States or stepped up their anti-Iranian rhetoric, while Iranians reacted to such episodes with greater venom. Somehow, Carter should have sought to move the crisis out of prime time, off the front pages, and into the hands of professional diplomats. He later realized the problems with his approach: "I think the issue would have died down a lot more if I had decided to ignore the fate of the hostages or if I had decided just to stop any statements on the subject."[48] One means of bringing about a more subdued approach was suggested by Deputy Secretary Christopher, who recommended turning over the day-to-day handling of the crisis to an interagency task force for quiet study, reflection, and summary, thus freeing the president for attention to other matters. The result might have been better government, better diplomacy, and, perhaps, an earlier return of the hostages. It also might have led to Carter's reelection.

Be that as it may, one cannot escape the conclusion that negotiation, and even concession of America's previous errors in Iran, represented the most sensible, most humane, way to terminate the crisis. The use of military power would have invoked too many imponderables, both regionally and internationally, and, unhappily, as the Reagan administration's experience was to show, would not have deterred further terrorist acts. The record, in fact, indicates that violence begets more violence especially when used against religious or ideological zealots. Difficult as it may be for hard-line policymakers and a sizable sector of public opinion to accept, the American experience with hostage situations throughout the twentieth century suggests that negotiations and conciliation, backed by a reserve of military power, have been the preferred and most sensible and effective tactics.

NOTES

1. For the documentary evidence on the declaration and its background, see memorandum by John Jernegan, January 23, 1943, U.S. Department of State, *Papers Relating to the Foreign Relations of the United States, 1943* (Washington, DC: Government Printing Office, 1965), 4:331–36 (hereafter cited as *FRUS*, followed by the appropriate year). Minister in Iran to secretary of state, April 14, 1943, ibid., 355–59; secretary of state to Roosevelt, August 16, 1943, ibid., 377–78; "Declaration Regarding Iran," December 1, 1943, ibid., 413–14.

2. See, for example, Bruce R. Kuniholm, *The Origins of the Cold War in the Near East: Great Power Conflict and Diplomacy in Iran, Turkey, and Greece* (Princeton, NJ: Princeton University Press, 1980).

3. For a good account of Iranian developments and U.S. policy through 1953 see James A. Bill, *The Eagle and the Lion: The Tragedy of American-Iranian Relations* (New Haven, CT: Yale University Press, 1988), 57–97. Former CIA director Richard Helms, who later served as U.S. ambassador to Tehran from 1973 to 1977, believed that bringing back the shah was popular in Iran. See William Burr's July 10, 1985, interview with Helms (p. 4), Oral History Collection of the Foundation for Iranian Studies, Bethesda, Maryland.

4. E. A. Bayne, *Persian Kingship in Transition* (New York: American Universities Field Staff, 1968), 50; Homa Katouzian, *The Political Economy of Modern Iran: Despotism and Pseudo-Modernism, 1926–1979* (New York: New York University Press, 1981), 216.

5. During this period those dissidents who began speaking out in opposition to the shah's program began to feel the blows of his increasingly powerful police force, SAVAK. Bill, *Eagle and Lion*, 192–200. Sir Peter Ramsbotham, the British ambassador to Iran from 1971 to 1974, once noted that the shah was not a bad listener but "seldom took advice." See Shusha Assar's January 20, 1986, inter-

view with Ramsbotham (p. 15), Oral History Collection of the Foundation for Iranian Studies, Bethesda, Maryland.

6. William Burr's July 24, 1985, interview with Richard Helms (p. 60), Oral History Collection of the Foundation for Iranian Studies, Bethesda, Maryland.

7. A good account of these arms sales is provided in U.S. Congress, Senate Committee on Foreign Relations, Subcommittee Staff Report, *U.S. Military Sales to Iran*, 94th Cong., 2nd sess. (Washington, DC: Government Printing Office, July 1976).

8. Cyrus Vance, *Hard Choices: Critical Years in America's Foreign Policy* (New York: Simon and Schuster, 1983), 317.

9. See President Carter's comments on the revolutionary events then transpiring in Tehran, *New York Times*, January 1, 1978.

10. Bill, *Eagle and Lion*, 243–48.

11. Ibid., 237.

12. Anthony Parsons, *The Pride and the Fall: Iran, 1974–1979* (London: Jonathan Cope, 1984), 150.

13. The following books by U.S. officials demonstrate the rivalry existing in policy circles: William H. Sullivan, *Mission to Iran* (New York: W. W. Norton and Company, 1981); Gary Sick, *All Fall Down: America's Tragic Encounter with Iran* (New York: Random House, 1985); Zbigniew Brzezinski, *Power and Principle: Memoirs of the National Security Advisor, 1977–1981* (New York: Farrar, Straus and Giroux, 1983); Jimmy Carter, *Keeping Faith: Memoirs of a President* (New York: Bantam Books, 1982); and Vance, *Hard Choices*.

14. Brzezinski, *Power and Principle*, 363.

15. Michael A. Ledeen and William Lewis, *Debacle: The American Failure in Iran* (New York: Alfred A. Knopf, 1981), 216–17.

16. Precht quoted in Bill, *Eagle and Lion*, 276.

17. Robert D. McFadden, Joseph B. Treaster, and Maurice Carroll, *No Hiding Place: N.Y. Times Inside Report on the Hostage Crisis* (New York: Times Books, 1981), 151–54.

18. Ibid., 155–64. The journalists provide a colorful account of the shah's movements and his friends' interventions on his behalf. Carter, *Keeping Faith*, 452–56.

19. Bill, *Eagle and Lion*, 324–25; McFadden, Treaster, and Carroll, *No Hiding Place*, 170.

20. Sick, *All Fall Down*, 195–216.

21. Ibid., 217–49. See also Waheed-uz-Zaman, "The American Hostages in Iran: The Crucial 444 Days," *Journal of South Asian and Middle Eastern Studies* 9 (Summer 1986): 29.

22. Sick, *All Fall Down*, 225–26.

23. Robert Carswell and Richard J. Davis, "The Economic and Financial Pressures: Freeze and Sanctions," in Warren Christopher et al., *American Hostages in Iran* (New Haven, CT: Yale University Press, 1985), 173–92.

24. For the discussions on arranging a new "home" for the shah, see Hamilton Jordan, *Crisis: The Last Year of the Carter Presidency* (New York: G. P. Putnam's Sons, 1982), 72–98.

25. Carter, *Keeping Faith*, 465; U.S. Congress, Report to House Committee on Foreign Affairs, Research Service, Library of Congress, *The Iran Hostage*

Crisis: A Chronology of Daily Developments, 97th Cong., 1st sess. (Washington, DC: Government Printing Office, 1981), 40–43.

26. Harold H. Saunders, "Diplomacy and Pressure, November 1979–May 1980," in Christopher et al., *American Hostages*, 107–11.

27. Ibid., 112; Carter, *Keeping Faith*, 483.

28. Sick, *All Fall Down*, 250–68.

29. Ibid., 268–70.

30. Carter, *Keeping Faith*, 501.

31. Ibid., 501–4. Carter strenuously and unconvincingly argues that he did not time his announcement to influence the Wisconsin primary.

32. Ibid., 506–7.

33. A great deal has been written about the rescue attempt. See Carter, *Keeping Faith*, 507–18, for his personal recollection; and Sick, *All Fall Down*, 284–99. For an evolution of the mission from the standpoint of decision-making models see Martin Hollis and Steve Smith, "Roles and Reasons in Foreign Policy Decision-Making," *British Journal of Political Science* 16 (July 1986): 269–86; and Bill, *Eagle and Lion*, 301–2.

34. Saunders, "Diplomacy and Pressure," 140; Carter, *Keeping Faith*, 505–6. Carter wrote to Precht congratulating him for the conciseness and clarity of his language.

35. Saunders, "Diplomacy and Pressure," 148.

36. Waheed-uz-Zaman, "American Hostages in Iran," 47.

37. Ibid., 48.

38. *Tehran Times*, June 12, 1980.

39. Ibid., August 28, September 4, and September 11, 1980.

40. Saunders, "Beginning of the End," in Christopher et al., *American Hostages*, 289.

41. Ibid., 291.

42. Gary Sick, *October Surprise: America's Hostages in Iran and the Election of Ronald Reagan* (New York: Random House, 1991), 11. Interestingly, Sick also states that the Carter administration "severely underestimated Iran's anxiety about the possibility of war with Iraq"; ibid., 102.

43. It is worthwhile to note the inconclusive nature of Sick's evidence and to point out the extensive scrutiny that this issue received during the 1992 presidential election. Attempts were made to link President George Bush, who had been Reagan's running mate in the fall of 1980, with the deal.

44. For a sample of the hostages' recollection of their treatment see Moorhead Kennedy, *The Ayatollah in the Cathedral: Reflections of a Hostage* (New York: Hill and Wang, 1986); Barbara and Barry Rosen with George Feifer, *The Destined Hour: The Hostage Crisis and One Family's Ordeal* (Garden City, NY: Doubleday, 1982); and Bruce Laingen, *Yellow Ribbon: The Secret Journal of Bruce Laingen* (Washington, DC: Brassey's, 1992). Laingen, the U.S. chargé d'affaires, his deputy and political counselor, Victor Tomseth, and a security officer, Michael Howland, spent their captivity in the Foreign Ministry where Laingen had gone to keep an appointment with the director general for political affairs.

45. Lieutenant Commander William F. Hickman, "Did It Really Matter?" *Naval War College Review* 36, no. 2 (March–April 1983): 22–24.

46. Jordan, *Crisis*, 44–45.

47. A representative sample of the criticism of President Carter's handling of the crisis is provided by Joseph W. Bishop, Jr., professor of law at the Yale Law School. He argued that "what the President should have done, of course, was to deliver an ultimatum and then, if the hostages were not released by a specified date, resort to force. . . . At the very least, he should have recognized that in certain instances the lives of diplomats, like those of soldiers, are at risk; and he should have honored the basic principle that a government should never make any concessions to terrorists." Joseph W. Bishop, Jr., "Carter's Last Capitulation," *Commentary* 71, no. 3 (March 1981): 33.

48. Quoted in Terence Smith, "Putting the Hostages' Lives First," *New York Times Magazine* (May 17, 1981): 101. Carter notes in his memoirs that "it was very likely that I had been defeated and would soon leave office as President because I had kept those hostages and their fate at the forefront of the world's attention." Carter, *Keeping Faith*, 594.

Chapter 8

Dealing with Brigands and Believers: An Appraisal

On July 15, 1979, in an address on energy and national goals, President Jimmy Carter identified a "crisis of confidence" in the United States that struck "at the very heart and soul and spirit of our national will. We can see this crisis in the growing doubt about the meaning of our own lives and in the loss of unity of purpose for our Nation. The erosion of our confidence in the future is threatening to destroy the social and the political fabric of America."[1] Presidents may be no more adept than other informed observers at capturing the mood of the nation, but Carter was surely on to something. The late 1970s was a time of palpable national self-doubt, of "malaise," a time when U.S. institutions and behavior were being questioned. The military came in for the lion's share of the criticism for its cost and for its alleged excesses in Vietnam. So, too, did the Central Intelligence Agency (CIA), as demonstrated in the congressional hearings of the mid-1970s. An investigative mania stemming from the Watergate affair dominated the news media as well. Voters had turned to Jimmy Carter in some measure because they saw in him the antithesis of the imperial presidents of the Cold War/Vietnam/Watergate era. Recent oil embargoes and the Iranian hostage crisis highlighted apparent American vulnerabilities by the end of the decade.

The election of Ronald Reagan in the fall of 1980 heralded the advent of "morning in America," both in the new administration's rhetoric and in the hearts of his admirers, if nowhere else.[2] It also heralded an enormous military buildup and a commitment to a two-dimensional approach to terrorism: no negotiation with terrorists and "swift and effective retribution."[3] What this meant and how President Reagan's policies compared to those of his predecessors are critical points to ponder, as is the question of the wisdom and efficacy of a non-negotiating position toward terrorism.

In the first instance of a terroristic act during the Reagan years the new approach stood up reasonably well, not so much because

191

of anything the administration did but due to effective police work. Brigadier General James L. Dozier was kidnapped on December 17, 1981, by a group of Italian renegades calling themselves the Red Brigades. Reagan's people put together a small force of advisers to assist the Italian police in locating Dozier, and Lieutenant Colonel Oliver North of the National Security Council (NSC) staff asked H. Ross Perot, the Texas billionaire, computer magnate, and proponent of daring rescue operations, for $500,000 as reward money for information on the kidnappers.[4] It was the Italian police, however, after forty-two days of relentless pursuit and with the assistance of American intelligence, who rescued the general unharmed. Neither the United States nor Italy engaged in negotiations, and the Italians thereafter attacked the Red Brigades with a vengeance, soon putting them out of business. "No negotiation and retribution" seemed to be working.

IT SHOULD HAVE been as easy to deal with Middle Eastern terrorists. After Israel invaded Lebanon in June 1982 to destroy the Palestine Liberation Organization (PLO), the United States decided, against the wishes of Secretary of Defense Caspar Weinberger but at the urging of Secretary of State Alexander Haig, Jr., to send U.S. Marines as part of a multinational force to establish stability in Leba-

Rescue workers carry the body of a U.S. Marine killed in the bombing of the Marine Operations Center on October 23, 1983. *Courtesy Associated Press*

non.[5] As the troops increasingly became engaged in support of the Beirut government, an array of resentful, radical Muslim groups carried out a series of terroristic acts in the hope of driving them out of the country. Some of these activists, particularly those of the Shiite faction, received support from Iran, which had sent nearly a thousand Revolutionary Guards into the Bekaa valley east of Beirut to help train followers of the Ayatollah Khomeini's brand of Muslim fundamentalism.

On April 18, 1983, a van loaded with at least two hundred pounds of dynamite slammed into the front of the U.S. embassy in Beirut, killing seventeen Americans and fifty Lebanese. Apart from increasing security and reducing the size of the embassy staff, the Reagan administration did virtually nothing. Negotiation obviously could not have taken place, and it was impossible to determine against whom to retaliate.

Over the next six months the killing of several Marines led to active American military participation in defense of the Lebanese army. Part of the assignment was to maintain the security of the Beirut airport, where also most of the Marines were quartered in a four-storey, fortified concrete barracks. The reinforcement was not

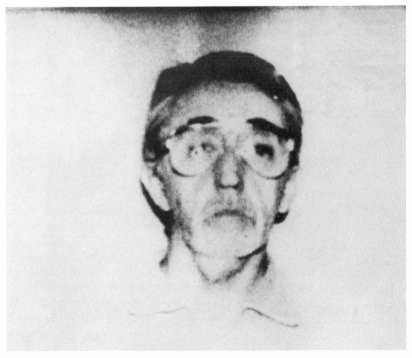

William Buckley, CIA station chief in Lebanon, 1984. *Courtesy Associated Press*

strong enough, for early in the morning of October 23 a truck loaded
with TNT sped through the front gate and into the building, killing
the driver and 241 of the Marines. Although evidence of Tehran's
complicity in the attack quickly became evident, Reagan administration officials apparently did not consider it so incontrovertible
as to justify an attack on Iran—again, no retribution.[6] Moreover,
despite a study blaming the tragedy on U.S. unpreparedness, Reagan
did nothing to assign responsibility. However, owing to political
pressure and fear of further loss of life, he did pull the remaining
Marines out of Lebanon in February 1984.[7]

If the nature of Middle Eastern terrorism through 1983 made
negotiation impossible and retribution difficult, its character beginning in early 1984 made retribution virtually impossible. Bombing attacks continued, as at the new U.S. embassy annex in Beirut
on September 20, where terrorists, again with Iranian connections,
detonated a truck loaded with explosives, killing two Americans
and fourteen others—but the primary problem was hostages. Four
Americans, including the CIA station chief in Lebanon, William
Buckley, were abducted in 1984. Buckley was tortured and killed.
CIA director William Casey found this kidnapping particularly difficult to accept, and he, along with Secretary of State George Shultz,
began pushing during 1984 for a more "active" policy, including
covert action that presumably included assassinations.[8] Although
documentation is inadequate for a definitive assessment, as the first
Reagan term came to an end one could find only modest evidence
of success, either in preventing further terrorism through forceful
retribution or in recovering hostages. In early 1985 several more
Americans in Lebanon were seized, bringing the total number in
captivity to six by that summer.[9]

That Reagan's policy had brought him embarrassment seems
apparent. To compensate he stepped up his rhetoric. Blaming others for his failures, he made a public statement in the fall of 1984
criticizing the Democrats in Congress and the Carter administration for causing a deterioration in U.S. intelligence-gathering
capabilities. This lack of intelligence, he said, had made it hard for
him to choose appropriate targets for retribution.[10]

In his remaining years in office, Reagan's policy in hostage
situations consisted of the use of sufficient retributive force to satisfy the requirements of international theater (but how many terroristic acts it deterred cannot yet be determined) and, to his credit,
the assiduous pursuit of a more flexible approach, including negotiating with kidnappers. The latter course brought his actions into
accord with those of every other twentieth-century president who
faced similar hostage situations and into line with sound judgment.[11]

Reaction to an aircraft hijacking is a case in point. The commandeering of a TWA flight bound from Athens to Rome on June 14, 1985, with 122 Americans on board, resulted in administration pressure on the government of Israel to release many of the 766 Shiites held in an Israeli jail and thus satisfy the main demand of the hijackers. (The plane, after forced flights to several Mediterranean cities, finally put down at Beirut.) This indirect negotiation allowed the administration to maintain an appearance of non-negotiation but did not fool anybody, least of all Middle Eastern terrorists.[12] American involvement in the bargaining, although behind the scenes, proved critical in the successful conclusion of the deal. Apart from one sailor, whom the kidnappers presumably killed in order to prove their credibility, no Americans lost their lives in the incident. Dealing with terrorists, hard as it was for Reagan officials to admit, in this instance saved a great many lives.[13] Whether it compromised national honor or encouraged further such incidents is impossible to say.

Another incident was brought to a successful conclusion through negotiation in 1985, only on this occasion the Egyptians did the bargaining, and the outcome received enthusiastic public endorsement because the United States captured the hijackers. This was the case of the seizure on October 7 of the *Achille Lauro*, an Italian cruise ship taken hostage by four members of the PLO who demanded as ransom the release of some fifty members of their organization from an Israeli jail. Finally docking in Port Said, Egypt, and realizing the futility of their effort, they sought a deal with the Egyptians in which they would release the passengers (except Leon Klinghoffer, an elderly American confined to a wheelchair, whom they had killed) in return for safe passage to Tunis. Egypt completed this deal, and then to the great satisfaction of the American people the United States was able to use fighter aircraft from the USS *Saratoga* to intercept the plane carrying the terrorists to Tunis. The fighter planes forced the aircraft to land in Sicily, where the Italian government arrested the hostage-takers.[14] The ending would have been happier if the Italians, worried about PLO retaliation against their own citizens abroad, had not set free the organizer of the hijacking and had been willing to extradite the others.

Concern for American hostages in Beirut prompted President Reagan to pursue further deals with hostage-takers and led him, finally, into ill-fated sales of arms to Tehran in return for Iranian influence in the release of these hostages. The "arms-for-hostages" trades, conducted (despite Reagan's protestations later to the contrary) at the president's instance, have been addressed in great detail elsewhere.[15] The deals almost destroyed the Reagan presidency as assertions of executive befuddlement and "loose cannons" within the NSC certainly tarnished its image. The public eventually became aware of an operation, run by Lieutenant Colonel North out of a White House basement office in conjunction with CIA director Casey, in which the United States made six different deliveries of arms to Iran (the first sale actually completed by Israel). Americans in general were displeased that North and others involved in the sales had received kickbacks of some of the profits and, especially, that North had violated a congressional proscription against aid to the Contra rebels in Nicaragua by surreptitiously using some of these monies to provide such assistance.

Although this effort at negotiating with hostage-takers achieved only limited success in that the release of three hostages was soon followed by the seizing of three others, it should not be condemned as either generally symptomatic of what happens when one deals with kidnappers or a bad idea on its face. President Reagan, like his predecessors, had come to understand, despite his rhetoric to the contrary, that deals with terrorists were often necessary. He also knew that Iran played a guiding role in the Beirut terroristic activity. When he and his subordinates authorized the sale of arms, they did so with a number of considerations in mind, all of them justifiable at the time: that it was necessary as soon as possible to put American relations back on track with Iran, a regional power not to be ignored forever; that anything that the United States could do to encourage a change in the complexion of the Tehran regime should be considered; that there was no comfort for the United States in the prospect of an Iraqi victory in the ongoing war between Iran and Iraq (Saddam Hussein did not possess, as he later demonstrated all too clearly, the qualities that the United States desired in a dependable ally in the area); and that these were, after all, sales, not gifts, of arms.[16]

Simultaneously, Reagan carried out an action against Libya in April 1986 that may have enhanced his reputation among the American people as a no-nonsense, big stick-type opponent of terrorists, but it probably did little to deter terrorism. From the very beginning of his administration, the president had authorized the harassment of Libya through military overflights of its territory. On the theory that the government of Muammar Qaddafi regularly sponsored terroristic activity around the world, Reagan administration officials hoped to identify a Libyan action that would allow for American retaliation. They finally found such hard evidence in National Security Agency intercepts of directives from Qaddafi's government to its embassies in Europe to begin terroristic acts against the United States and in earlier Libyan support for terroristic killings at the Rome and Vienna airports on December 27, 1985. Included among the victims were some Americans. The result of the directive to the European embassies was the bombing of a West Berlin nightclub on April 5, 1986, in which two American servicemen were killed.[17]

On April 15 the United States bombed Libyan military installations and Qaddafi's headquarters and residence, in the process killing, among others, his adopted daughter. That this effort terrified the Libyan leader may be assumed, and that it led to a temporary abatement of Qaddafi-sponsored terrorism also seems clear. Among administration motives in launching the attack was surely the urge to punish Libya, but probably more important was the desire to send a signal around the world that the United States was a credible actor against international terrorism.[18]

Hungry for a decisive blow against gun-toting, bomb-wielding Muslim fanatics, the American people were all too happy to endorse the bombing and to credit the administration with success in its antiterrorist activity. They were too generous. The action put Qaddafi's terrorism in abeyance only briefly. Libyan agents played a part, subsequent investigations showed, in planning the bombing of Pan American Flight 103 over Lockerbie, Scotland, on December 21, 1988, which killed 259 people on board the plane and several more on the ground.[19]

BY ANY MEASURE, but particularly in terms of loss of life, President Reagan's policy against terrorists must be judged as having achieved far less than promised. Iran continued its attacks on Americans. Libya, in the Pan Am bombing, retaliated against the U.S. assault of April 1986. Six hostages remained in captivity in Beirut. Altogether, terroristic acts killed 550 Americans during Reagan's two terms in office.[20] Did he uphold the nation's honor or advance U.S. interests better than other presidents through his stated non-negotiation/forceful retribution approach? Perhaps, but it would be difficult to argue that proposition affirmatively.

Among those who consistently promoted the efficacy and wisdom of non-negotiation was Henry Kissinger, one of a multitude who accepted and continues to embrace this view. After the Iranian hostage crisis and throughout the 1980s, Kissinger became a regular guest on television interview programs, where he expressed his opinion that if the target governments of terrorism simply refused to reward it—that is, refused to negotiate or pay ransom—hostage-taking and other terrorist acts would eventually cease.

The no-ransom/no-negotiation argument has a compelling logic about it; it rests on some fundamental truths, and thus it appears to possess unchallengeable validity.[21] The first of these truths is that if a given behavior is not reinforced, the likelihood of its recurrence will diminish. Just as individuals usually repeat their actions in direct proportion to the psychological and material rewards derived from them, so, too, do terrorist groups. Moreover, while it might be argued that these groups often commit terroristic acts for secondary or hidden reasons, their behavior is strongly affected by the overall quality of the results they achieve, and one should always assume that hostage-takers are much more inclined to hold onto their captives when the outcome includes ransom than when it includes only the secondary or hidden benefits. Finally, if terrorists found that they could never extort ransom by taking hostages, it should stand to reason that they would either try some other activity or give up the effort. A corollary to the foregoing is that if potential terrorists are aware of the likelihood of punishment or capture, they will be less inclined to participate in terroristic activity.[22]

The arguments may be compelling, but they are also flawed. Military action is sometimes as likely to compel a desire for revenge as for surcease, particularly among fanatical terrorists with a lengthy litany of grievances. Military force creates martyrs. Owing to their history and to the veneration of martyrdom in their heritage, Shiite Muslims often invite violence against themselves; military action may give them what they want. Certainly, any examination of the actual use of military force against Middle Eastern terrorists would tend to inspire skepticism about its effectiveness. Although it is impossible to determine whether or not Israel might have suffered more rather than fewer terrorist attacks in the absence of military retaliation, it appears that nearly every Israeli military blow has provoked a terrorist response. In turn, of course, every terrorist response has provoked an Israeli military action; a seemingly interminable cycle of violence has ensued. Acts of American violence, as the Reagan experience demonstrated all too clearly, also have been met by counterviolence. This is not to say that narcoterrorists and others who would harm American citizens are necessarily anxious to martyr themselves and cannot be defeated through force or to argue that punishment has no place against terrorists. It is only to note that policy should be formulated on an ad hoc basis and that U.S. officials should exercise care in eschewing negotiation in favor of retribution.

After the Iranian hostage crisis, Moorhead Kennedy, a Foreign Service officer and one of the hostages held in Tehran in 1979–80, insightfully observed that mechanistic refusal to negotiate with hostage-takers, again particularly those in the Middle East, would bring in its wake significant loss of life and little practical benefit. Middle Eastern kidnapper/terrorists, he submits, usually possess as many as three major objectives—the stated end that they are seeking at the beginning of the crisis, the hidden aim that may be the most important of all (in the case of the Iranians and Khomeini's crowd, the revitalization of the revolution), and what they might in fact accept. He also notes the symbolic nature of a number of hostage seizures in which young men and women may accept the risk of taking hostages as a way of bonding with a particular cause and other proponents of that cause. Moreover, they may do so thinking, even hoping, that they might die. A refusal to negotiate does nothing but address the up-front and stated objective. It can do nothing to address the other reasons for terrorism and is therefore an illogical policy to adopt.[23]

It is especially illogical for a democracy to adopt such a course. For a policy of no ransom/no negotiation to be effective it must be credible. For it to be credible it must not cost too much to implement. However, terrorists, by determining the nature and number of hostages or the threat they will present to the target government, also determine the cost. If adhering to no ransom/no negotiation requires the payment of too high a price for the target government to bear—too high in lives or in some other respect—it will, just as the Reagan administration and other previous administrations amply proved, abandon the policy and risk its own credibility. It seems axiomatic that only a government that could abide by such a policy in all projected circumstances should adopt it.[24] No such democratic government, not even the Israeli one, fits this description.

No American president of the twentieth century has effectively practiced no ransom/no negotiation; none has utilized swift and "effective" retribution. Although his predilection may have been to avoid negotiation in favor of force, Theodore Roosevelt established the precedent for his successors by arranging the release of kidnapped Americans through peaceful means. He secured private funding through subscriptions to ransom Ellen Stone, the contributions to be reimbursed with government funds years after conclusion of the incident. Stung by newspaper criticism of his handling of the Stone affair, Roosevelt adopted a posture of bellicosity in pursuing the release of Ion Perdicaris, but the bellicosity did not affect the kidnapper and, ironically, it was not aimed at him. Once again third-party negotiation saved the day after Roosevelt applied pressure on the Moroccan government to satisfy Raisuli's demands.

Subsequent administrations likewise pursued a line of both negotiation and concession. Officials of the Wilson and Harding administrations gained the release of Americans held in Soviet Russia by providing food and medical relief to the Kremlin rather than through military intervention. President Harry Truman privately blustered about blockading the China coast but settled for patient diplomacy to free the Mukden consulate. Lyndon Johnson considered every possible military option against North Korea but secured release of the *Pueblo* crew, after months of discussion, by agreeing to an apology and a phony confession of guilt. Jimmy Carter lost an election and a great deal of prestige but traded little more than frozen Iranian assets for fifty-two American lives.

While nineteenth-century officials often vented their machismo in acts of retributive violence against "less civilized" people—acts that tell us a good deal about American values in the nineteenth century—it would be difficult to demonstrate that such expressions of violence enhanced the national interest or the national honor. Although they may have effectively avenged the many attacks on Americans living or doing business abroad, they were no more successful against hostage-takers than were their twentieth-century counterparts. The Barbary pirates, contrary to popular conception, did not receive their comeuppance primarily from the United States, nor did they cease and desist in their kidnappings because of American force. It took concerted action by the international community over an extended period of time to bring them to retreat and retire.

The historical record then, even that of the nineteenth century, does not recommend a policy of non-negotiation and retribution against terrorists. It suggests the opposite, that is, that negotiation to postpone bloodshed—postponement being the essence of diplomacy—also may promote a degree of understanding. It further suggests the wisdom of eschewing military policies in support of transitory definitions of national honor (the latter often, in any event, being equated with the egos of individual policymakers or the political fortunes of the administration in power) in favor of support for the protection of lives. National honor may be advanced in an alternative fashion by pursuing clearly defined vital interests abroad through the selective use of economic and military power, by formulating foreign policies respectful of the values and institutions of other societies, by maintaining a strong domestic economy, and by maintaining a just society that nourishes its free institutions and provides for those who cannot provide for themselves.

Unfortunately, the advancement of national honor, even through the creation of a just society, has little to do with the deterrence of terrorism. Indeed, it may be argued that in the twentieth century terrorism has occurred in inverse proportion to the degree of openness, democracy, or legitimacy of particular governments. Dictatorships or abusive authoritarian regimes, while not totally immune, have seldom been the targets of terrorists. Where the regime controls the press, where public awareness of hostage incidents and other terroristic acts is nearly nonexistent, and where no mechanism exists for registering opinion, it stands to reason that the regime's leadership will succumb to the terrorists' demands only to the extent that it chooses to pay their price—and where hostages are involved, only to the extent that it values the lives of those being held.

The United States is the world's richest and most powerful nation. In the aftermath of the Cold War it is the only superpower. Whether or not it follows a multilateral approach in the promotion of international stability and no matter how benign its motives in attempting to facilitate world peace and harmony, it will remain the most visible and obtrusive of nations. Its products will fill the world's markets; its popular culture will affect the lives of hundreds of millions of people in other countries; its business men and women will aggressively seek international access and opportunity; its corporations will exploit other nations' resources; it will station its troops in far-flung areas of the world; and it will forge alliances in accord with its interests and sentiments that may offend other peoples.

On the assumption that the United States will continue to engender international animosity and that violence against its citizens will never fully abate, the nation must have a strategy for dealing with terrorism. Such a strategy, if informed by historical experience, will include negotiation backed by political, economic, and military leverage (a willingness, in fact, occasionally to utilize punishing military power), support from the international community, sophisticated police and espionage activity, and, most importantly, foresight, where possible, in keeping Americans out of harm's way.

NOTES

1. Jimmy E. Carter, *Public Papers of the Presidents of the United States: Jimmy Carter, 1979* (Washington, DC: Government Printing Office, 1980), 2:1237.

2. Lou Cannon, *President Reagan: The Role of a Lifetime* (New York: Simon and Schuster, 1991), 20–22. See also Garry Wills, *Reagan's America: Innocents at Home* (New York: Doubleday and Company, 1987), 2–4; Edwin Meese III, *With Reagan: The Inside Story* (Washington, DC: Regnery Gateway, 1992), xiv–xv; Jane Blankenship and Janette Kenner Muir, "The Transformation of Actor to Scene: Some Strategic Grounds of the Reagan Legacy," in Michael Weiler and W. Barnett Pearce, eds., *Reagan and Public Discourse in America* (Tuscaloosa: University of Alabama Press, 1992), 150–53, 157–60; and William Ker Muir, Jr.,

The Bully Pulpit: The Presidential Leadership of Ronald Reagan (San Francisco: Institute for Contemporary Studies Press, 1992), 7–12.

3. Ronald Reagan, *Public Papers of the Presidents of the United States, Ronald Reagan, 1981* (Washington, DC: Government Printing Office, 1982), 42. Constantine Menges categorized this policy as "swift and sure retribution" in his *Inside the National Security Council: The True Story of the Making and Unmaking of Reagan's Foreign Policy* (New York: Simon and Schuster, 1988), 266. See also Caspar Weinberger, *Fighting for Peace* (New York: Warner Books, 1990), 356–57, 369; and George P. Shultz, *Turmoil and Triumph: My Years as Secretary of State* (New York: Charles Scribner's Sons, 1993), 328, 857–58. Shultz, however, also recommends "quiet, patient work to lower the value and raise the costs of taking and holding hostages." This strategy, he concedes, is difficult in a free and open society but one that proved successful in the case of the Iranians returning a *Wall Street Journal* correspondent in February 1987. Shultz also relates the impact that the Iranian hostage crisis had on President Reagan's decision to land U.S. forces on Grenada in October 1983.

4. Bob Woodward, *VEIL: The Secret Wars of the CIA, 1981–1987* (New York: Simon and Schuster, 1987), 408. In 1979, Ross Perot hired a seven-member commando team to rescue two of his employees held captive in Iran. This story is recounted in Ken Follett's best-selling *On Wings of Eagles* (New York: William Morrow and Company, 1983) and in a television movie. Perot's can-do approach, not to mention his considerable wealth, landed him a position on President Reagan's Foreign Intelligence Advisory Board in 1982. Several hundred thousand "perot dollars" were used by U.S. officials in their efforts to ransom American hostages held in Lebanon during the mid-1980s. See also Oliver North with William Novak, *Under Fire: An American Story* (New York: HarperCollins, 1991), 15.

5. Alexander M. Haig, Jr., *Caveat: Realism, Reagan, and Foreign Policy* (New York: Macmillan Company, 1984). See also Weinberger, *Fighting for Peace*, 159–60, 433–45. Weinberger's six-point statement on the proper use of force to combat terrorism, jokingly known as the Capgun Doctrine, is criticized by Shultz in *Turmoil and Triumph*, 649–51.

6. Shultz, *Turmoil and Triumph*, 330–32.

7. Ibid., 645. The former secretary of state describes the impact of the Long Commission's report to Congress. (The U.S. Department of Defense had appointed a commission of inquiry, headed by retired Admiral Robert L. J. Long, to examine all of the circumstances surrounding the October 23 attack on the Marine barracks and compound in Beirut.)

8. In a speech on June 24, 1984, Shultz stated: "It is time to think long, hard, and seriously about more active means of defense—about defense through appropriate preventive or preemptive actions against terrorists before they strike." Shultz, *Turmoil and Triumph*, 647. Woodward relates in *VEIL* (393–98) that Casey saw assassination as an appropriate self-defense mechanism against terrorists. See also Bill Moyers, "Send in the CIA," in his *The Secret Government: The Constitution in Crisis* (Cabin John, MD: Seven Locks Press, 1988), 53–61.

9. David C. Martin and John Walcott, *Best Laid Plans: The Inside Story of America's War on Terrorism* (New York: Harper and Row, 1988), 224–25. In early June 1985 the six were: CIA officer William Buckley, the Reverend Ben-

jamin Weir, Servite priest Lawrence Martin Jenco, journalist Terry Anderson, hospital administrator David Jacobsen, and agriculture professor Thomas Sutherland.

10. David Hoffman, "Reagan Ties Beirut Attack to Curb on Intelligence," *Washington Post*, September 27, 1984. Although it is true that the intelligence community had suffered as a result of the investigations of the mid-1970s, it is doubtful that Reagan would have been able to respond, except possibly with force against Iran, the known source of much of the terrorist activity. Woodward also describes a message from Casey to Reagan in November 1986 (*VEIL*, 497) warning the president that "you need a new pitcher!" Casey also named Shultz and "the Carterite bureaucracy" at the State Department as the culprits behind the growing public scandal over Iran-Contra. See Shultz, *Turmoil and Triumph*, 837, for the secretary's reaction.

11. Haynes Johnson, *Sleepwalking through History: America in the Reagan Years* (New York: W. W. Norton and Company, 1991), 289–91, 295–300.

12. Jonathan Marshall, Peter Scott, and Jane Hunter, "Irangate: The Israel Connection," in *The Iran-Contra Connection: Secret Teams and Covert Operations in the Reagan Era* (Boston: South End Press, 1987), 167–86.

13. Shultz, *Turmoil and Triumph*, 794.

14. Abraham D. Sofaer, "Terrorism and the Law," *Foreign Affairs* 64, no. 5 (Summer 1986): 910–12.

15. Lawrence E. Walsh, *Final Report of the Independent Counsel for Iran/ Contra Matters* (Washington, DC: U.S. Court of Appeals for the DC Circuit Division for the Purpose of Appointing Independent Counsel, 1994); John Tower, Edmund Muskie, and Brent Scowcroft, *Report of the President's Special Review Board* (Washington, DC: Government Printing Office, 1987); U.S. Congress, *Report of the Congressional Committees Investigating the Iran-Contra Affair* (Washington, DC: Government Printing Office, 1987); Peter Kornbluh and Malcolm Byrne, eds., *The Iran Contra Scandal: The Declassified History* (New York: The New Press, 1993), 213–325; William S. Cohen and George J. Mitchell, *Men of Zeal: A Candid Inside Story of the Iran-Contra Hearings* (New York: Viking Press, 1988); Meese, *With Reagan*; Donald Regan, *For the Record* (New York: Harcourt Brace Jovanovich, 1988); Robert C. McFarlane with Zofia Smardz, *Special Trust* (New York: Codell and Davies, 1994); Steve Emerson, *Secret Warriors: Inside the Covert Military Operations of the Reagan Era* (New York: Putnam Publishing Group, 1988); Theodore Draper, *A Very Thin Line: The Iran-Contra Affairs* (New York: Hill and Wang, 1991).

16. Michael A. Ledeen, *Perilous Statecraft: An Insider's Account of the Iran-Contra Affair* (New York: Scribner's, 1988), 91–193. See also Elliott Abrams, *Undue Process: A Story of How Political Differences Are Turned into Crimes* (New York: Free Press, 1993) for the more sympathetic view of the "Iran initiative."

17. President Reagan's June 18, 1985, news conference, *Weekly Compilation of Presidential Documents*, vol. 21, 1–25 (January–June 1985) (Washington, DC: Government Printing Office, 1986), 806–13; address to the American Bar Association, July 8, 1985, *Weekly Compilation of Presidential Documents*, vol. 21, 26–52 (July–December 1985), 876–82. Especially dubious and misleading is President Reagan's assertion at the June 18 press conference that "America will

never make concessions to terrorists—to do so would only invite more terrorism." See Ronald Reagan, *An American Life* (New York: Simon and Schuster, 1990), 516–20. See also George Bush, *Looking Forward* (New York: Doubleday and Company, 1987), 244. Bush drew several lessons from Iran-Contra before becoming the forty-first president of the United States. "Don't look for shortcuts," he wrote, "and don't try to circumvent the process." Most important, he concluded, was to adhere to two rules: follow the letter of the law and "never try to strike a bargain with terrorists."

18. Shultz, *Turmoil and Triumph*, 683–87; Weinberger, *Fighting for Peace*, 175–201.

19. Shultz, *Turmoil and Triumph*, 688. It is especially difficult to consider Shultz's "You've had it, pal [Qaddafi]" as the final word, especially in light of the overwhelming evidence linking the Christmas-week midair bombing of Pan Am Flight 103 as a retaliatory attack on Americans by Libya.

20. For a critical assessment of Ronald Reagan's policy on terrorism see Stansfield Turner, *Terrorism and Democracy* (Boston: Houghton Mifflin Company, 1991), 161–225. Turner was director of the Central Intelligence Agency during the Carter administration. See also Ann Wroe, *Lives, Lies, and the Iran-Contra Affair* (London: I. B. Tauris, 1991), 61–69, 82–94.

21. Shultz, *Turmoil and Triumph*, 688.

22. Nehemia Friedland, "Hostage Negotiations: Dilemmas about Policy," in Lawrence Zelic Freedman and Yonah Alexander, eds., *Perspectives on Terrorism* (Wilmington, DE: Scholarly Resources, 1983), 202–3.

23. Moorhead Kennedy, *The Ayatollah in the Cathedral: Reflections of a Hostage* (New York: Hill and Wang, 1986), 97–99.

24. Friedland, "Hostage Negotiations," 204–5.

Appendix

Major Hostage Incidents in U.S. History

Much of the information contained in this section is derived from several studies by the U.S. Department of State's Office of the Historian, Bureau of Public Affairs. One study in particular (Research Project #1246) lists many episodes in which U.S. citizens, whether as private individuals or public officials, were taken hostage while living or working abroad.[1] Assassinations, kidnappings, or instances of mob violence against American citizens and officials also have been included when the perpetrators either demanded a ransom or engaged in some form of exchange, whether diplomatic or military, with agencies of the U.S. government.

1785–1796, the Barbary States
In 1785 the dey of Algiers captured two U.S. ships, the *Maria* and the *Dauphin*, and demanded $6,000 in ransom for each of the three captains aboard the ships, $4,000 each for the two mates and the two passengers, and $1,400 each for the fourteen seamen. Ensuing negotiations collapsed because the American emissary was authorized to pay only $200 for each man. These prisoners and others were not freed until 1796. They were released according to the terms of a treaty between the United States and Algiers that provided for the former to pay $585,000 for the release of the captives. The U.S. Treasury estimated the price paid for this treaty at $992,463.25.

1802, 1805, 1814, the Barbary States
In 1802, Tripolitanians captured an American merchantman, the *Franklin*, and its crew of nine, freeing them a few months later upon payment of $6,500 to the bey of Tripoli. The 1805 peace treaty that ended the war between Tripoli and the United States called for the latter to ransom about three hundred American prisoners for $60,000 and return about one hundred Tripolitanians then in American hands. Finally, in 1814 the United States paid the dey of Algiers $8,000 for the ransom of six Americans captured the previous year aboard the *Edwin*.

1831–32, Dutch East Indies/Sumatra

On February 7, 1831, three crewmen of the U.S. merchant vessel *Friendship* were killed while the ship was being ransacked by armed natives in the port of Kuala Batu. President Andrew Jackson ordered Captain John Downes and the USS *Potomac* to Kuala Batu to seek retribution from and chastisement of the perpetrators. However, Captain Downes's invasion there in February 1832 led to a constitutional crisis between Congress and President Jackson. In the summer of 1832 his authorization and use of naval and marine forces in the Indian Ocean became a topic of heated debate in the nation's capital.

1831–1833, Argentina and the Falkland Islands/Malvinas

In August 1831 the Argentine governor in the Falklands/Malvinas seized three American fishing schooners. President Jackson sent a squadron to the South Atlantic to protect American fishing rights in the region. Commander Silas Duncan and the USS *Lexington* entered Soledad (East Falkland) harbor several months later and took temporary military control of the islands. Throughout the summer of 1832 the matter developed into a diplomatic debate between the United States and Argentina over the legal status of the islands, to be resolved only by the military intervention of Great Britain in January 1833.

1852–53, Turkey

In the late fall of 1852 a young Hungarian national, Martin Koszta, on business in Turkey with official U.S. papers recognizing his intent to become an American citizen, was kidnapped by the Austrian consul general in Smyrna. Koszta was held prisoner aboard the Austrian ship *Hussar* in preparation for probable transit to Austria for trial and execution as a result of his alleged insurrectionary activity back in Austria-Hungary in 1848–49. The State Department tried diplomatic channels to win Koszta's release but to no avail. Fortuitously for the would-be American citizen, the USS *St. Louis* was in port at the time. Her commander, Captain Duncan Ingraham, applied some on-the-scene naval persuasion, and with encouragement from the U.S. chargé in Constantinople he gave the Austrian commander an ultimatum. Koszta was released to the French consul general in Smyrna, where he remained for several months until his return to the United States in the late fall of 1853.

1891–92, Chile

On October 16, 1891, sailors on shore leave from the USS *Baltimore* were attacked by a mob of Chilean nationals in the port of

Valparaiso. Three seamen from the American warship—Charles Riggin, John Talbot, and William Turnbull—were killed as a result of the mayhem, while seventeen others were injured. President Benjamin Harrison made an issue of the attack in his annual message to Congress in January 1892; he called for "prompt reparation" and implied a request to Congress for authority to take military action against Chile if necessary. On January 25 the Chilean foreign minister promised that his government would pay the death and injury amounts determined by arbitration.

1900, China
In July a large force of antiforeign fanatics, the Boxers, and soldiers of the moribund Manchu dynasty attacked the legation quarter in Peking (now Beijing), placing all foreign diplomats and their families in peril for over a month. Legation defenders at first put up resistance, but concerted international action was required to break the siege in early August. Americans lost their lives during the incident and also participated in the military expedition to end it.

1901–02, Bulgaria
On September 3, 1901, Macedonian brigands abducted Ellen Stone, an American missionary, while she was traveling to Djumabala in Turkish European territory. She was released on February 23, 1902, upon payment of $66,000 raised by private subscription. The State Department cooperated in the efforts to obtain Stone's release, and Congress reimbursed her benefactors by authorizing payment on May 21, 1912.

1904, Morocco
On May 18 a Moroccan chieftain named Raisuli seized Ion Perdicaris, who claimed to be an American citizen, and his stepson, a British subject, at their villa near Tangier and held them for ransom. Naval vessels were sent to the area. Although arrangements already had been made to release the two men, President Theodore Roosevelt concurred with Secretary of State John Hay's open instructions to the American consul general at Tangier to demand "Perdicaris alive or Raisuli dead." After the Moroccan sultan paid $70,000, assured the immunity of Raisuli, and released some of the chieftain's supporters from prison, Perdicaris and his stepson were freed.

1912, Nicaragua
During a civil war in Nicaragua in 1912, Lieutenant E. H. Conger was held hostage temporarily while on a mission for the U.S.

embassy. The American ambassador publicly requested that the military officer be allowed to proceed to his destination or else start back to the legation. Before any more action became necessary, Lieutenant Conger returned to Managua.

1918–19, Russia
On March 15, 1918, the U.S. consul at Tashkent in Turkestan, Roger C. Tredwell, was detained by Bolshevik forces during their siege of the city. This detention lasted only five hours. After the active U.S. participation in the Allied intervention to bring Russia back into World War I, however, and in response to the Allies holding a Soviet official in the Caucasus, the Soviet government officially arrested Tredwell on October 20. This time, he remained a prisoner at Tashkent for over five months. This incarceration served both as a retaliation against Allied intervention and as an attempt to force other nations to negotiate with the newly constituted Soviet regime. The Soviets finally transported Tredwell, with eighteen other foreigners, in a special railcar on a 2,500-mile trip from Tashkent to Finland, where he was freed on April 27, 1919.[2]

1919, Mexico
On October 19 the U.S. consular agent in Puebla, William O. Jenkins, was abducted by Zapatista rebels. He was held for a ransom of three hundred thousand pesos, to be paid only by the government of Venustiano Carranza. The kidnappers also informed the U.S. embassy in Mexico City that the abduction was not an act of banditry but only proof that the Carranza government could not protect foreign nationals. In view of Jenkins's weakening physical condition the rebels decided to accept payment of the ransom from private sources and released the U.S. official on October 26. On November 15, however, Jenkins was arrested by Mexican authorities on charges of collusion with his former captors. On December 5, responding to an American ultimatum, the Carranza government released Jenkins on bail without dropping the charges against him.

1923, China
In early May, bandits kidnapped nineteen foreign travelers, including twelve Americans, from an express train in Shantung Province. After prolonged negotiations the last prisoners were let go on June 12. The terms of the agreement included incorporation of the bandits into the Chinese military forces, with guaranteed pay for three years. An American, Roy Anderson, assisted in arranging the release of the prisoners. Others taking part in the negotiations were American diplomatic personnel and officials of the Chinese gov-

ernment. This case revealed the weakness of the central government and resulted in demands on the part of the foreign powers for an agreement on compensation, guarantees, and sanctions.

1932, China
On January 16 sixteen bandits described as "communists" kidnapped an American riverboat master on the Yangtze (now Yangzi) River in Hupeh Province. He was released on May 31 after a ransom was paid. A British subject conducted the negotiations, and payment was made in cash and with American wheat from famine-relief supplies in the country through the auspices of the U.S. National Flood Relief Commission. The State Department favored payment of the ransom by the Chinese government as the best means of effecting the prompt and safe release of the American.

1948–49, China
Although several Americans were held against their will in areas of China recently overrun by armies of the Chinese Communist Party, the most prominent hostage incident was the taking of the U.S. consulate in Manchuria at Mukden. On November 20, 1948, Consul General Angus Ward, his wife, and his staff were all taken prisoner and remained incommunicado for a year. The incident seriously complicated American consideration of the recognition of the Chinese Communist government and exposed the limitations of even a nuclear power in hostage situations. At one point during the standoff, Ward and four staff members were tried and convicted for mistreating the consulate's Chinese employees. Their sentences of four to six months were all commuted, however, to deportation, with back payment and severance pay for the hostages' employees. After months of negotiations with Chinese officials, Ward and his entourage were released on November 21, 1949. They closed the Mukden consulate on December 7 and journeyed to Tianjin, where on December 11 they boarded a ship for the United States.

1951, the Philippines
On March 29, John Hardie, an American living in the Philippines, and his wife were murdered at their farm near Manila by the Huks (Hukbalahap), a leftist guerrilla organization attempting to discredit the Philippine government. On October 25 the Huks killed two more Americans near Olongapo.

1952–1955, People's Republic of China (PRC)
Between September 1952 and April 1953 four American airmen were shot down while flying missions for the United Nations (UN)

in Korea and were imprisoned in the PRC. In November 1952 two additional Americans, John T. Downey and Richard G. Fecteau, were captured by the Communist Chinese while on a mission for the Central Intelligence Agency (CIA).

On November 23, 1954, Beijing Radio announced that another eleven American airmen, as well as Downey and Fecteau, had been convicted of espionage and sentenced to prison terms ranging from four years to life. (The eleven airmen were Colonel John K. Arnold and his crew, whose B-29 had been shot down in January 1953 while on a leaflet-dropping mission under UN Command in Korea.)

On December 4 the United States requested UN action concerning the airmen. On December 10 the General Assembly adopted Resolution 906 (IX), which requested Secretary-General Dag Hammarskjöld to seek the release of the eleven servicemen and any others who were still being detained. Hammarskjöld arrived in Beijing on January 5, 1955, for discussions with Premier Zhou Enlai (Chou En-lai). As a result of these meetings in early January, the U.S. citizens were released that summer as a prelude to the PRC's inclusion in the Geneva Conference of 1955.[3]

1958, East Germany/USSR

On June 7 a U.S. Army helicopter strayed across the border into East Germany and was forced to land. After surrendering, the crew of nine Americans was turned over to Soviet Army officials. In an attempt to use the airmen as pawns, the Soviets insisted that the United States recognize the East German Communist government by negotiating with it directly for the release of the hostages. Moscow reported that the U.S. airmen were under the jurisdiction of East German officials and that they could only be released after Washington recognized the regime in East Berlin as the legal government.

In early July the East German government put the nine airmen on public display at a restricted news conference. The servicemen complained that they were being held as political hostages. They were released later that month.[4]

1958, Cuba

In June, Cuban rebels, on orders from Fidel Castro's brother Raul, kidnapped fifty persons including forty-three Americans, at various sites around the country. Raul Castro demanded, as conditions for their release, that the United States make no more arms shipments to the Batista government in Cuba and that it give assurances that its naval base at Guantanamo Bay would not be used for supplying fuel or arms. Washington replied, publicly and through Derek Wellam (the American consul at Santiago de Cuba, who had established contact with Raul Castro), that its decision of March 1958 not to ship arms to Cuba was unchanged and that the Guantanamo base was not being used to supply fuel or arms. Meanwhile, the first of the prisoners had been freed.

Raul Castro tried to delay releasing the remainder of the prisoners until he had received further assurances from the United States. After another meeting between Wellam and Raul Castro, the rest were released by July 16. It was subsequently confirmed that he had seized the Americans without the knowledge of Fidel Castro, who probably was responsible for allowing the prisoners to be returned without pressure to satisfy the rebels' demands.

1963–64, Venezuela

On November 27, 1963, members of the Army of National Liberation (FALN) kidnapped Colonel James K. Chenault, deputy chief of the U.S. military mission in Caracas. The FALN made no demands, claiming that it merely wanted publicity. Chenault was quickly released, but he reported that his captors had tried to indoctrinate him.

On October 3, 1964, members of the FALN kidnapped Colonel Michael Smalen, deputy chief of the U.S. Air Force mission in Venezuela. Colonel Smalen was released on October 12. His captors made no demands on the Venezuelan government, again claiming to want only publicity. Five members of the FALN were later arrested in connection with the case.

1963, Bolivia

On December 7 tin miners, who were antagonists of the Bolivian government, seized four Americans and other foreigners as hostages in an attempt to obtain the release of imprisoned union leaders. The lives of the captives were in danger for several days. Bolivian troops surrounded their place of detention while U.S. officials vainly offered their assistance to the government. The captives finally were freed after nine days, primarily through the efforts of Vice President Juan Lechin.

1963–64, North Korea

In early 1963 two American helicopter pilots, who had been patrolling along the Korean Demilitarized Zone (DMZ), were forced down over North Korea by hostile ground fire. Jailed for nearly a year on spy charges, the two servicemen finally were released in May 1964 to the UN Military Armistice Commission following a formal apology on the part of the United States. Five years later this apology would serve as the framework for an agreement between North Korea and the United States that brought about the return of the crew of the USS *Pueblo*.

1968, Guatemala

On August 28 members of the Rebel Armed Forces (FAR) killed U.S. ambassador John Gordon Mein in Guatemala City. After forcing his car off the highway, they shot him as he tried to flee. FAR guerrillas claimed responsibility, stating that they had intended to kidnap Mein and demand the release of imprisoned leftist leader Camilo Sanchez.

1968–69, North Korea

On January 23, 1968, two North Korean submarine chasers and four torpedo boats surrounded the USS *Pueblo*, an intelligence ship engaged in electronic espionage roughly three miles outside North Korean territorial waters to the east of Wonsan. When the ship tried to flee, the North Koreans opened fire, killing one crewman and wounding three others, including Commander Lloyd M. Bucher. As the crew attempted to destroy highly classified intelligence machinery and documents, ten armed North Korean sailors boarded the *Pueblo* and took its surviving eighty-two crewmen prisoner. The North Koreans towed the ship into Wonsan harbor and proceeded to hold the men captive for eleven months, forcing them to sign numerous confessions and savagely brutalizing them. After months of negotiations the U.S. government agreed to sign a statement of guilt and accept sole responsibility for the incident. On December 23, 1968, as the document was signed, the eighty-two crew members were released to American custody.

1969, Brazil

On September 4 leftist urban guerrillas kidnapped U.S. ambassador C. Burke Elbrick in Rio de Janeiro and demanded that the Brazilian government release fifteen political prisoners and broadcast a revolutionary manifesto. The government, encouraged by the State Department in Washington, met the demands. Elbrick was freed on September 7 after the political prisoners had been flown to Mexico.

1969, Ethiopia

On September 9 members of the Eritrean Liberation Front (ELF) kidnapped Consul General Murray E. Jackson while he was driving between Agordat and Keren. He was released two hours later, after his captors had him sign a statement that he had listened to their views and had not been mistreated.

1970, Guatemala
On March 6 members of the FAR kidnapped U.S. labor attaché Sean M. Holly in Guatemala City. He was released two days later, after the government had freed three political prisoners.

1970, Dominican Republic
On March 24 terrorists kidnapped Lieutenant Colonel Donald J. Crowley, the U.S. air attaché, in Santo Domingo. He was released two days later, after the Dominican government had freed twenty political prisoners and flown them to Mexico.

1970, Ethiopia
On April 21 members of the ELF removed Peace Corpsman Jack Fry and his wife from a train. They were released on April 26, with no ransom demand.

1970, Jordan
On June 7 members of the Popular Front for the Liberation of Palestine (PFLP) captured Morris Draper, head of the political section of the U.S. embassy in Jordan. His captors reportedly demanded the release of comrades who had been captured by the Jordanian army the day before. Draper was released after twenty-two hours. On the same day, Army captain Robert Potts and his wife were wounded when Palestinian commandos fired on their car at a roadblock. Potts was assigned to the defense attaché's office in Amman.

In early June the PFLP also seized sixty hostages, among them American, British, Canadian, and German citizens, at the Inter-Continental and Philadelphia hotels in Amman to protest the bombardment of Palestinian refugee camps by the Jordanian army. The hostages were released on June 12, the day after a cease-fire was arranged in Amman between the army and the Palestinian guerrillas. They then joined five hundred foreigners who were being evacuated to Beirut in an airlift by the International Red Cross.

On June 10, Major Robert Perry, a U.S. military attaché, was killed in Amman when a band of Palestinians tried to break into his house. In a separate incident, two fedayeen ransacked the homes of two American officials in Amman and raped their wives. Yasir Arafat, leader of the Palestine Liberation Organization (PLO), later announced that the fedayeen did not belong to either al-Fatah or the PFLP and that the two men had been executed on June 13.

On September 9 the PLO kidnapped Staff Sergeant Ervin Graham of the defense attaché's office in Amman. There was no ransom demand, and Graham was released eight days later.

On September 11 in Amman the PLO kidnapped Jon Stewart, a cultural affairs officer with the U.S. Information Agency (USIA), and interrogated him. He was released the next day; there was no ransom demand.

1970, Western Europe/Israel/Egypt/Jordan

On September 6 the PFLP attempted to hijack four aircraft, all of which were engaged in international flights originating in Europe with several U.S. citizens aboard. The crew of an Israeli El Al airliner was able to overpower the hijackers. The passengers on the other three flights, however, were not as fortunate. One of the three aircraft, a Pan American plane with 177 aboard, landed safely in Cairo, Egypt, but was destroyed by fuse explosives moments after the evacuation of all the passengers. The other two aircraft, owned by Swissair and Trans World Airways (TWA), were forced to land at Jordan's Dawson Field, outside of Zarqu near the Iraqi border; the hijackers demanded the release of Palestinian prisoners held in Israeli, Swiss, British, and West German jails. On September 9 a British airliner also was hijacked and flown to the same airstrip. Although these three aircraft were destroyed by the hijackers, the hostages were released between September 25 and 29. On September 30 seven terrorists were released in Germany, Switzerland, and England, while Israel released some prisoners for "humanitarian" reasons.

1970–71, Uruguay

On July 31, 1970, U.S. Agency for International Development (AID) official Dan A. Mitrione was kidnapped by Tupamaro guerrillas, who demanded the release of all political prisoners in Uruguay. The government refused to negotiate, and Mitrione was found dead in Montevideo on August 10.

On August 7, Claude L. Fly, an AID agricultural expert, was kidnapped by Tupamaros. The Uruguayan government refused the terrorists' demands to publish the text of a revolutionary manifesto, but Fly was released on March 2, 1971, after suffering a heart attack.

1971, Turkey

On February 15 fifteen members of the Turkish People's Liberation Army held Sergeant James R. Finley for seventeen hours. He had reportedly come upon them as they were trying to steal arms from a U.S. Air Force base outside Ankara.

On March 4 five members of the Turkish People's Liberation Army kidnapped four Air Force personnel shortly after they left a radar station outside Ankara. The captors demanded a $400,000 ransom and the release of all political prisoners in Turkey. The Ankara government refused to negotiate, and Turkish police arrested a suspect on March 4. The four Americans, Sergeant James Sexton and Airmen Larry Heavner, Richard Caraszi, and James Gholson, were released unharmed on March 8.

1973, Haiti

On January 23 three Haitians kidnapped U.S. ambassador Clinton E. Knox in Port-au-Prince. Their initial demands were for the release of thirty-one political prisoners and a $500,000 ransom. Consul General Ward L. Christensen voluntarily joined Knox in captivity during the negotiations. The terrorists later reduced their demands to the release of sixteen political prisoners, a ransom of $70,000, and safe conduct to Mexico. Knox and Christensen were released after the Haitian government met the reduced demands. The terrorists and the released prisoners, accompanied by the Mexican ambassador, were flown to Mexico, where the ransom money was taken from them and returned to Haiti. Mexico refused to accept the political prisoners, who then proceeded to Chile.

1973, Mexico

On May 4 members of the People's Revolutionary Armed Forces kidnapped Terrence G. Leonhardy, the American consul general in Guadalajara. They demanded freedom for thirty political prisoners, passage to Cuba, publication of a communiqué, and suspension of a police search for them. Leonhardy was freed on May 7 after the Mexican government met the demands and Mrs. Leonhardy paid $80,000. Five persons were later arrested in connection with the case.

1973, the Sudan

On March 1 eight members of the Palestinian terrorist group Black September seized the Saudi embassy in Khartoum during a farewell reception for the American chargé d'affaires, George Moore. They took ten hostages, including Moore, incoming U.S. ambassador Cleo A. Noel, Jr., the Saudi ambassador and his family, and the Belgian and Jordanian chargés. They demanded the release of al-Fatah leader Abu Daoud, other Palestinians held by Jordan and

Israel, Sirhan Sirhan (the assassin of Robert F. Kennedy), and members of the Baader-Meinhof Gang imprisoned in Germany. All of the hostages except Noel, Moore, and the Belgian chargé, Guy Eid, were released, and the terrorists reduced their demands to the release of Abu Daoud and sixteen Palestinians held by Jordan. The government of the Sudan refused to negotiate, and all of the remaining hostages were killed. The terrorists surrendered on March 6.

The Sudanese government denounced the incident and banned further operations in the country by Palestinian organizations. The terrorists were convicted of murder on June 24 and sentenced to life imprisonment, but President Jaafar al-Nimeiry commuted their sentence to seven years and released them to the PLO the next day. The terrorists were then flown to Cairo, where Egyptian authorities imprisoned them.

1974, Argentina

On April 12 members of the People's Revolutionary Army (ERP) kidnapped USIA director Alfred A. Laun in Córdoba. Laun, who was seriously wounded when captured, was released several hours later.

1974, the Philippines

On April 13 the New People's Army claimed responsibility for the murders of three U.S. Navy personnel near Subic Bay Naval Base. Killed were Commander Leland Dobler, Captain J. T. Mitchell, and Lieutenant Charles Jeffries.

1974, Dominican Republic

On September 27 members of the January 12 Liberation Movement kidnapped USIA director Barbara Hutchison in Santo Domingo. The terrorists demanded the release of thirty-eight political prisoners and a ransom of $1 million. The Dominican government refused to comply with the demands, and Hutchison was freed on October 9 in return for safe conduct to Panama for her captors.

1974, Mexico

On March 22 members of the People's Liberation Army kidnapped American vice consul John Patterson near Hermosillo. They demanded a ransom of $500,000. Mrs. Patterson claimed that all of her attempts to deliver the ransom had been unsuccessful. Patterson was found dead in the desert on July 8.

The "PLA" turned out to be a hoax. Bobbie Joe Keesee of San Diego, who had hijacked a small plane from Thailand to North Vietnam in September 1970, was arrested and charged with planning the kidnapping, and Greg Curtis Fielden was named as an unindicted coconspirator. Keesee was sentenced to twenty years in prison in 1975 for conspiracy to kidnap a diplomat.

1975, Argentina

On February 26, Montoneros guerrillas kidnapped John P. Egan, a retired businessman serving as the American honorary consul in Córdoba. They demanded that four captured guerrillas be shown on national television or Egan would be killed. He was found dead the next day.

1975–76, Lebanon

On March 13, 1975, three Palestinians kidnapped Michael Konner, a Foreign Service officer, in a Beirut marketplace. They released him fourteen hours later after questioning and beating him. Konner was not seriously injured.

On April 16, John McKay of the U.S. Drug Enforcement Agency was held for two days at the Sabra refugee camp near Beirut. His Palestinian captors made no ransom demand and released him after interrogation.

On June 29, Palestinian guerrillas captured Army colonel Ernest R. Morgan in Beirut as he returned to Turkey from Central Treaty Organization (CENTO) exercises in Pakistan. They demanded that the U.S. embassy donate food, clothing, and building materials to a Muslim district of Beirut that had been heavily damaged in the Lebanese civil war. Both the PLO and the PFLP denied responsibility for the kidnapping. Colonel Morgan was released on July 12, after the Lebanese government had distributed free rice and sugar in the Al Masklakh quarter of Beirut.

On October 22 in Beirut, members of the PFLP captured Charles Gallagher and William Dykes of the USIA. They were released on February 25, 1976, at the home of Kamal Jumblatt, a Lebanese leftist leader. Their captors' demands ranged from ransom to the release of Palestinian guerrillas held in Lebanon or in Israel. Lebanese sources claimed that Israel had released two Palestinians in exchange for Gallagher and Dykes, but U.S. and Israeli sources denied any connection between the two releases.

1975, Cambodia

On May 12 a Cambodian gunship seized the U.S. merchant ship *Mayaguez* near the island of Koh Tang. Thirty-nine seamen were taken prisoner. After two days of diplomatic talks, U.S. military forces were ordered to rescue the Americans and retake the merchant ship. The assault against Koh Tang cost the lives of eighteen Marines, with another twenty-three American servicemen killed in a helicopter accident in Thailand while preparing to take part in the assault. The thirty-nine seamen were rescued from a Cambodian boat carrying them from the mainland back toward the *Mayaguez.* The Cambodians had broadcast their offer to release the ship, and probably its crew as well, prior to the Marines' assault.

1975, Tanzania
On May 19 members of the Zaire People's Revolution Party (PRP) kidnapped a Dutch student and three American students from Stanford University from Gombe Stream Research Center. One student was released on May 26 to deliver the PRP's demand for $500,000, arms and ammunition, and the release of his two comrades held in Tanzania. The Tanzanian government refused to meet the terrorists' demands, and efforts by American diplomats and the families of the hostages to contact them were unsuccessful. Two hostages were released on June 28 and the last on July 27 after their families and Stanford University reportedly paid a ransom of $40,000.

1975, Malaysia
On August 4 five members of the Japanese Red Army seized the consular sections of the American and Swedish embassies in Kuala Lumpur and took fifty-two hostages, including the Swedish chargé d'affaires and the American consul, Robert S. Stebbins. The hostages were freed after Japan agreed to release five other members of the Red Army. All ten departed for Libya on August 8.

1975–76, Ethiopia
On September 12, 1975, members of the ELF kidnapped Army Specialist 5 David Strickland and Navy Electronics Technician Thomas Bowodowicz near Asmara. Both were released in the Sudan on January 9, 1976.

1976, Lebanon
On June 16, Ambassador Francis E. Meloy, Jr., and Economic Counselor Robert O. Waring were kidnapped in Beirut while on their way to meet with President-elect Elias Sarkis. Meloy, Waring, and their Lebanese chauffeur were found dead near a beach several hours later. No demands were made, and the assassins remain unknown. The U.S. government urged its citizens to leave Lebanon on

June 18. Twenty of the thirty-two remaining embassy personnel were evacuated by sea on July 27.

1976, Yugoslavia/United States/France/Great Britain

On September 10 six Croatian nationalists hijacked a TWA 727 on a domestic flight from New York to Chicago. The hijackers released all of their hostages in Paris after authorities in the United States, Great Britain, and France complied with their demands that a communiqué in support of Croatian independence from Yugoslavia be published in those countries' major newspapers and that propaganda leaflets be dropped over Montreal, London, and Paris. They also directed the New York City police to a bomb that they had placed in a subway locker at Grand Central Station. The bomb exploded prematurely, however, killing one policeman and severely injuring several others. French officials extradited the hijackers to the United States for prosecution.

1977–1980, Colombia

On February 14, 1977, guerrillas belonging to the Colombian Revolutionary Army (FARC) raided the town of La Macarena and kidnapped Peace Corpsman Richard Starr, whom they accused of being a CIA operative. He was released on February 11, 1980, after American journalist Jack Mitchell paid a ransom of $250,000. Mitchell worked for Washington-based columnist Jack Anderson.

1977, United States

On March 9, Muslim gunmen seized three buildings in Washington, DC, and held 134 persons hostage. The gunmen surrendered two days later, after their propaganda communiqué was aired.

1979, Afghanistan

On February 14 four Islamic fundamentalists opposed to the Afghan government kidnapped U.S. ambassador Adolph Dubs in Kabul and demanded the release of various "religious figures" held by the government. Dubs was killed when Afghan police stormed the hotel room where he was being held. Washington criticized Kabul for not having tried to secure Dubs's release peaceably.

1979–1981, Iran

On February 14, 1979, two hundred militants occupied the U.S. embassy in Tehran for two hours before Iranian government forces persuaded them to leave. An Iranian employee of the embassy and the son of another local employee were killed. Marine sergeant

Kenneth Kraus, who had been wounded and captured during the takeover, was not released until February 22.

On November 4 a mob of students stormed the U.S. embassy in Tehran and captured sixty-six Americans, all but two of them embassy personnel. On November 7 the Iranians demanded the return of the deposed shah, who had been admitted to the United States for medical treatment, as a precondition for the release of the hostages. Washington stopped delivery of military supplies (November 9), suspended imports of Iranian oil (November 12), froze Iranian assets (November 14), and began to assemble naval forces in the Indian Ocean.

Iran released one woman and two black Marine security guards on November 19 and four women and six blacks the next day. The remaining hostages were threatened at various times with trial as spies. Six members of the embassy staff had escaped from the consular section during the takeover and found shelter at the Canadian embassy. Canada closed its embassy on January 28, 1980, and brought the six Americans out the next day.

The United States broke relations with Iran on April 7, 1980, and banned travel to that country on April 20. An attempt to rescue the hostages failed on April 25, resulting in the deaths of eight American military personnel. Secretary of State Cyrus Vance resigned shortly thereafter. Following the death of the former shah in Egypt on June 27, the Iranians modified their demands to include the return of the shah's wealth, the cancellation of American claims against Iran, the unfreezing of assets, and a promise of noninterference in the country's affairs. Richard Queen, a consular officer, was released on July 10 due to ill health.

On November 3 the Iranian militants turned the hostages over to the government. Negotiations leading to their release began in Algiers on November 10. Despite support from the United Nations and two favorable rulings by the International Court of Justice, the United States was unable to secure the release of the hostages until minutes before President Jimmy Carter left office on January 20, 1981.

1979, Yugoslavia/United States

On June 20 a Serbian nationalist belonging to the Freedom of the Serbian Fatherland (SEPO) hijacked an American Airlines flight between New York and Chicago. The lone gunman demanded the release of a Serbian priest, also a member of the SEPO and at the time held in a Chicago jail for a December 1975 bombing targeting an assistant of the Yugoslav consul. Although the priest was not released, the hijacker freed all 127 passengers and five of the plane's eight crewmembers at Chicago's O'Hare Airport. With the remaining crew the hijacker flew to New York where he transferred by gunpoint over to a larger airliner that took him to Shannon, Ireland, on June 21. Irish authorities immediately returned the gunman to the United States.

1979, Belgium/Germany/United States
On June 25 near Brussels, the North Atlantic Treaty Organization (NATO) Supreme Commander, General Alexander Haig, was the target of an assassination attempt by the ultraleft Red Army Faction (RAF) when a bomb prematurely exploded seconds before his car drove by the site of detonation.

1980, Colombia
On February 27 members of the M-19 guerrilla group seized the embassy of the Dominican Republic in Bogotá, capturing thirty diplomats from seventeen countries, including fifteen chiefs of mission. Ambassador Diego Ascencio was the only American among them. The terrorists initially demanded the release of 311 political prisoners, a $50-million ransom, and government publication of their manifesto. They gradually reduced their demands and released all but eighteen of their captives. The remaining hostages, including Ascencio, were released on April 27 in return for a $2.5-million ransom and passage to Cuba.

1981, West Germany
On August 31 a bomb exploded at Ramstein Air Base, near Kaiserslautern, within several yards of the headquarters of the U.S. Air Force in Europe, detonating in an abandoned automobile and injuring twenty people, including eighteen U.S. servicemen. The ultraleft RAF, which was believed to have received training and support from the PLO in Lebanon, claimed responsibility for the early morning attack. Among the RAF's demands was that the United States abandon its plans to deploy Pershing II medium-range nuclear missiles in Western Europe.

On September 15 the RAF also attempted to assassinate the commander in chief of the U.S. Army in Europe, General Frederick Kroesen, who escaped serious injury after his automobile was hit by a rifle-launched grenade as he left his headquarters in Heidelberg. This attack was the year's tenth on U.S. military personnel or property in West Germany.

1981–82, Italy

On December 17, 1981, four members of the Red Brigades kidnapped Brigadier General James L. Dozier from his apartment in Verona. General Dozier, deputy chief of staff for logistics and administration for NATO ground forces in southern Europe, became the first non-Italian victim of the Red Brigades. During his forty-two-day captivity, the American was threatened with "trial" and "execution" for his military service in Vietnam. On January 28, 1982, Italian police raided an apartment in Padua, rescued General Dozier, and arrested five of his captors.

1982, France

On January 18, U.S. military attaché Lieutenant Colonel Charles R. Ray was gunned down outside his home in Paris by terrorists belonging to the Christian group Lebanese Armed Revolutionary Factions (FARL).

1982, Honduras

In April leftist terrorists of the Lorenzo Zelaya Popular Revolutionary Forces (FRP-LZ) attacked the American, Argentine, Chilean, and Peruvian embassies in Tegucigalpa. Several members were captured and imprisoned. Then, on April 28, four members of the FRP-LZ hijacked a Honduran Air Service plane and demanded a ransom of $1 million and the release of thirty-two political prisoners. The siege ended on May 1 when ten of the passengers, eight of whom were American, escaped. The hijackers then flew on to Cuba after releasing the remaining eleven passengers.

1982, Lebanon

On July 19 pro-Ayatollah Ruholla Khomeini Iranian "revolutionary guards" kidnapped David S. Dodge, acting president of the American University in Beirut. Dodge spent a year in captivity, much of it in Tehran.

1983, Lebanon

On April 18 a Shiite fundamentalist, thought to be with a pro-Iranian group known as the Islamic Jihad, rammed a van loaded with several hundred pounds of TNT into the front of the U.S. embassy in West Beirut. Sixty-seven people were killed. Seventeen of the dead were Americans, including several CIA officers and the CIA's top adviser on the Middle East, Robert C. Ames.

On October 23 another suicide driver crashed directly into the four-storey barracks where U.S. Marines, stationed in Beirut as part of a multinational force (MNF) to protect the city's airport, were billeted. Two hundred forty-one American personnel, most of them asleep, were killed in this attack. (Four other Marines had been killed earlier by Druze batteries in two separate mortar attacks against the American positions near the Beirut airport.) Simultaneously, the French MNF contingent suffered a suicide bombing that caused fifty-nine casualties. The Islamic Jihad and a new Islamic group, the Hezbollah (Party of God), were implicated in these dawn attacks.

1983, Grenada

On October 25, President Ronald Reagan sent military forces to this Caribbean island to protect some eleven hundred Americans from an ongoing Marxist coup that was actively supported by Cuban military "advisers." After securing the country's airport on October 26, American troops began evacuating U.S. citizens.

1983, Kuwait

On December 12, in a coordinated, ninety-minute series of bombings, six targets in Kuwait were hit, including the American and French embassies. Five people were killed and some eighty-six injured. The Kuwaitis apprehended and convicted seventeen men for the bombings. Fourteen of them were members of al-Dawa, an Iranian-backed Shiite Muslim group, and the other three were from Beirut, where they had close family ties to the Hezbollah. These seventeen men became known as the Dawa prisoners.

1984, Lebanon/Syria

On January 3, Lieutenant Robert O. Goodman, Jr., a U.S. Navy pilot, was released by Syria after the Reverend Jesse Jackson made a personal appeal to President Hafez al-Assad. Goodman's plane had been downed on December 4, 1983, during a bombing raid over Syrian-occupied East Beirut.

On January 18, Malcolm Kerr, president of the American University in Beirut, was killed by two gunmen outside his office. Frank Regier, chairman of the university's Department of Electrical Engineering, became the first captive in a wave of hostage-taking carried out by Islamic fundamentalists in Lebanon. The kidnappers demanded both that the United States get out of Lebanon completely and that the seventeen Dawa prisoners jailed in Kuwait be released and flown to Iran.

On September 20 a truck loaded with explosives crashed through security forces and detonated within several feet of the new U.S. embassy annex in East Beirut. Two Americans were among the fourteen people killed in the attack, which effectively ended U.S. embassy operations in Lebanon.

1984, Italy

On February 14, Leamon Hunt, an American diplomat and the director general of the Multinational Peacekeeping Force in the Sinai, was assassinated in Rome by FARL terrorists.

1984, Iran

On December 4 four gunmen hijacked a Kuwaiti Airways jet during a flight from Kuwait to Pakistan. Six Americans, including three auditors employed by the AID, were among the 162 persons aboard. Shortly after the plane landed at Tehran, the hijackers shot and killed AID auditor Charles F. Hegna and released forty-four women and children, two of whom were Americans. They then threatened to blow up the plane unless the government of Kuwait released seventeen persons, including fourteen members of the militant al-Dawa Shiite group.

The Kuwaiti government refused to meet these demands. Although the hijackers gradually released most of their hostages, they killed a second American AID official, William L. Stanford, on December 6 and severely beat and tortured the remaining U.S. and Kuwaiti passengers. On December 9, Iranian security forces stormed the plane, captured the hijackers, and freed the remaining seven hostages, including AID auditor Charles Kapar and American businessman John Costa. Kapar and Costa were flown to an American hospital in Germany for medical treatment before returning to the United States.

The hijackers, who did not identify themselves, were believed to have been affiliated with either the Hezbollah, the Lebanese Shiite faction, or to al-Dawa. The Iranian government refused to extradite the hijackers to Kuwait but announced on December 18 that they would be tried according to Islamic law.

1984–1986, Lebanon

On March 16, 1984, political officer William Buckley was kidnapped by three gunmen outside his Beirut apartment. On May 9 the Islamic Jihad claimed to be holding him. On January 28, 1985, Buckley was shown in a videotape holding a Beirut newspaper dated January 22; he stated that he and two other Americans were being held as hostages. According to those other Americans, Buckley died in captivity on June 3, 1985. His captors, however, kept his death a secret until October 1985 when they reported that he was executed in retaliation for the Israeli bombing of PLO headquarters that month in Tunis.

Peter Kilburn, a librarian at Beirut's American University, was kidnapped on December 3, 1985, and killed in April 1986, apparently in retaliation for the American raid on Libya. The Libyans are reported to have ransomed Kilburn for this purpose.

1985, Lebanon/Algeria/Syria

On June 14 two Shiite fundamentalists belonging to the Islamic Jihad, armed with grenades and pistols, hijacked TWA Flight 847 to Beirut after it had departed Athens on a scheduled flight to Rome. Of the 153 passengers and crew aboard, 122 were Americans. Over the next fifty-three hours, the pilot, Captain John L. Testrake, was forced to fly some 8,300 miles in two round trips between Beirut and Algiers. Global media attention was at full frenzy especially after one of the passengers, 23-year-old U.S. Navy diver Robert Stethem, was brutally beaten, shot to death, and dropped on the tarmac of Beirut's airfield. The hijackers demanded that Israel free 766 Shiite Lebanese and Palestinian prisoners being held in Israel and the seventeen Dawa prisoners behind bars in Kuwait. After two weeks of intense media coverage, the last thirty-nine hostages were released in Damascus on June 30 following mediation efforts by both Nabih Berri, Lebanon's minister of justice and the political leader of the Lebanese Shiite community, and Syrian president Hafez al-Assad. Although Israel released thirty-one prisoners on June 24, it insisted that the decision was in no way connected to the hijacking as it had long intended to release the prisoners.

1985, Germany/United States

On August 8 the RAF detonated a car bomb at the Rhein-Main Air Base near Frankfurt, West Germany. The blast killed two Americans and injured seventeen others. The terrorists had killed an off-duty American serviceman the previous night and used his military identification to gain access to the base.

On November 25 a bomb exploded at a major U.S. military shopping center in Frankfurt, possibly set by a member of an Iranian-sponsored organization in West Germany.

1985, Italy/Egypt

On October 7 the Italian cruise liner *Achille Lauro* was seized in the Mediterranean off the coast of Egypt by four gunmen who were reported to be members of the Palestinian Liberation Front, a splinter group of the PLO. The gunmen were apparently planning a terrorist raid against the ship's next port of call, Ashdod, Israel. The four

commandeered the ship prematurely, however, after they were discovered cleaning their weapons in their cabin by a ship steward.
The hijackers killed a handicapped American passenger, 69-year-
old Leon Klinghoffer, and threw him overboard before surrendering to the Egyptian authorities on October 9. As part of the surrender
pact the gunmen were to be flown to Tunisia, but their plane was
intercepted by U.S. fighters and forced to land in Sicily, which resulted in the Palestinians being brought to trial in Italy.

1985–1991, Lebanon
In February 1985, CNN Beirut bureau chief Jeremy Levin, who
had been taken hostage eleven months earlier, escaped from his
abductors, apparently with some assistance from Syria. By mid-
June, five Americans were being held as hostages by the Hezbollah:
the Reverend Benjamin Weir (in captivity since May 8, 1984) and
Father Lawrence Jenco (taken January 8); Terry Anderson, Beirut's
Associated Press bureau chief (captured March 16); American University hospital administrator David Jacobsen (kidnapped May 28);
and Thomas Sutherland, an agriculture professor at the American
University of Beirut (abducted June 9).

Three hostages were released in 1985–86 during the course of
several U.S. arms-for-hostages deals with Iran: Weir was returned
on September 14, 1985; Father Jenco was released on July 24, 1986;
and Jacobsen was freed on November 2, 1986, the day before the
arms-for-hostages operation became public. Three more Americans
were abducted in 1986: Frank H. Reed, headmaster of the Lebanese International School in South Beirut (September 9); Joseph J.
Cicippio, acting comptroller of the American University (September 12); and Edward Austin Tracy, a writer (October 21).

Four Americans were kidnapped in 1987. On January 24 three
professors working in Beirut—Jesse Turner, Alann Steen, and Robert Pohill—were seized by the Islamic Holy War for the Liberation
of Palestine. On June 17 a journalist, Charles Glass, was kidnapped
by a faction of the Hezbollah, the Organization for the Defense of
Free People. Glass, however, was able to escape from his captors
two months later on August 17.

The hostage-holders continued to demand the release of the
Dawa prisoners held in Kuwait in exchange for Anderson, Sutherland, Reed, Cicippio, and Tracy. Reed was the first to be released,
on April 30, 1990. When the Dawa prisoners became "free" after
the Iraqi invasion of Kuwait in August 1990, the negotiated release
of the remaining captives became possible. UN special envoy
Giandomenico Picco helped to arrange for the freedom of the last
American hostages: Cicippio on December 2, 1991, and Anderson

two days later. Anderson's ordeal of 2,455 days in captivity made it the longest such episode in U.S. history.[5]

1986, Italy/Greece/Great Britain/Berlin/Libya
On April 2 an explosion aboard a TWA jetliner flying from Rome to Athens caused four persons, including a nine-month-old infant, to be swept through a gaping hole in the fuselage and to plunge to their deaths. A group calling itself the Arab Revolutionary Cells claimed that it had planted the bomb to retaliate for U.S. attacks on March 24 on Libyan missile sites and vessels in the Gulf of Sidra.

On April 5 a West Berlin nightclub, La Belle, was bombed. This attack, in which a U.S. serviceman and a Turkish woman were killed, provoked a crisis with Libya that resulted in an American air strike on Tripoli and Benghazi on April 15 in which two airmen were killed.

1987, Honduras
On August 8 twelve people, among them six Americans, were injured in Comayuga when a pipe bomb exploded outside a popular restaurant frequented by U.S. servicemen deployed at nearby Palmerola Air Base.

1987, Greece
On August 10 ten American airmen from Hellenikon Air Base were injured near Athens when a bomb detonated under their bus. Revolutionary Organization 17 November claimed responsibility.

1987, the Philippines
On October 26 two U.S. servicemen were assassinated by the New People's Army's "Sparrow Squads" at Clark Air Base near Manila.

1987, Spain
On December 26 a hand grenade killed one American serviceman and injured nine others at a United Service Organizations (USO) bar in Barcelona. Two Catalan separatist groups, the Catalan Red Army and Terra Lliure, claimed responsibility for the attack.

1988, Italy
On April 14 a car bomb detonated outside a USO club in Naples, killing an American sailor and four other people. Responsibility for the attack, which took place just one day short of the second anniversary of the U.S. air raid on Libya, was claimed by a Japanese Red Army front group, the Organization of the Jihad Brigades.

1988, Peru
On June 13 two contract employees of the AID were ambushed and murdered near Lima by leftist Sendero Luminoso terrorists.

1988, Greece
On June 28 the military attaché at the U.S. embassy in Athens, Captain William Nordeen, was killed by a car bomb set by Revolutionary Organization 17 November.

1988, Honduras
On July 17, Cinchoneros (a splinter group of the Honduran Communist Party) claimed responsibility for a terrorist attack in San Pedro Sula that injured several American servicemen.

1988, Bolivia
On August 8 a bomb exploded as the motorcade carrying Secretary of State George Shultz sped along a highway near La Paz. The Simón Bolívar Commando group is believed to be responsible.

1988, United Kingdom
On December 21, Pan Am Flight 103 exploded in midair over Lockerbie, Scotland, killing all 259 people on board (eleven perished on the ground as the aircraft's flaming debris fell onto the village). The Frankfurt-London-New York Boeing 747 was probably destroyed by a bomb concealed inside a radio-cassette player that was loaded in the cargo bay in Frankfurt, West Germany. Libyan intelligence agents, possibly working with Iranian financial assistance, are believed to be responsible for the bombing.

1988–89, Lebanon
On February 17, 1988, Lieutenant Colonel William R. Higgins, a U.S. Marine attached to the UN truce-monitoring force in southern Lebanon, was kidnapped by the Organization for the Oppressed of the Earth, a faction of the Iranian-backed Hezbollah. In late July 1989, Higgins's ongoing captivity presented President George Bush with his first hostage crisis, precipitated by the abduction of a prominent pro-Iranian Muslim cleric, Sheikh 'Abd-al Karim Obeid, on July 28. In a late-night raid, Israeli commandos had kidnapped the Lebanese Shiite leader together with two associates from his home in southern Lebanon. The Israeli government offered to exchange the sheikh and three hundred other Shiite prisoners for three Israeli soldiers and seventeen Western hostages, including Higgins and eight other Americans, held in Lebanon. Three days later, however, Higgins's kidnappers announced that he had been hanged in retali-

ation for the Israeli commando raid against the Muslim cleric. The kidnappers released a grisly videotape to prove that they had killed Higgins and threatened to kill other hostages. President Bush sought to resolve the crisis by diplomatic rather than military means. Negotiations with Iran and its new president, Ali Akbar Hashemi Rafsanjani, temporarily defused the dangerous standoff, and on August 3 the Revolutionary Justice Organization announced the suspension of threats to execute another U.S. hostage, Joseph Cicippio.

1989, Iran/United States

On March 10, as Sharon Rogers was driving her family's van near the U.S. Naval Base at San Diego, California, a pipe bomb exploded within the vehicle. Mrs. Rogers, the wife of the commanding officer of the USS *Vincennes*, Captain Will C. Rogers, escaped serious injury and survived. The attack, however, sparked fears of deliberate, Iranian-sponsored terrorist attacks against American civilians within the United States itself.

The explosion was believed to have been the work of such terrorists in retaliation for the *Vincennes*'s downing of an Iranian airliner over the Persian Gulf on July 3, 1988. The *Vincennes* had misidentified the passenger airliner as an attacking fighter-bomber and fired two radar-guided missiles at Iran Air Flight 655, killing all 290 persons aboard.[6]

1989, the Philippines

On April 21 terrorists of the New People's Army murdered an American military adviser, Lieutenant Colonel James N. Rowe, in Manila.

1989, Panama

On December 16, Panamanian soldiers shot and killed an unarmed American Marine, Lieutenant Robert Paz. Panama's strongman, Manuel Noriega, on the previous day had declared his country to be at war with the United States. On December 20, President Bush dispatched combat forces to protect Americans and the Panama Canal and to seize Noriega, who was under indictment in the United States as a narcoterrorist. Noriega sought refuge in the Vatican's embassy in Panama City but eventually surrendered to American soldiers on January 3, 1990.

1990, Ecuador

In April members of a Colombian guerrilla group calling themselves the People's Liberation Army kidnapped Scott Heimdal. He was later released after the citizens of his hometown, Peoria, Illinois, raised $60,000 in ransom.

1990, the Philippines
On May 14 two American airmen were shot and killed as they waited for a taxi outside the gates of Clark Air Base. The New People's Army is thought to be responsible for the murders.

On June 13 a Peace Corps volunteer, Timothy Swanson, was kidnapped by the New People's Army. He was released, along with a kidnapped Japanese aid worker, on August 2.

On September 26 two American businessmen were murdered by six gunmen just outside Clark Air Base. The attack coincided with a visit to Manila by Vice President Dan Quayle.

1990, Chile
On November 4 eight people, including three U.S. Navy sailors, were injured when a bomb exploded in a crowded seaside restaurant near Valparaiso. Thirteen days later, during a softball game between the United States and Chile, a bat loaded with dynamite exploded, killing one person and injuring five others. Conflicting callers claimed responsibility for the attacks on Americans.

1993, United States
On February 26 a midday explosion in a parking garage on a subterranean level beneath one of the twin World Trade Center buildings in New York City killed five Americans. Because of dense smoke and the lack of electrical power, hundreds of others suffered the effects of smoke inhalation while some fifty thousand people evacuated the buildings. Officials later charged several Muslim extremists with the bombing.

1993, Somalia
On October 3 eighteen U.S. soldiers were killed and seventy-four wounded in a gun battle against the forces of the Somalian warlord Muhammad Farah Aydid. One of the wounded soldiers, Chief Warrant Officer Michael Durant, was captured by the Aydid militia and paraded before the international press on October 4. He was released to American officials in Mogadishu several days later. The capture of Durant and the televised display of dead American soldiers stripped and dragged through the streets of Mogadishu prompted both a reevaluation of Washington's Operation Restore Hope and a schedule for the withdrawal of U.S. forces from Somalia.

1993, Yemen

On November 25 the head of the USIA, Haynes Mahoney, was kidnapped by rebel tribesmen. Five gunmen intercepted his car in San'a and held him for several days in the desert region of Gahm. Mahoney was returned unharmed within a week after Yemen's interior minister negotiated with the kidnappers' chieftains for the diplomat's release.[7]

1994, North Korea

On December 17 two U.S. Army pilots were forced down by North Korean forces after they strayed some ten miles into the DMZ in their OH-58 helicopter. The crew was on a routine reconnaissance mission along the DMZ when it "deviated from the route" and was fired upon by North Korean forces. Chief Warrant Officer (CWO) Bobby Hall was captured immediately after his helicopter went down, but his co-pilot, CWO David Michael Hilemon, was killed in the crash.

While Hilemon's body was returned to U.S. authorities within a week, Hall was detained by the North Koreans pending an investigation of the incident. Thomas Hubbard, a U.S. State Department diplomat, was dispatched in late December to gain Hall's release amid concerns that the incident would jeopardize a fragile agreement over North Korea's nuclear program. On December 29, following a personal appeal from President Bill Clinton, U.S. and North Korean officials agreed to a written apology by Hall that acknowledged that the helicopter had "accidentally strayed into North Korea." He was released the following day.[8]

1995, Pakistan

On March 9 two American government workers were killed and another wounded in an ambush as they were being driven to the U.S. consulate in Karachi. The assassinations were linked to radical Islamic fundamentalists attempting to embarrass the pro-American government of Prime Minister Benazir Bhutto. The killings, which preceded a visit to Pakistan by First Lady Hillary Rodham Clinton by several weeks, also were believed to be connected to the Pakistani-American extradition a month earlier of Ramzi Yousef, the alleged mastermind of the February 1993 bombing of the World Trade Center building in New York City.

1995, Iraq

On March 13 two Americans, William Barloon and David Daliberti, strayed across the Iraqi-Kuwaiti border near Umm Qasr. The men, employees of a U.S. defense contractor in Kuwait, were trying to visit a friend working with the United Nations near the border when they were arrested by Iraqi police. Polish diplomats in Baghdad, on behalf of the United States, monitored the treatment and trial of the two Americans, who were sentenced on March 25 to eight years in prison for illegal entry into Iraq. On April 30 the wives of the two men visited their imprisoned husbands and made a personal plea for clemency to Iraqi President Saddam Hussein.[9]

NOTES

1. U.S. Department of State, *Bulletin* 81, #2048 (March 1981), 23–28, and *Bulletin* 81 #2049 (April 1981), 34–37; *Bulletin* 82, #2062 (May 1982), 63–64, and *Bulletin* 85, #2097 (April 1985), 65–66.

2. "Tredwell Set Free by the Bolsheviki," *New York Times*, May 4, 1919.

3. U.S. Department of State, *Papers Relating to the Foreign Relations of the United States, 1955–1957*, vol. 2, *China* (Washington, DC: Government Printing Office, 1986), 6–7, n. 4. See also *Public Papers of the Secretaries-General of the U.N.*, vol. 2, *Dag Hammarskjöld, 1953–1956*, ed. Andrew W. Cordier and Wilder Foote (New York: Columbia University Press, 1972), 415–59.

4. Jeffrey D. Simon, *The Terrorist Trap: America's Experience with Terrorism* (Bloomington: Indiana University Press, 1994), 53–59.

5. George P. Shultz, *Turmoil and Triumph: My Years as Secretary of State* (New York: Charles Scribner's Sons, 1993), 643–88, 783–813; Stansfield Turner, *Terrorism and Democracy* (Boston: Houghton Mifflin, 1991), 208–9; Terry Anderson, *Den of Lions: Memoirs of Seven Years* (New York: Crown Publishing, 1993).

6. Marilyn J. Young, "When the Shoe Is on the Other Foot: The Reagan Administration's Treatment of the Shootdown of Iran Air 655," in *Reagan and Public Discourse in America*, eds. Michael Weiler and W. Barnett Pearce (Tuscaloosa: University of Alabama Press, 1992), 203–24.

7. "Efforts Under Way to Free U.S. Envoy," *Knoxville News Sentinel*, November 28, 1993, A-8.

8. "North Koreans Release U.S. Helicopter Pilot: Negotiators for Both Sides Agree Flight Not a Spy Mission," ibid., December 30, 1994, A-1.]

9. "Iraq Sentences 2 Americans: Pair Facing 8-year Prison Terms," ibid., March 26, 1995, A-1.

Bibliography

ARCHIVES AND MANUSCRIPT COLLECTIONS

Foundation for Iranian Studies, 4343 Montgomery Avenue, Bethesda, Maryland
  Oral History Interviews of Archie Bolster, Farah Ebrahimi,
    Theodore Eliot, Mansur Farhang, Richard Helms, William
    Lehfeldt, John Macy, Jack Miklos, Charles Naas, Earnest Oney,
    Sir Anthony Parsons, and Sir Peter Ramsbotham
National Archives, Washington, DC
  Record Group 59. General Records of the Department of State
    Consular Dispatches—Sofia
      Bulgarian Series, 1901–1904
  Record Group 84. Records of the Foreign Service Posts of the
    Department of State
  National Archives Microfilm Publications (NAMP)
    Notes from the Legation of Tunis
    Diplomatic Instructions—American States
    Diplomatic Instructions—Turkey
    Diplomatic Instructions—Chile
    Diplomatic Instructions—China
    Notes to Foreign Legations—Chile
    Russia and the Soviet Union, 1910–1929
University of Arkansas Library, Fayetteville, Arkansas
  Papers of J. William Fulbright

GOVERNMENT DOCUMENTS

Carter, Jimmy E. *Public Papers of the Presidents of the United States: Jimmy Carter, 1979.* 2 vols. Washington, DC: Government Printing Office, 1980.

Harrison, Benjamin. *Public Papers and Addresses of Benjamin Harrison, Twenty-third President of the United States, March 4, 1889–March 4, 1893.* Washington, DC: Government Printing Office, 1893.

Reagan, Ronald. *Public Papers of the Presidents of the United States, Ronald Reagan, 1981.* Washington, DC: Government Printing Office, 1982.

———. *Public Papers of the Presidents of the United States, Ronald Reagan, 1983–1986.* Washington, DC: Government Printing Office, 1984–1987.

Roosevelt, Theodore. *Theodore Roosevelt Papers*. Presidential Papers Microfilm. (Roosevelt-Hay Letters, 1897–1905) Washington, DC: Library of Congress, 1967.

Tower, John, Edmund Muskie, and Brent Scowcroft. *Report of the President's Special Review Board*. Washington, DC: Government Printing Office, 1987.

U.S. Congress. House and Senate. *Report of the Congressional Committees Investigating the Iran-Contra Affair* (H.Rept.100-433/S.Rept.100-216). Washington, DC: Government Printing Office, 1987.

U.S. Congress. House. *Register of Debates in Congress*. 22d Cong., 1st sess., 1831–32. Washington, DC: Gales and Seaton, 1832.

―――. ―――. Committee on Claims. *Repayment of Ransom of Ellen Stone*. Report 807, 62d Cong., 2d sess., May 31, 1912. Washington, DC: Government Printing Office, 1912.

―――. ―――. Report of the Special Subcommittee on the U.S.S. *Pueblo*. *Inquiry into the U.S.S. Pueblo and EC-121 Plane Incidents*. 91st Cong., 1st sess., July 28, 1969. Washington, DC: Government Printing Office, 1969.

―――. ―――. Report to House Committee on Foreign Affairs, Research Service, Library of Congress. *The Iran Hostage Crisis: A Chronology of Daily Developments*. 97th Cong., 1st sess. Washington, DC: Government Printing Office, 1981.

U.S. Congress. Senate. Committee on Foreign Relations. *Ransom of Miss Ellen M. Stone*. 63d Cong., 1st sess., document no. 29, May 14, 1913. Washington, DC: Government Printing Office, 1913.

―――. ―――. Committee on Foreign Relations. Subcommittee Staff Report. *U.S. Military Sales to Iran*. 94th Cong., 2nd sess., July 1976. Washington, DC: Government Printing Office, 1976.

U.S. Department of State. *American State Papers*. 38 vols. Washington, DC: Gales and Seaton, 1832–1861.

―――. *Papers Relating to the Foreign Relations of the United States*: 1891; 1900; 1902; 1904; 1918 (*Russia*, vols. 1–3); 1919; 1920; 1921; 1943; 1945 (*Europe*, vol. 5); 1945 (*The Conferences at Malta and Yalta*); 1948 (vols. 1–9); 1949 (vols. 1–8). Washington, DC: Government Printing Office, 1892–1976.

―――. *Bulletin*. December 1949; January 1969; March 1981; April 1981; May 1982; April 1985.

―――. OSS/State Department, Office of Intelligence and Research Reports. Washington, DC: Government Printing Office, 1949.

Walsh, Lawrence E. *Final Report of the Independent Counsel for Iran/ Contra Matters*. 3 vols. Washington, DC: U.S. Court of Appeals for the District of Columbia Circuit Division for the Purpose of Appointing Independent Counsel, 1994.

Weekly Compilation of Presidential Documents. Vol. 21 (January–June 1985). Washington, DC: Government Printing Office, 1986.

BOOKS

Abel, Elie, and W. Averell Harriman. *Special Envoy to Churchill and Stalin, 1941–1946*. New York: Random House, 1975.

Abrams, Elliott. *Undue Process: A Story of How Political Differences Are Turned into Crimes*. New York: Free Press, 1993.

Acheson, Dean. *Present at the Creation: My Years in the State Department*. New York: W. W. Norton and Company, 1969.

Adams, Henry. *The Education of Henry Adams*. Boston: Houghton Mifflin Company, 1961.

Afkhami, Gholam Reza, and Seyyed Vali Reza Nasr, eds. *The Oral History Collection of the Foundation for Iranian Studies*. Bethesda, MD: Foundation for Iranian Studies, 1991.

Allen, Gardner W. *Our Navy and the Barbary Corsairs*. Boston: Houghton Mifflin Company, 1905.

Alliluyeva, Svetlana. *Only One Year*. New York: Harper and Row, 1969.

Allison, Graham, and Gregory Treverton, eds. *Rethinking America's Security: Beyond the Cold War to New World Order*. New York: W. W. Norton and Company, 1992.

Ambrosius, Lloyd E. *Wilsonian Statecraft: Theory and Practice of Liberal Internationalism during World War I*. Wilmington, DE: Scholarly Resources, 1991.

———. *Woodrow Wilson and the American Diplomatic Tradition: The Treaty Fight in Perspective*. New York: Cambridge University Press, 1987.

Anderson, Terry. *Den of Lions: Memoirs of Seven Years*. New York: Crown Publishing, 1993.

Armbrister, Trevor. *A Matter of Accountability: The True Story of the Pueblo Affair*. New York: Coward-McCann, 1970.

Bailey, Thomas. *The Pugnacious Presidents: White House Parade*. New York: Free Press, 1980.

Bamford, Paul W. *The Barbary Pirates: Victims and the Scourge of Christendom*. Minneapolis: University of Minnesota Press, 1972.

Bani-sadr, Abol Hassan. *My Turn to Speak: Iran, the Revolution, and Secret Deals with the U.S.* Washington, DC: Brasseys, 1991.

Barnby, H. G. *The Prisoners of Algiers*. London: Oxford University Press, 1966.

Battistini, Lawrence H. *The Rise of American Influence in Asia and the Pacific*. East Lansing: Michigan State University Press, 1960.

Bauer, K. Jack, ed. *The New American State Papers, Naval Affairs, 1789–1860*. Vol. 2, *Diplomatic Activities*. Wilmington, DE: Scholarly Resources, 1981.

Bayne, E. A. *Persian Kingship in Transition*. New York: American Universities Field Staff, 1968.

Beale, Howard K. *Theodore Roosevelt and the Rise of America to World Power*. Baltimore, MD: Johns Hopkins University Press, 1956.

Beckwith, Charlie A., and Donald Knox. *Delta Force: The Army's Elite Counterterrorist Unit.* New York: Dell Publishing Company, 1985.

Bell, J. Bowyer. *Transnational Terror.* Washington, DC: American Enterprise Institute for Public Policy Research, 1975.

Belohlavek, John M. *Let the Eagle Soar: The Foreign Policy of Andrew Jackson.* Lincoln: University of Nebraska Press, 1985.

Bemis, Samuel F., ed. *The American Secretaries of State and Their Diplomacy.* 10 vols. New York: Cooper Square Publishers, 1963.

Bill, James A. *The Eagle and the Lion: The Tragedy of American-Iranian Relations.* New Haven, CT: Yale University Press, 1988.

Billington, Ray Allen. *Westward Expansion: A History of the American Frontier.* 5th ed. New York: Macmillan Company, 1982.

Bixler, Raymond. *The Open Door on the Old Barbary Coast.* New York: Pageant Press, 1959.

Blum, Robert M. *Drawing the Line: The Origins of the American Containment Policy in East Asia.* New York: W. W. Norton and Company, 1982.

Bohlen, Charles E. *Witness to History.* New York: W. W. Norton and Company, 1973.

Borg, Dorothy, and Waldo Heinrichs, eds. *Uncertain Years: Chinese-American Relations, 1947–1950.* New York: Columbia University Press, 1980.

Borisov, O. B., and B. T. Koloskov. *Soviet-Chinese Relations, 1945–1970.* Bloomington: Indiana University Press, 1975.

Boyd, Julian P., et al., eds. *The Papers of Thomas Jefferson.* 24 vols. Princeton, NJ: Princeton University Press, 1950–1992.

Bradley, John. *Allied Intervention in Russia.* New York: Basic Books, 1968.

Brandt, Ed. *The Last Voyage of the U.S.S. Pueblo.* New York: W. W. Norton and Company, 1969.

Brzezinski, Zbigniew. *Power and Principle: Memoirs of the National Security Advisor, 1977–1981.* New York: Farrar, Straus and Giroux, 1983.

Bucher, Lloyd, with Mark Rascovich. *Bucher: My Story.* Garden City, NY: Doubleday and Company, 1970.

Buhite, Russell D. *Decisions at Yalta: An Appraisal of Summit Diplomacy.* Wilmington, DE: Scholarly Resources, 1986.

———. *Soviet-American Relations in Asia, 1945–1954.* Norman: University of Oklahoma Press, 1981.

Burgess, John W. *Reconstruction and the Constitution, 1866–1876.* New York: Charles Scribner's Sons, 1901.

———. *Political Science and Comparative Constitutional Law.* 2d ed. Boston: Ginn and Company, 1890.

Bush, George. *Looking Forward.* New York: Doubleday and Company, 1987.

Byrnes, James. *All in One Lifetime.* New York: Harper, 1958.

Cannon, Lou. *President Reagan: The Role of a Lifetime.* New York: Simon and Schuster, 1991.

Carlson, Kurt. *One American Must Die: A Hostage's Personal Account of the Hijacking of Flight 847*. Chicago: Congdon and Weed, 1986.

Carter, Jimmy. *Keeping Faith: Memoirs of a President*. New York: Bantam Books, 1982.

Cathcart, James Leander, and J. B. Cathcart Newkirk. *The Captives: Eleven Years a Prisoner in Algiers*. La Porte, IN: Herald Point, 1899.

Chang, Gordon H. *Friends and Enemies: The United States, China, and the Soviet Union, 1948–1972*. Stanford, CA: Stanford University Press, 1990.

Christopher, Warren, et al. *American Hostages in Iran: The Conduct of a Crisis*. New Haven, CT: Yale University Press, 1985.

Churchill, Winston S. *Triumph and Tragedy*. Vol. 6, *The Second World War*. New York: Houghton Mifflin, 1986.

Clubb, O. Edmund. *China and Russia: The "Great Game."* New York: Columbia University Press, 1971.

Clyde, Paul H., ed. *United States Policy toward China: Diplomatic and Public Documents, 1839–1939*. 2d ed. New York: Russell and Russell, 1964.

Cohen, Warren I., ed. *The Cambridge History of American Foreign Relations*. 4 vols. New York: Cambridge University Press, 1993.

Cohen, William S., and George J. Mitchell. *Men of Zeal: A Candid Inside Story of the Iran-Contra Hearings*. New York: Viking Press, 1988.

Conklin, Paul K. *Prophets of Prosperity: America's First Political Economists*. Bloomington: Indiana University Press, 1980.

Cooling, Benjamin F. *Benjamin Franklin Tracy: Father of the Modern American Fighting Navy*. Hamden, CT: Archon, 1973.

Cooper, John M., Jr. *The Warrior and the Priest: Woodrow Wilson and Theodore Roosevelt*. Cambridge, MA: Harvard University Press, 1983.

Crapol, Edward P. *America for Americans: Economic Nationalism and Anglophobia in the Late Nineteenth Century*. Westport, CT: Greenwood Press, 1973.

Cray, Ed. *General of the Army: George C. Marshall, Soldier and Statesman*. New York: W. W. Norton and Company, 1990.

Crelinsten, Ronald, and Denis Szabo. *Hostage-Taking*. Lexington, MA: D. C. Heath and Company, 1979.

Crenshaw, Martha, ed. *Terrorism, Legitimacy, and Power: The Consequences of Political Violence*. Hanover, NH: University Press of New England, 1983.

Curtis, James C. *Andrew Jackson and the Search for Vindication*. Boston: Little, Brown and Company, 1976.

Dallin, Alexander. *German Rule in Russia*. New York: St. Martin's Press, 1957.

Deane, John R. *The Strange Alliance: The Story of Our Efforts at Wartime Cooperation with Russia*. New York: Viking Press, 1947.

DeConde, Alexander, ed. *Encyclopedia of American Foreign Policy: Studies of the Principal Movements and Ideas*. 3 vols. New York: Charles Scribner's Sons, 1978.

DeVoto, Bernard, ed. *Mark Twain in Eruption*. New York: Harper and Brothers, 1940.

Dingley, Edward Nelson. *The Life and Times of Nelson Dingley, Jr.* Kalamazoo, MI: Ihling Brothers and Everand, 1902.

Dobson, Christopher, and Ronald Payne. *The Never-Ending War: Terrorism in the 80s*. New York: Facts on File Publications, 1987.

Draper, Theodore. *A Very Thin Line: The Iran-Contra Affairs*. New York: Hill and Wang, 1991.

Duiker, William J. *Cultures in Collision: The Boxer Rebellion*. San Rafael, CA: Presidio Press, 1978.

Dulles, Foster R. *American Policy toward Communist China, 1949–1969*. Arlington Heights, IL: Harlan Davidson, 1972.

Earle, Peter. *Corsairs of Malta and Barbary*. London: Sidgwick and Jackson, 1970.

Elliot, Mark R. *Pawns of Yalta: Soviet Refugees and America's Role in Their Repatriation*. Urbana: University of Illinois Press, 1982.

Emerson, Steve. *Secret Warriors: Inside the Covert Military Operations of the Reagan Era*. New York: Putnam Publishing Group, 1988.

———, and Brian Duffy. *The Fall of Pan Am 103: Inside the Lockerbie Investigation*. New York: Putnam Publishing Group, 1990.

Esherick, Joseph W. *The Origins of the Boxer Uprising*. Berkeley: University of California Press, 1987.

Evans, Henry C., Jr. *Chile and Its Relations with the United States*. Durham, NC: Duke University Press, 1927.

Fairbank, John K., ed. *The Missionary Enterprise in China and America*. Cambridge, MA: Harvard University Press, 1974.

Farrell, William R. *The U.S. Government Response to Terrorism, 1972–1980: In Search of an Effective Strategy*. Boulder, CO: Westview Press, 1982.

Feis, Herbert. *Churchill, Roosevelt, Stalin: The War They Waged and the Peace They Sought*. Princeton, NJ: Princeton University Press, 1957.

Ferrell, Robert H. *Woodrow Wilson and World War I: Nineteen Seventeen to Nineteen Twenty-one*. New York: HarperCollins, 1985.

Field, James A. *America and the Mediterranean World, 1776–1882*. Princeton, NJ: Princeton University Press, 1969.

Fiske, John. *The Destiny of Man*. Boston: Houghton Mifflin Company, 1881.

Fleming, Peter. *The Siege of Peking*. New York: Harper and Brothers, 1959.

Follett, Ken. *On Wings of Eagles*. New York: William Morrow and Company, 1983.

Ford, Gerald R. *A Time to Heal: The Autobiography of Gerald R. Ford*. New York: Harper and Row, 1979.

Foster, John W. *American Diplomacy in the Orient*. Boston: Houghton Mifflin Company, 1903.

Fredrickson, George. *The Inner Civil War: Northern Intellectuals and the Crisis of the Union*. New York: Harper and Row, 1965.

Freedman, Lawrence Zelic, and Yonah Alexander, eds. *Perspectives on Terrorism*. Wilmington, DE: Scholarly Resources, 1983.

Friedlander, Robert A. *Global Terrorism in the Dangerous Decade*. Vol. 6. New York: Oceana Publications, 1992.

Fuller, Graham E. *The Center of the Universe: The Geopolitics of Iran*. Boulder, CO: Westview Press, 1991.

Gaddis, John Lewis. *The Long Peace: Inquiries into the History of the Cold War*. New York: Oxford University Press, 1987.

―――. *Strategies of Containment: A Critical Appraisal of Postwar American National Security Policy*. New York: Oxford University Press, 1982.

Gallery, Daniel V. *The Pueblo Incident*. New York: Doubleday and Company, 1970.

Gardner, Lloyd C. *Safe for Democracy: The Anglo-American Response to Revolution, 1913–1923*. New York: Oxford University Press, 1987.

Gilderhus, Mark T. *Diplomacy and Revolution: U.S.-Mexican Relations under Wilson and Carranza*. Tucson: University of Arizona Press, 1977.

Gittings, John. *The World and China, 1922–1972*. New York: Harper and Row, 1974.

Goebel, Julius, Jr. *The Struggle for the Falkland Islands*. New Haven, CT: Yale University Press, 1927.

Goetzmann, William H. *When the Eagle Screamed: The Romantic Horizon in American Diplomacy, 1800–1860*. New York: John Wiley and Sons, 1966.

Goldberg, Joyce. *The Baltimore Affair*. Lincoln: University of Nebraska Press, 1986.

Goldhurst, Richard. *The Midnight War: The American Intervention in Russia, 1918–1920*. New York: McGraw-Hill, 1978.

Graber, Doris A. *Crisis Diplomacy: A History of U.S. Intervention Policies*. Washington, DC: Public Affairs Press, 1959.

Griffin, Eldon. *Clippers and Consuls: American Consular and Commercial Relations with Eastern Asia, 1845–1860*. Ann Arbor: University of Michigan Press, 1938.

Haig, Alexander M., Jr. *Caveat: Realism, Reagan, and Foreign Policy*. New York: Macmillan Company, 1984.

Halberstam, David. *The Best and the Brightest*. New York: Fawcett Books, 1973.

Han, Henry H., ed. *Terrorism and Political Violence: Limits and Possibilities of Legal Control*. Vol. 2, *Terrorism: Documents of International and Local Control*. New York: Ocean Publications, 1993.

Hanle, Donald J. *Terrorism: The Newest Face of Warfare*. Washington, DC: Pergamon-Brassey's, 1989.

Harbaugh, William Henry. *Power and Responsibility: The Life and Times of Theodore Roosevelt*. New York: Farrar, Straus and Cudahy, 1961.

Harding, Harry, and Yuan Ming, eds. *Sino-American Relations, 1945–1955: A Joint Reassessment of a Critical Decade*. Wilmington, DE: Scholarly Resources, 1989.

Hastings, Max, and Simon Jenkins. *The Battle for the Falklands.* New York: W. W. Norton and Company, 1983.

Hatcher, William. *Edward Livingston: Jeffersonian Republican and Jacksonian Democrat.* Baton Rouge: Louisiana State University Press, 1940.

Hay, John. *Letters of John Hay and Extracts from His Diary.* 2 vols. Staten Island, NY: Gordian Press, 1969.

Hilsman, Roger. *The Politics of Policymaking in Defense and Foreign Affairs: Conceptual Models and Bureaucratic Politics.* 3d ed. Englewood Cliffs, NJ: Prentice-Hall, 1993.

Hoffman, Fritz L., and Olga M. Hoffman. *Sovereignty in Dispute: The Falklands/Malvinas, 1493–1982.* Boulder, CO: Westview Press, 1984.

Hourani, Albert. *A History of the Arab Peoples.* Cambridge, MA: Harvard University Press, 1991.

Howard, Lawrence, ed. *Terrorism: Roots, Impact, and Responses.* New York: Praeger, 1992.

Hunt, Michael H. *Ideology and U.S. Foreign Policy.* New Haven, CT: Yale University Press, 1987.

Huyser, Robert E. *Mission to Tehran.* New York: Harper and Row, 1986.

Iriye, Akira. *The Cold War in Asia: A Historical Introduction.* Englewood Cliffs, NJ: Prentice-Hall, 1974.

Irwin, Ray W. *The Diplomatic Relations of the United States with the Barbary Powers, 1776–1816.* Chapel Hill: University of North Carolina Press, 1931.

Janis, Irving L. *Crucial Decisions: Leadership in Policymaking and Crisis Management.* New York: Free Press, 1989.

Jervis, Robert, and Jack Snyder. *Dominoes and Bandwagons: Strategic Beliefs and Great Power Competition in the Eurasian Rimland.* New York: Oxford University Press, 1991.

Johnson, Haynes. *Sleepwalking through History: America in the Reagan Years.* New York: W. W. Norton and Company, 1991.

Johnson, Lyndon B. *The Vantage Point.* New York: Popular Library, 1971.

Jones, Elizabeth, ed. *Declassified Documents Reference System.* 7 vols. Washington, DC: Carrollton Press, 1975–1981.

Jordan, Hamilton. *Crisis: The Last Year of the Carter Presidency.* New York: G. P. Putnam's Sons, 1982.

Katouzian, Homa. *The Political Economy of Modern Iran: Despotism and Pseudo-Modernism, 1926–1979.* New York: New York University Press, 1981.

Kegley, Charles W., ed. *International Terrorism: Characteristics, Causes, Controls.* New York: St. Martin's Press, 1990.

Kennan, George F. *The Decision to Intervene.* Princeton, NJ: Princeton University Press, 1958.

———. *Russia Leaves the War.* Princeton, NJ: Princeton University Press, 1956.

———. *Russia and the West under Lenin and Stalin.* New York: New American Library, 1962.

Kennedy, Moorhead. *The Ayatollah in the Cathedral: Reflections of a Hostage.* New York: Hill and Wang, 1986.

Klay, Andor. *Daring Diplomacy: The Case of the First American Ultimatum.* Minneapolis: University of Minnesota Press, 1957.

Koen, Ross Y. *The China Lobby in American Politics.* 2d ed. New York: Harper and Row, 1974.

Korn, David A. *Assassination in Khartoum.* Bloomington: Indiana University Press, 1993.

Kornbluh, Peter, and Malcolm Byrne, eds. *The Iran Contra Scandal: The Declassified History.* New York: New Press, 1993.

Kuniholm, Bruce R. *The Origins of the Cold War in the Near East: Great Power Conflict and Diplomacy in Iran, Turkey, and Greece.* Princeton, NJ: Princeton University Press, 1980.

Kupperman, Robert, and Jeff Kamen. *Final Warning: Averting Disaster in the New Age of Terrorism.* New York: Doubleday and Company, 1989.

Laingen, Bruce. *Yellow Ribbon: The Secret Journal of Bruce Laingen.* Washington, DC: Brassey's, 1992.

Laqueur, Walter. *The Age of Terrorism.* New York: Little, Brown and Company, 1987.

Ledeen, Michael A. *Perilous Statecraft: An Insider's Account of the Iran-Contra Affair.* New York: Scribner's, 1988.

―――, and William Lewis. *Debacle: The American Failure in Iran.* New York: Alfred A. Knopf, 1981.

Lee, Luke T. *The Vienna Convention on Consular Relations.* Leiden, the Netherlands: A. W. Sijthoff, 1966.

Leffler, Melvyn. *A Preponderance of Power: National Security, the Truman Administration, and the Cold War.* Stanford, CA: Stanford University Press, 1992.

Levitt, Geoffrey M. *Democracies against Terror: The Western Response to State-Supported Terrorism.* New York: Praeger, 1988.

Link, Arthur S. *Woodrow Wilson: Revolution, War, and Peace.* Arlington Heights, IL: Harlan Davidson, 1979.

Livingston, Marius H., ed. *International Terrorism in the Contemporary World.* Westport, CT: Greenwood Press, 1978.

Livingston, Steven. *The Terrorism Spectacle.* Boulder, CO: Westview Press, 1994.

Lockhart, R. H. Bruce. *British Agent.* Garden City, NY: Doubleday and Company, 1933.

Long, David E. *Anatomy of Terrorism.* New York: Free Press, 1990.

Long, David F. *Gold Braid and Foreign Relations: Diplomatic Activities of U.S. Naval Officers, 1798–1883.* Annapolis, MD: Naval Institute Press, 1988.

MacWillson, Alastair C. *Hostage-Taking Terrorism: Incident-Response Strategy.* New York: St. Martin's Press, 1991.

Maddox, Robert J. *The Unknown War with Russia: Wilson's Siberian Intervention.* San Rafael, CA: Presidio Press, 1977.

Malone, Dumas. *Jefferson and the Rights of Man.* Boston: Little, Brown and Company, 1951.

Manning, William R. *Diplomatic Correspondence of the United States: Inter-American Affairs, 1831–1860.* 12 vols. Washington, DC: Carnegie Endowment, 1932–1939.

Mao Zedong. *On People's Democratic Dictatorship.* Beijing: Foreign Language Press, 1952.

Marks, Frederick W. *Independence on Trial: Foreign Affairs and the Making of the Constitution.* 1973. Reprint, Wilmington, DE: Scholarly Resources, 1986.

———. *Velvet on Iron: The Diplomacy of Theodore Roosevelt.* Lincoln: University of Nebraska Press, 1979.

Martin, David C., and John Walcott. *Best Laid Plans: The Inside Story of America's War on Terrorism.* New York: Harper and Row, 1988.

Martin, Edwin W. *Divided Counsel: The Anglo-American Response to Communist Victory in China.* Lexington: University Press of Kentucky, 1986.

May, Ernest R. *The Truman Administration and China, 1945–1949.* Philadelphia: J. B. Lippincott, 1975.

———, and Richard E. Neustadt. *Thinking in Time: The Uses of History for Decision Makers.* New York: Free Press, 1986.

May, Henry F. *The End of American Innocence: A Study of the First Years of Our Time, 1912–1917.* New York: Alfred P. Knopf, 1959.

Mayers, David. *Cracking the Monolith: U.S. Policy against the Sino-Soviet Alliance, 1949–1955.* Baton Rouge: Louisiana State University Press, 1986.

McFadden, Robert D., Joseph B. Treaster, and Maurice Carroll. *No Hiding Place: N.Y. Times Inside Report on the Hostage Crisis.* New York: Times Books, 1981.

McFarlane, Robert C., with Zofia Smardz. *Special Trust.* New York: Codell and Davies, 1994.

Meese, Edwin, III. *With Reagan.* Washington, DC: Regnery Gateway, 1992.

Menges, Constantine. *Inside the National Security Council: The True Story of the Making and Unmaking of Reagan's Foreign Policy.* New York: Simon and Schuster, 1988.

Merk, Frederick. *Manifest Destiny and Mission in American History: A Reinterpretation.* New York: Alfred A. Knopf, 1963.

Merli, Frank J., and Theodore A. Wilson, eds. *Makers of American Diplomacy: From Benjamin Franklin to Henry Kissinger.* New York: Scribner's, 1974.

Miller, Abraham H. *Terrorism and Hostage Negotiations.* Boulder, CO: Westview Press, 1980.

Miller, Nathan. *Theodore Roosevelt: A Life.* New York: William Morrow and Company, 1992.

Millett, Allan R. *Semper Fidelis: The History of the United States Marine Corps.* New York: Macmillan Company, 1980.

————, and Peter Maslowski. *For the Common Defense: A Military History of the United States, 1607–1983.* New York: Free Press, 1984.

Miroff, Bruce. *Icons of Democracy: American Leaders as Heroes, Aristocrats, Dissenters, and Democrats.* New York: Basic Books, 1993.

Moore, John Bassett. *A Digest of International Law.* 8 vols. Washington, DC: Government Printing Office, 1886–1906.

Morison, Elting E., ed. *The Letters of Theodore Roosevelt.* 8 vols. Cambridge, MA: Harvard University Press, 1951–1954.

Mowry, George E. *Era of Theodore Roosevelt, 1900–1912.* New York: Harper and Row, 1958.

Moyers, Bill. *The Secret Government: The Constitution in Crisis.* Cabin John, MD: Seven Locks Press, 1988.

Muir, William Ker, Jr. *The Bully Pulpit: The Presidential Leadership of Ronald Reagan.* San Francisco: Institute for Contemporary Studies Press, 1992.

Nagai, Yonosuke, and Akira Iriye, eds. *The Origins of the Cold War in Asia.* New York: Columbia University Press, 1977.

North, Oliver, with William Novak. *Under Fire: An American Story.* New York: HarperCollins, 1991.

Norton, Augustus R. *International Terrorism: An Annotated Bibliography and Research Guide.* Boulder, CO: Westview Press, 1980.

Nuechterlein, Donald. *National Interests and Presidential Leadership: The Setting of Priorities.* Boulder, CO: Westview Press, 1978.

Ochberg, Frank M., and David A. Soskis, eds. *Victims of Terror.* Boulder, CO: Westview Press, 1982.

O'Connor, Richard. *The Spirit Soldiers: A Historical Narrative on the Boxer Rebellion.* New York: Putnam Publishing Group, 1973.

Osgood, Robert. *Ideals and Self-Interest in America's Foreign Relations.* Chicago: University of Chicago Press, 1953.

Pahlavi, Mohammad Reza. *Answer to History.* New York: Stein and Day, 1980.

Parsons, Anthony. *The Pride and the Fall: Iran, 1974–1979.* London: Jonathan Cope, 1984.

Paterson, Thomas G. *On Every Front: The Making of the Cold War.* New York: W. W. Norton and Company, 1979.

Perkins, Bradford. *The First Rapprochement: England and the United States, 1795–1805.* Philadelphia: University of Pennsylvania Press, 1955.

Perry, Duncan M. *The Politics of Terror: The Macedonian Revolutionary Movements, 1893–1903.* Durham, NC: Duke University Press, 1988.

Peterson, Harold F. *Argentina and the United States, 1810–1960.* New York: State University of New York Press, 1964.

Peterson, Merrill D., ed. *The Political Writings of Thomas Jefferson.* Monticello, VA: Thomas Jefferson Memorial Foundation, 1993.

Pike, Fredrick B. *Chile and the United States, 1880–1962: The Emergence of Chile's Social Crisis and the Challenge to U.S. Diplomacy.* Notre Dame, IN: Notre Dame University Press, 1963.

Pringle, Henry. *Theodore Roosevelt: A Biography*. New York: Harcourt, Brace and Company, 1931.

Purcell, Victor. *The Boxer Uprising: A Background Study*. London: Archon, 1963.

Qiang Zhai. *The Dragon, the Lion, and the Eagle: Chinese-British-American Relations, 1949–1958*. Kent, OH: Kent State University Press, 1994.

Rapoport, David C., and Yonah Alexander. *The Morality of Terrorism: Religious and Secular Justifications*. 2d. ed. New York: Columbia University Press, 1989.

Reagan, Ronald. *An American Life: The Autobiography*. New York: Simon and Schuster, 1990.

Regan, Donald. *For the Record: From Wall Street to Washington*. New York: Harcourt Brace Jovanovich, 1988.

Remini, Robert V. *Andrew Jackson*. 3 vols. New York: Harper and Row, 1977–1984.

Reynolds, Jeremiah. *Voyage of the United States Frigate Potomac during the Circumnavigation of the Globe, 1831–1834*. New York: Harper and Brothers, 1835.

Rhodes, Benjamin D. *The Anglo-American Winter War with Russia, 1918–19: A Diplomatic and Military Tragicomedy*. New York: Greenwood Press, 1988.

Richardson, James D., comp. *A Compilation of the Messages and Papers of the Presidents, 1789–1902*. Vol. 2. Washington, DC: Bureau of National Literature and Art, 1903.

Roosevelt, Theodore. *Theodore Roosevelt: An Autobiography*. New York: Macmillan Company, 1913.

Rosen, Barbara, and Barry Rosen, with George Feifer. *The Destined Hour: The Hostage Crisis and One Family's Ordeal*. Garden City, NY: Doubleday and Company, 1982.

Rourke, John. *Congress and the Presidency in U.S. Foreign Policymaking: A Study of Interaction and Influence, 1945–1982*. Boulder, CO: Westview Press, 1983.

Rubin, Barry. *Secrets of State: The State Department and the Struggle over U.S. Foreign Policy*. New York: Oxford University Press, 1987.

Rusk, Dean, and Richard Rusk. *As I Saw It*, ed. Daniel S. Papp. New York: W. W. Norton and Company, 1990.

Scalapino, Robert A., and Chong-Sik Lee. *Communism in Korea*. 2 vols. Berkeley: University of California Press, 1973.

Schiller, Daniel. *Objectivity and the News: The Public and the Rise of Commercial Journalism*. Philadelphia: University of Pennsylvania Press, 1981.

Schlesinger, Arthur M., Jr. *The Imperial Presidency*. Boston: Houghton Mifflin Company, 1973.

Schley, Winfield S. *Forty-Five Years under the Flag*. New York: D. Appleton, 1904.

Schmid, Alex P. *Political Terrorism: A Research Guide to Concepts, Theories, Data Bases, and Literature.* 2d ed. New Brunswick, NJ: Transaction Publications, 1988.

Schumacher, F. Carl, Jr., and George C. Wilson. *Bridge of No Return: The Ordeal of the U.S.S. Pueblo.* New York: Harcourt Brace Jovanovich, 1971.

Sellers, Charles. *The Market Revolution: Jacksonian America, 1815–1846.* New York: Oxford University Press, 1992.

Shafritz, Jay, E. F. Gibbons, Jr., and Gregory Scott. *Almanac of Modern Terrorism.* New York: Facts on File Publications, 1991.

Sherman, Laura M. *Fires on the Mountain: The Macedonian Revolutionary Movement and the Kidnapping of Ellen Stone.* New York: Columbia University Press, 1980.

Sherman, William R. *The Diplomatic and Commercial Relations of the United States and Chile, 1820–1914.* Boston: Gorham Press, 1926.

Shultz, George P. *Turmoil and Triumph: My Years as Secretary of State.* New York: Charles Scribner's Sons, 1993.

Sick, Gary. *All Fall Down: America's Tragic Encounter with Iran.* New York: Random House, 1985.

———. *October Surprise: America's Hostages in Iran and the Election of Ronald Reagan.* New York: Random House, 1991.

Simon, Jeffrey D. *The Terrorist Trap: America's Experience with Terrorism.* Bloomington: Indiana University Press, 1994.

Smith, Culver H. *The Press, Politics, and Patronage: The American Government's Use of Newspapers.* Athens: University of Georgia Press, 1977.

Spencer, Ivor D. *The Victor and the Spoils: A Life of William L. Marcy.* Providence, RI: Brown University Press, 1959.

Stavrianos, Leften Stavros. *The Balkans since 1453.* New York: Reinhart, 1958.

Steiger, George Nye. *China and the Occident: The Origin and Development of the Boxer Rebellion.* New York: Russell and Russell, 1966.

Stohl, Michael, and George A. Lopez, eds. *Terrible beyond Endurance? The Foreign Policy of State Terrorism.* Westport, CT: Greenwood Press, 1988.

Strong, Josiah. *Our Country: Its Possible Future and Its Present Crisis.* Rev. ed. New York: Baker and Taylor, 1891.

Stuart, Graham H. *American Diplomatic and Consular Practice.* 2d ed. New York: Irvington, 1952.

Stuart, John Leighton. *Fifty Years in China: The Memoirs of John Leighton Stuart, Missionary and Ambassador.* New York: Random House, 1954.

Sullivan, William H. *Mission to Iran.* New York: W. W. Norton and Company, 1981.

Tang Tsou. *America's Failure in China, 1941–1950.* Chicago: University of Chicago Press, 1963.

Thorpe, Francis N., ed. *The Statesmanship of Andrew Jackson, as Told in His Writings and Speeches.* New York: Tandy-Thomas Company, 1909.

Topping, Seymour. *Journey between Two Chinas*. New York: Harper and Row, 1974.

Truman, Harry S. *Memoirs*. 2 vols. Garden City, NY: Doubleday and Company, 1955–56.

Tucker, Glenn. *Dawn Like Thunder: The Barbary Wars and the Birth of the U.S. Navy*. Indianapolis: Bobbs-Merrill, 1963.

Tucker, Nancy B. *Patterns in the Dust: Chinese-American Relations and the Recognition Controversy, 1949–50*, ed. William E. Leuchtenburg. New York: Columbia University Press, 1983.

Tulchin, Joseph S. *Argentina and the United States: A Conflicted Relationship*. New York: Macmillan Company, 1990.

Turner, Stansfield. *Terrorism and Democracy*. Boston: Houghton Mifflin Company, 1991.

Tyler, Alice F. *The Foreign Policy of James G. Blaine*. 1927. Reprint, Hamden, CT: Archon, 1965.

Uldricks, Teddy. *Diplomacy and Ideology: The Origins of Soviet Foreign Relations, 1917–1930*. London: Sage Publications, 1979.

Unterberger, Betty M. *The United States, Revolutionary Russia, and the Rise of Czechoslovakia*. Chapel Hill: University of North Carolina Press, 1989.

Vance, Cyrus. *Hard Choices: Critical Years in America's Foreign Policy*. New York: Simon and Schuster, 1983.

Varg, Paul A. *Foreign Policies of the Founding Fathers*. East Lansing: Michigan State University Press, 1963.

Vollmar, R. D., ed. *Declassified Documents Reference System*. 13 vols. Woodbridge, CT: Research Publications, 1982–1994.

Volwiler, Albert T., ed. *The Correspondence between Benjamin Harrison and James G. Blaine, 1882–1893*. Philadelphia: The American Philosophical Society, 1940.

Von Glahn, Gerhard. *Law among Nations: An Introduction to Public International Law*. 2d ed. Toronto: Macmillan and Company, 1970.

Wardlaw, Grant. *Political Terrorism: Theory, Tactics, and Countermeasures*. New York: Cambridge University Press, 1982.

Warriner, Francis. *Cruise of the U.S. Frigate Potomac Round the World, 1831–1834*. New York: Leavith, Lord and Company, 1835.

Weiler, Michael, and W. Barnett Pearce, eds. *Reagan and Public Discourse in America*. Tuscaloosa: University of Alabama Press, 1992.

Weinberger, Caspar. *Fighting for Peace*. New York: Warner Books, 1991.

Wells, Tim. *444 Days: The Hostages Remember*. San Diego: Harcourt Brace Jovanovich, 1985.

Whipple, A. B. C. *To the Shores of Tripoli: The Birth of the U.S. Navy and Marines*. New York: William Morrow and Company, 1991.

Wilkinson, Paul, and Alastair M. Stewart, eds. *Contemporary Research on Terrorism*. Aberdeen: Aberdeen University Press, 1987.

Wills, Garry. *Reagan's America: Innocents at Home*. New York: Doubleday and Company, 1987.

Wilson, R. Jackson. *In Quest of Community: Social Philosophy in the United States, 1860–1920*. New York: John Wiley and Sons, 1968.

Woodward, Bob. *VEIL: The Secret Wars of the CIA, 1981–1987.* New York: Simon and Schuster, 1987.

Wright, Louis B. *The First Americans in North Africa: William Eaton's Struggle for a Vigorous Policy against the Barbary Pirates, 1799–1805.* Princeton, NJ: Princeton University Press, 1945.

Wright, Robin. *Sacred Rage: The Wrath of Militant Islam.* New York: Simon and Schuster, 1985.

Wroe, Ann. *Lives, Lies, and the Iran-Contra Affair.* London: I. B. Tauris, 1991.

Yergin, Daniel. *Shattered Peace: Origins of the Cold War and the National Security State.* Boston: Houghton Mifflin Company, 1980.

———. *The Prize: The Epic Quest for Oil, Money, and Power.* New York: Simon and Schuster, 1991.

Young, Marilyn. *The Rhetoric of Empire: American China Policy, 1895–1901.* Cambridge, MA: Harvard University Press, 1968.

ARTICLES

Andonov-Polyanski, Hristo. "Miss Ellen Stone and the American Diplomatic Papers." *Macedonian Review* 8, no. 1 (1978): 42–52.

Armbruster, William A. "The Pueblo Crisis and Public Opinion." *Naval War College Review* 23, no. 7 (1971): 84–110.

Aston, Clive. "Hostage-Taking: A Conceptual Overview." In *Contemporary Terror: Studies in Sub-State Violence*, ed. David Carlton and Carlo Schaerf. New York: St. Martin's Press, 1981.

Baker, Liva. "Cathcart's Travels or a Dey in the Life of an American Sailor." *American Heritage* 26, no. 4 (June 1975): 53–85.

Beers, Burton. "Protection of American Citizens Abroad." In *Encyclopedia of American Foreign Policy*, 3 vols., ed. Alexander DeConde, 3:827–35. New York: Charles Scribner's Sons, 1978.

Belohlavek, John M. "Andrew Jackson and the Malaysian Pirates: A Question of Diplomacy and Politics." *Tennessee Historical Quarterly* 36 (Spring 1977): 19–29.

———. " 'Let the Eagle Soar!' Democratic Constraints on the Foreign Policy of Andrew Jackson." *Presidential Studies Quarterly* 10, no. 1 (1980): 36–50.

Bevans, Charles I., and Jerome H. Silber. "Contemporary Practice of the United States Relating to International Law." *American Journal of International Law* 62 (1968): 756–57.

Bishop, Joseph W., Jr. "Carter's Last Capitulation." *Commentary* 71, no. 3 (March 1981): 33–35.

Blankenship, Jane, and Janette Kenner Muir. "The Transformation of Actor to Scene: Some Strategic Grounds of the Reagan Legacy." In *Reagan and Public Discourse in America*, ed. Michael Werler and W. Barnett Pearce, 135–60. Tuscaloosa: University of Alabama Press, 1992.

Blum, Robert M. "The Peiping Cable." *New York Times*, August 13, 1978.

Borchard, Edwin M. "How Far Must We Protect Our Citizens Abroad?" *New Republic* 50 (13 April 1927): 214–16.

Brandt, Ed. "Seizure of Vessel Scored in Capital." *New York Times*, January 24, 1968.

Buhite, Russell D. "Soviet-American Relations and the Repatriation of Prisoners of War, 1945." *The Historian* 35, no. 3 (May 1973): 384–97.

Cantor, Milton. "Joel Barlow's Mission to Algiers." *The Historian* 25, no. 2 (February 1963): 172–94.

Carr, James A. "John Adams and the Barbary Problem: The Myth and the Record." *American Neptune* 26, no. 4 (October 1966): 231–57.

Carswell, Robert, and Richard J. Davis. "The Economic and Financial Pressures: Freeze and Sanctions." In Warren Christopher et al., *American Hostages in Iran: The Conduct of a Crisis*, 173–200. New Haven, CT: Yale University Press, 1985.

Clifford, J. Garry. "Bureaucratic Politics." In *Explaining the History of American Foreign Relations*, ed. Michael J. Hogan and Thomas G. Paterson, 141–50. New York: Cambridge University Press, 1991.

Curtis, James C. "Andrew Jackson: Symbol of What Age?" *Reviews in American History* 8 (1980): 194–99.

Cumberland, Charles C. "The Jenkins Case and Mexican-American Relations." *Hispanic American Historical Review* 31 (November 1951): 586–607.

Davis, Harold E. "The Citizenship of Ion Perdicaris." *Journal of Modern History* 13 (December 1941): 517–26.

Davis, Vincent. "A Commentary on the Pueblo Affair." *Aerospace Historian* 18, no. 2 (1971): 81–83.

Dickens, Paul D. "The Falkland Islands Dispute between the United States and Argentina." *Hispanic American Historical Review* 9 (1929): 471–87.

Earl, Robert L. "A Matter of Principle." *U.S. Naval Institute Proceedings* 109, no. 2 (February 1983): 29–36.

"Efforts Under Way to Free U.S. Envoy." *Knoxville News Sentinel*, November 28, 1993.

Etzold, Thomas. "Protection or Politics? 'Perdicaris Alive or Raisuli Dead.' " *The Historian* 37 (February 1975): 297–304.

Fiske, John. "Manifest Destiny." *Harper's Magazine*, 1885.

Fitzhugh, David. "Terrorism and Diplomacy." *Foreign Service Journal* (February 1977): 14–17.

Fork, P. J. "In the Clutches of the Barbary Corsairs." *Illinois Catholic Historical Review* 9 (1926): 162–76.

Friedland, Nehemia. "Hostage Negotiations: Dilemmas about Policy." In *Perspectives on Terrorism*, ed. Lawrence Zelic Freedman and Yonah Alexander, 201–11. Wilmington, DE: Scholarly Resources, 1983.

Gaddis, John Lewis. "Containment: A Reassessment." *Foreign Affairs* 56 (July 1977): 873–87.

Gazit, Shlomo. "Risk, Glory, and the Rescue Operation." *International Security* 6, no. 1 (Summer 1981): 111–35.

Glaser, David. "1919: William Jenkins, Robert Lansing, and the Mexican Interlude." *Southwestern Historical Quarterly* 74 (January 1971): 337–56.

Goldstein, Stephen M. "Chinese Communist Policy toward the United States: Opportunities and Constraints, 1944–1950." In *Uncertain Years: Chinese-American Relations, 1947–1950*, ed. Dorothy Borg and Waldo Heinrichs, 235–78. New York: Columbia University Press, 1980.

Grzybowski, Kazimierz. "The Regime of Diplomacy and the Tehran Hostages." *International and Comparative Law Quarterly* 30 (January 1981): 42–58.

Gwertzman, Bernard. "The Hostage Crisis—Three Decades Ago." *New York Times Magazine* (May 4, 1980): 41.

Hamm, Michael. "The Pueblo and Mayaguez Incidents: A Study of Flexible Response and Decision Making." *Asian Survey* 17 (June 1977): 545–55.

Hickman, William F. "Did It Really Matter?" *Naval War College Review* 36, no. 2 (March–April 1983): 22.

Hoffman, David. "Reagan Ties Beirut Attack to Curb on Intelligence." *Washington Post*, September 27, 1984.

Hollis, Martin, and Steve Smith. "Roles and Reasons in Foreign Policy Decision Making." *British Journal of Political Science* 16 (July 1986): 269–86.

Hourihan, William J. "Marlinspike Diplomacy: The Navy in the Mediterranean, 1904." *U.S. Naval Institute Proceedings* 105 (January 1979): 42–51.

Humphrey, David C. "NSC Meetings during the Johnson Presidency." *Diplomatic History* 18, no. 1 (Winter 1994): 29–45.

Hyde, Charles C. "The Temporary Protection of Domiciled Aliens Declaring an Intention to Become American Citizens." In *International Law*, 686–88. Boston: Little, Brown and Company, 1922.

Klafter, Craig Evan. "United States Involvement in the Falkland Islands Crisis of 1831–33." *Journal of the Early Republic* 4 (Winter 1984): 395–420.

Koh, B. C. "The *Pueblo* Incident in Perspective." *Asian Survey* 9 (April 1969): 264–80.

Kunz, Diane B. "When Money Counts and Doesn't: Economic Power and Diplomatic Objectives." *Diplomatic History* 18 (Fall 1994): 451–62.

Laqueur, Walter. "Reflections on Terrorism." *Foreign Affairs* 64 (Fall 1986): 86–100.

Larson, David L. "The American Response to the Iranian Hostage Crisis." *International Social Science Review* 57 (Autumn 1982): 195–209.

Lentner, Howard H. "The Pueblo Affair: Anatomy of a Crisis." *Military Review* 49, no. 7 (July 1969): 55–66.

Lewis, Winston B. "The Birth of a Navy." *U.S. Naval Institute Proceedings* 101, no. 10 (1975): 18–65.

Lillich, Richard B. "The Diplomatic Protection of Nationals Abroad: An Elementary Principle of International Law under Attack." *American Journal of International Law* 69, no. 2 (1975): 359–65.

Lissakers, Karin. "Money and Manipulation." *Foreign Policy* 44 (1981): 107–26.

Long, David F. "Martial Thunder: The First Official American Armed Intervention in Asia." *Pacific Historical Review* 42 (May 1973): 143–62.

Long, John W. "American Intervention in Russia: The North Russian Expedition, 1918–19." *Diplomatic History* 6 (Winter 1982): 45–67.

Machado, Manuel A., Jr., and James T. Judge. "Tempest in a Teapot? The Mexican-United States Intervention Crisis of 1919." *Southwestern Historical Quarterly* 74 (July 1970): 1–23.

Marshall, Jonathan, Peter Scott, and Jane Hunter. "Irangate: The Israel Connection." In *The Iran-Contra Connection: Secret Teams and Covert Operations in the Reagan Era*, 167–86. Boston: South End Press, 1987.

Martin, John. "The Media's Role in International Terrorism." *Terrorism* 8, no. 2 (1985): 127–46.

McKee, Delbert. "The Boxer Indemnity Remission." *Society for Historians of American Foreign Relations Newsletter* 23, no. 1 (March 1992): 1–19.

McMahon, Robert J. "United States Relations with Asia in the Twentieth Century: Retrospect and Prospect." In *American Foreign Relations: A Historiographical Review*, ed. Gerald K. Haines and J. Samuel Walker, 273–70. Westport, CT: Greenwood Publishing Group, 1981.

Mineo, Nakajima. "The Sino-Soviet Confrontation in Historical Perspective." In *The Origins of the Cold War in Asia*, ed. Yonosuke Nagai and Akira Iriye, 203–23. New York: Columbia University Press, 1977.

Moore, John Bassett. "The Koszta Case." In *A Digest of International Law*. Vol. 3, 820–54. Washington, DC: Government Printing Office, 1906.

Moyers, Bill. "Send in the CIA." In *The Secret Government: The Constitution in Crisis*, 53–61. Cabin John, MD: Seven Locks Press, 1988.

Neu, Charles E. "The Rise of the National Security Bureaucracy." In *The New American State: Federal Bureaucracies and Policies since World War II*, ed. Louis Galambos, 85–108. Baltimore: Johns Hopkins University Press, 1987.

"North Koreans Release U.S. Helicopter Pilot: Negotiators for Both Sides Agree Flight Not a Spy Mission." *Knoxville News Sentinel*, December 30, 1994.

Roeling, B. V. A. "Aspects of the Case Concerning United States Diplomatic and Consular Staff in Tehran." *Netherlands Yearbook of International Law* 11 (1980): 125–53.

Rosati, Jerel A. "Developing a Systematic Decision Making Framework." *World Politics* 33 (1981): 234–51.

Ross, Frank E. "Mission of Joseph Donaldson to Algiers, 1795–1797." *Journal of Modern History* 7, no. 4 (December 1935): 422–33.

———, and M. A. Washington. "The Mission of John Lamb to Algiers, 1785–86." *Americana* 28 (July 1934): 287–94.

Sapin, Burton M. "Isn't It Time for a Modest Presidency in Foreign Affairs?" *Presidential Studies Quarterly* 10 (Winter 1980): 19–28.

Saunders, Harold H. "Beginning of the End." In Warren Christopher et al., *American Hostages in Iran*, 281–96. New Haven, CT: Yale University Press, 1985.

———. "Diplomacy and Pressure, November 1979–May 1980." In Warren Christopher et al., *American Hostages in Iran*, 72–143. New Haven, CT: Yale University Press, 1985.

Schachter, Oscar. "Self-Help in International Law: U.S. Action in the Iranian Hostages Crisis." *Journal of International Affairs* 37, no. 2 (1984): 231–46.

Schratz, Paul R. "A Commentary on the Pueblo Affair." *Military Affairs* 35 (October 1971): 93–95.

Shewmaker, Kenneth. "Congress Only Can Declare War." *Diplomatic History* 12 (Fall 1988): 383–409.

Smith, Gaddis. "The U.S. vs. International Terrorists." *American Heritage* 28, no. 5 (August 1977): 37–43.

Smith, Terence. "Putting the Hostages' Lives First." *New York Times Magazine* (May 17, 1981): 76–101.

Sofaer, Abraham D. "Terrorism and the Law." *Foreign Affairs* 64, no. 5 (Summer 1986): 901–22.

Stebbins, Richard, and Elaine Adam. "The Pueblo Incident." In *Documents on American Foreign Relations, 1968–69*, ed. Richard Stebbins and Elaine Adam, 292–302. New York: Simon and Schuster, 1972.

Stein, Ted L. "Contempt, Crisis, and the Court: The World Court and the Hostage Rescue Attempt." *American Journal of International Law* 76, no. 3 (1982): 499–531.

Stokes, William N. "The Future between America and China." *Foreign Service Journal* (January 1968): 14–16.

Stone, Ellen. "Six Months among Brigands." *McClure's Magazine* 19, no. 5 (September 1902): 464–71.

Sweezy, Paul. "Cold War, Inflation, and Controls." *Monthly Review* 31, no. 10 (March 1980): 1–9.

Tatsumi, Okabe. "The Cold War and China." In *The Origins of the Cold War in Asia*, ed. Yonosuke Nagai and Akira Iriye, 224–51. New York: Columbia University Press, 1977.

"Tredwell Set Free by the Bolsheviki." *New York Times*, May 4, 1919.

Tsilka, Katerina. "Born among Brigands." *McClure's Magazine* 19, no. 4 (August 1902): 290–300.

Tuchman, Barbara W. "Perdicaris Alive or Raisuli Dead." *American Heritage* 10 (August 1959): 18–21, 98–101.

Unterberger, Betty M. "Woodrow Wilson and the Bolsheviks: The 'Acid Test' of Soviet-American Relations." *Diplomatic History* 11 (Spring 1987): 71–91.

Waheed-uz-Zaman. "The American Hostages in Iran: The Critical 444 Days." *Journal of South Asian and Middle Eastern Studies* 9 (Summer 1986): 26–57.

Ward, Angus. "The Mukden Affair." *American Foreign Service Journal* 27 (February 1950): 15.

Weinberger, Caspar. "U.S. Defense Strategy." *Foreign Affairs* 64 (Spring 1986): 675–97.

Whipple, A. B. C. "Jefferson vs. the Barbary Pirates." *Constitution* (Fall 1989): 4–14.

Wilkinson, Paul. "After Tehran." *Contemporary Review* 238, no. 1385 (June 1981): 281–90.

Wilson, Gary E. "American Hostages in Moslem Nations, 1784–1796: The Public Response." *Journal of the Early Republic* 2, no. 2 (Summer 1982): 123–41.

———. "The First American Hostages in Moslem Nations, 1784–1789." *American Neptune* 41 (July 1981): 214–23.

Wohlstetter, Roberta. "Kidnapping to Win Friends and Influence People." *Survey* 20, no. 4 (1971): 1–40.

Woods, Randall B. "Terrorism in the Age of Roosevelt: The Miss Stone Affair." *American Quarterly* 31 (Fall 1979): 478–95.

———. "The Miss Stone Affair." *American Heritage* 32, no. 6 (1981): 26–29.

Yang Kuisong. "The Soviet Factor and the CCP's Policy toward the United States in the 1940s." *Chinese Historians* 5, no. 1 (Spring 1992): 17–34.

Young, Marilyn J. "When the Shoe Is on the Other Foot: The Reagan Administration's Treatment of the Shootdown of Iran Air 655." In *Reagan and Public Discourse in America*, ed. Michael Weiler and W. Barnett Pearce, 203–24. Tuscaloosa: University of Alabama Press, 1992.

Zimmerman, William. "Iran: Consequences of the Abortive Attempt to Rescue the American Hostages." *Conflict* 3, no. 1 (1981): 55–77.

PERIODICALS

Atlanta Constitution. 1902 (Ellen Stone), 1904 (Ion Perdicaris).
Chicago Tribune. 1901.
Christian Herald. 1901.
Current Digest of the Soviet Press. 1949.
Harper's Magazine. 1885.
Houston Post. 1901–02.
Knoxville News Sentinel. 1993, 1994, 1995.
Los Angeles Times. 1968.
Louisville Courier-Journal. 1901 (Ellen Stone), 1904 (Ion Perdicaris).

The Nation. 1902, 1904.
National Intelligencer. 1832.
New Orleans Daily Picayune. 1904.
Newsweek. 1968.
New York Daily Tribune. 1892.
New York Herald Tribune. 1949.
New York Times. 1901, 1904, 1919, 1921, 1945, 1949, 1968–69, 1978, 1985.
New York Times Magazine. 1981.
New York Tribune. 1902, 1948–49.
New York Weekly Tribune. 1853.
The Tampa Tribune-Times. 1989.
Tehran Times. 1980.
Washington Bee. 1901.
Washington Globe. 1832.
Washington Post. 1901–02, 1980, 1984.

UNPUBLISHED MATERIAL

Wilson, Gary E. "American Prisoners in Barbary Nations, 1784–1816." Ph.D. diss., North Texas State University, 1979.

INTERVIEW

Crowe, Admiral William, retired chairman of the Joint Chiefs of Staff. Interviewed by the author. Washington, DC, July 19, 1991.

Index

China (Manchu): declares war
against foreigners (1900), 46;
U.S. policy toward, 50–51,
207–9. *See also* Beijing; Boxer
Rebellion
China (People's Republic): civil war,
117; Cultural Revolution, 142;
relations with North Korea, 139,
143; Sino-American relations,
117–18, 128–30; Sino-Soviet
relations, 126–28; Ward incident,
118–24. *See also* Mao Zedong
China lobby (U.S.): influence of,
124–25
Christensen, Ward L., 215
Christopher, Warren: Iranian hostage
crisis and, 168–69, 182–83, 185–
86
Churchill, Winston: on Poland,
107–8; relationship with
Roosevelt and Stalin, 106
Cicippio, Joseph, 226, 229
Clark, Ramsey: mission to Iran,
173
Clarke, J. F., 60
HMS *Cleo*, 29
Clifford, Clark, 149
Clinton, Bill: terrorist incident and,
231
Clinton, Hillary Rodham: visit to
Pakistan, 231
Clubb, Edmund, 121, 131; Zhou's
demarche and, 123, 126
Cold War: Communist China and,
17; consensus and credibility,
157–58; dispute over Iran and,
161–63; end of, 201; origins of,
101–2, 112–13; *Pueblo* crisis
and, 150
Colombia: terrorism in, 219
Conger, E. H., 207–8
Congress (U.S.): China policy, 125;
commissioners to Algiers and,
5–6; creates U.S. Navy, 9; policy
toward piracy, 16; ransom
payments and, 15; Stone ransom
and, 69, 72
Constantinople (Istanbul), 3, 31. *See
also* Ottoman Empire
Containment: strategy of, 112
Contra rebels. *See* Nicaragua; North,
Oliver

USS *Coral Sea*: *Pueblo* incident and,
150
Corsairs: Barbary states and, 3, 5
Costa, John, 224
Croatia: hostage crisis in, 219
Cromie, Francis N.A., 96
Crowley, Donald J., 213
Curzon Line (Poland), 107
Czech Legion: in Siberia, 90–92

Dagu Forts (China): attack on, 46–
47, 49, 51
Dale, Richard, 12
Daliberti, David: arrested in Iraq,
231–32
Dallin, Alexander, 110
Daoud, Abu, 215–16
Dauphin (ship): seizure of, 4–6, 9–
10, 205
Davies, John, 124
Dawa, al- (Shiite group), 223–26
Deane, John R.: repatriation and,
102, 104–5, 108, 112
Debs, Eugene, 97
Decatur, Stephen, 12, 15
Democratic party (Democrats): two-
China policy, 124–25
Depew, Chauncey, 80
Derne (Tripoli/Libya): capture of, 13
Dickinson, Charles: Stone negotia-
tions and, 63, 65–68
Dingley, Nelson, 43
Diplomacy: as response to hostage-
taking, 15; diplomatic immunity,
120–21, 123–24; in Iranian
hostage-taking, 173–75; in
release of hostages in Soviet-
occupied Poland, 100–101; in
Stone affair, 67–69; in TWA
hijacking, 195; in Ward affair,
132; prescription for hostage
release, 200–201
Dobler, Leland, 216
Dodge, David S., 222
Dominican Republic: acts of
terrorism in, 213, 216
Donaldson, Joseph, Jr., 9–10
Downes, John, 23–25, 206
Downey, John T., 210
Dozier, James: kidnapping of, 192,
222
Draper, Morris, 213

ISBN 0-8420-2552-9

90000>

9 780842 025522